PSYCHOL(

2nd

An informa.

PSYCHOLOGY & YOU

2nd edition

AN INFORMAL INTRODUCTION

Julia C. Berryman
University of Leicester

David J. Hargreaves
University of Leicester

Kevin Howells
*Edith Cowan University, and Justice and
Forensic Services, Perth, Australia*

Elizabeth M. Ockleford
University of Leicester

BPS Blackwell

350 Main Street, Malden, MA 02148-5018, USA
108 Cowley Road, Oxford OX4 1JF, UK
550 Swanston Street, Carlton South, Melbourne, Victoria 3053, Australia
Kurfürstendamm 57, 10707 Berlin, Germany

First published in 1987 by BPS Books, The British Psychological Society, St Andrews House, 48 Princess Road East, Leicester LE1 7DR, UK in association with Routledge, 11 New Fetter Lane, London EC4P 4EE, UK.

New revised edition 1997 published by BPS Books, The British Psychological Society, St Andrews House, 48 Princess Road East, Leicester LE1 7DR, UK and 22883 Quicksilver Drive, Stirling, VA 20166, USA.

First published as a BPS Blackwell book 2002 by Blackwell Publishing Ltd
Reprinted 2002

Library of Congress Cataloging-in-Publication Data on file.

ISBN 1-85433-226-0

A catalogue record for this title is available from the British Library.

Set by Poole Typesetting (Wessex) Ltd
Printed and bound in the United Kingdom
by T. J. International Ltd, Padstow, Cornwall

For further information on
Blackwell Publishing, visit our website:
http://www.blackwellpublishing.com

CONTENTS

Start reading this book at the point, chapter or sub-heading that interests you most. Each chapter is self-contained but refers you to other related chapters as appropriate. A glossary at the end defines all the technical terms. We hope that by dipping in here and there you will soon find that you have read the whole book.

N.B. REFERENCES

References are included at the end of each chapter. For ease of reading the text, we have not always cited the author of every study to which we have referred. However, should you want to find the source material, we have annotated each reference to indicate the parts of the text to which it is relevant. Thus, we recommend that readers scan the annotations to references in a chapter in which a particular study of interest to them occurs. For example, Lorenz in Chapter 5 is not referenced directly but is included in the annotation to the Sluckin reference. Similarly, a quotation cited in the text, but not directly referenced, will be referred to in an annotation. We trust that this system will enable enthusiastic readers to follow up references, without making the book too heavy to read by citing numerous authors.

LIST OF EXERCISES

LIST OF TABLES AND FIGURES

PREFACE AND ACKNOWLEDGEMENTS TO THE SECOND EDITION

Psychology and You has been written with you, the reader, very much in mind. The purpose of this book is to introduce psychology in a lively and accessible way – linking the subject matter to people's everyday experiences. The original idea for the book came out of my experience of teaching psychology in the Department of Adult Education, at Leicester University, UK. I became aware of the need for a broad-based introduction to the subject which introduced topics from the viewpoint of the reader, taking into account the everyday interests of the person rather than the needs of a particular course syllabus. Most people have a grounding in subjects such as history, geography, mathematics and the physical sciences, but psychology, a subject of immediate relevance to us all, rarely forms part of the school curriculum. Yet it is surprisingly difficult to find a book that introduces psychology to adults in an up-to-date manner whilst also starting at the point that interests them. We have tried to bring together all the topics that our teaching experience has shown are intriguing and relevant to everyday life. We hope that this book will be the beginning of a life-long interest in psychology for you, and with this in mind we have included recommended reading and references. We also hope that all those who teach psychology will find the book a 'user-friendly' introduction for their students and will find the exercises helpful in stimulating interest in each topic. Psychologists have certainly not found all the answers in their attempts to explain human behaviour, thoughts and feelings, but we hope that you, the reader, will find that the topics which we have considered will enhance your understanding of yourself and others.

In the second edition our intention has been to add new topics and up-to-date references as appropriate and to amend the text to bring in new developments and perspectives. The extent to which each chapter has been updated varies according to the way in which each subject area has changed since the first edition. Many new exercises have been included.

The following people have all played a vital part in the preparation of this book. Firstly, the students whose questions and comments were the initial stimulus for producing this book. Secondly, our families who have played in an invaluable role in supporting us in various ways whilst we researched and wrote the book, so particular thanks are due to: Philip Drew, and Ruby and Eric Berryman for many helpful comments on drafts of the text; to Linda Hargreaves, for providing information and valuable help with one of the chapters; to Marguerite. '... all the sun long it was running, it was lovely ...'; to Colin Ockleford for his patience and Kirsty Ockleford for her work on the diagrams for Chapters 8 and 9. Thirdly, to those who assisted in the production of the manuscript: to Rebekah Szucik for her great care and efficiency in word processing the text and Julie Evans for additional word processing. Our sincere thanks to them all.

Julie C Berryman

Introduction: Beginning to Understand You

'Why did you do it?'

'What were you thinking?'

'How did you feel?'

These three questions sum up what psychologists are striving to explain in their quest to understand people. They are also questions that we *all* find ourselves trying to answer when another's behaviour, thoughts and feelings baffle us; if we know someone well we expect to be able to predict what they will do, think, or feel in many everyday situations.

If someone in your family is slow to wake in the morning, but is bright-eyed at midnight, you soon learn to discuss important topics with them in the evening rather than at breakfast. You come to expect him or her to eat little at breakfast, nod rather than talk, and through the experience of many mornings together you are able to predict a whole host of other things about that person's behaviour. In a sense, we are all amateur psychologists because we observe our friends' and partner's behaviour carefully and discover rules by which they seem to act. This ability is not unique

1

to adults. In a family it is likely that the children and the dog have also learned to make these predictions about each other.

Perhaps, you are thinking, this is all just common sense. But we hope that this book shows that psychology goes well beyond what can be answered by common sense. It is a subject which has developed a variety of methods to assist in answering questions about human behaviour, thoughts and feelings, and these methods are illustrated by examples throughout this book.

WHAT IS PSYCHOLOGY?

What does psychology mean to you? When people who have not studied the subject are asked to say what comes into their mind when the words 'psychology' or 'psychologists' are mentioned, a whole ragbag of answers is given:

'Psychologists know what you are thinking.'
'They analyse you like Freud did.'
'They measure I. Q. and personality.'
'Psychologists deal with problems like phobias and depression.'
'They use lie detectors.'
'They do devious experiments.'

The commonest answers deal with uncovering the hidden aspects of people and their psychological problems and, as these answers show, there is often more than a certain wariness about psychologists and their profession. Sigmund Freud's name is often mentioned in connection with psychology and his ideas have certainly influenced psychologists, but what did he actually do?

Was Freud a psychologist?

Sigmund Freud, often referred to as 'the father of psychoanalysis', was not a psychologist. Freud (1856–1939) was a Viennese physician who became interested in the role of unconscious mental processes in influencing people's behaviour and, in particular, their psychological problems. He was interested in exploring human behaviour, feelings and thoughts, but his ideas were based on his clinical work. He built up a view of what makes humans 'tick' from his deductions about the causes of the problems he saw in his patients. Thus his view of human nature was shaped

Figure 1.1: Sigmund Freud (1856–1939).

by observing and trying to help those who had problems; he was not concerned with the 'normal' or average person, but just a small number of rather unhappy people.

Essentially Freud believed that a large part of the mind was unconscious, and that our behaviour was 'driven' by instincts housed in this unconscious area of the mind. The expression of these instincts was, he suggested, shaped by our early life experiences: so, for example, a person who was deprived of adequate breast feeding, or mother love, might later show neurotic patterns of behaviour such as a craving for comfort, food or love.

In attempting to find the causes of psychological problems, Freud's approach, in psychoanalytic therapy, was to use a variety of techniques which were intended to give insights into a person's unconscious mental processes. Two of these techniques were *free association* and *dream analysis*. In the former, a patient would lie on a couch and be asked to say freely whatever thoughts or feelings came to mind; in dream analysis the contents of the patient's dreams were explored using free association with a dream event as the initial stimulus. Freud believed that these techniques led him to the source of a patient's problems, and, by bringing that source out into the open into conscious awareness, the emotional release (or *catharsis*) induced would assist in helping the patient towards a solution of the problem.

But being based on clinical evidence, which is open to a variety of interpretations, Freud's ideas cannot easily be tested or verified in the way that modern psychologists believe to be essential. So although Freud's views of the human mind and behaviour have influenced psychological thinking, they are not, as we shall see, central to it.

Three different approaches

The distinction between *psychoanalysis, psychiatry* and *psychology* needs to be clarified, because it is not a simple one. Psychiatry is a branch of medicine and, as such, psychiatrists are concerned largely with the treatment of mental *illnesses* and psychological *problems.* Any qualified physician may choose to specialize and take a further qualification in psychiatry, just as he or she might select gynaecology or surgery. Psychiatrists, like physicians (or general practitioners), may use drugs in the treatment of mental illness, or they may use other methods such as behaviour therapy – a technique also used by psychologists.

Psychologists train by taking a degree course in psychology in which all aspects of behaviour and its underlying causes – in both humans and other animals – are studied. One distinction between psychologists, psychiatrists and psychoanalysts is that the former are concerned with all people, while the latter two are concerned solely with those who cannot cope, and who are unwell. Clinical psychologists, however, also make the *patient* the main focus of their work, but the treatment methods used by them involve therapies which do not rely on the prescription of drugs.

Psychoanalysts have their own training which is quite separate from that of both psychologists and psychiatrists. This training usually involves the would-be analyst first undergoing psychoanalysis themselves in order to gain increased insight. Psychologists and psychiatrists sometimes undergo further training in order to become psychoanalysts, and thus it is perhaps not surprising that there is sometimes confusion, in the minds of the public, about these three professions.

In this book we are concerned with psychology, which has developed its own rigorous methods of studying humans, quite distinct from the techniques of psychoanalysis. Indeed, at the height of Freud's influence at the turn of the century, psychologists showed a marked disregard for subjective reports of mental processes (*introspection*) as the major source of data. Overt behaviour became the focus of attention and psychology became known as the 'science of behaviour'; thoughts and feelings were largely ignored, being intangible and unobservable. Speculations about the causes of human behaviour based on introspection were thought to be unhelpful and misleading.

PSYCHOLOGY AND COMMON SENSE

Psychologists are often said to be studying the obvious, spending years trying to find the answers to questions that common sense can tell us. We, as psychologists, believe this to be an unfair comment, and to test your common sense we should like you to answer the following questions using just your own ideas – please don't refer to books to find the answers. (You will find the answers on pp.12–14.)

Question 1
How long do dreams last? In *A Midsummer Night's Dream* (I.i), Lysander says that true love is 'brief' and 'momentary', like a dream. Do dreams really come and go in an instant as Shakespeare apparently believed? Do you think a typical dream lasts:

(a) a fraction of a second;
(b) a few seconds;
(c) a minute or two;
(d) many minutes;
(e) a few hours?

Take a bonus point for correctly answering the following question about yourself. How often do you dream?:

(f) hardly ever or never;
(g) about once every few nights;
(h) about once a night;
(i) several times every night.

Question 2
John's childish curiosity led him to the kitchen where his mother was baking a cake for his ninth birthday. On the kitchen table were two identical bottles of milk. He watched his mother open one of the bottles and pour the contents into a wide glass bowl. His eyes roved from the bowl to the bottle that was still full of milk and back to the bowl. His mother suddenly remembered something that she had read in a psychology book, 'Tell me, clever boy,' she said, 'is there more milk in the bottle or the bowl?' Is John likely to have thought that:

(a)   the bottle contained more milk;
(b)   the bowl contained more milk;
(c)   the bottle and the bowl contained the same amount of milk?

Question 3
Chapter 9 of the Gospel According to Saint John in the Bible is devoted entirely to an episode in which Jesus restored the sight of a man 'which was blind from his birth'. More recently, surgical, rather than miraculous, methods have occasionally been used to restore the sight, late in life, of people born blind. During the first few days after the bandages are removed, do you think such people:

(a)   see nothing at all;
(b)   see only a blur;
(c)   see only vague shapes moving about;
(d)   recognize familiar objects without touching them;
(e)   recognize objects by sight only after touching and looking at them simultaneously;
(f)   see everything upside-down?

Question 4
A group of friends decided to put some money into a kitty and spend it at the race track on Derby Day. Before each race they wrote down their private opinions about the bet that ought to be placed. Then the group assembled to discuss their individual opinions and to arrive at a group decision. On each race, the most cautious decision was not to place a bet at all, a more risky decision was to place a small bet on a horse with favourite odds of winning, and a very risky decision was to place a large bet on an outsider. Compared to the average of the individual decisions, are the group decisions likely to have been:

(a)   more cautious;
(b)   more risky;
(c)   neither more cautious nor more risky?

Question 5
The influential philosopher Friedrich Nietzsche (1844–1900) suffered from insanity and general ill-health for the last 20 years of
his life. The great physicist Albert Einstein (1879–1955), on the
other hand was quite sane and enjoyed good health through most
of his three score years and sixteen. Are exceptionally intelligent
people in general:

(a)   less physically and mentally healthy than others;
(b)   more physically and mentally healthy than others;
(c)   similar to others in physical and mental health;
(d)   less mentally healthy but similar to others in physical health;
(e)   less physically healthy but similar to others in mental health?

Figure 1.2: Albert Einstein (1879–1955). Are exceptionally intelligent
people healthier than others?

THE PSYCHOLOGIST'S APPROACH

Today psychologists base their conclusions about humans on both observations of the behaviour of many people, and reports from those people themselves. It is more than the 'science of behaviour', because people's own unique experiences also form part of the data.

Psychologists use a wide range of equipment to measure both easily observable and unobservable bodily changes. The well-known lie detector or polygraph is one example: this measures a variety of physiological changes, including heart rate and skin moistness, but psychologists would rarely use this to detect lies. Indeed, most psychologists are well aware of its fallibility in this respect. What is fascinating about the polygraph is that it can reveal minute changes in emotional arousal.

Read the following words:

TABLE, COFFEEPOT, PAGE, CROSS, FATHER, CLOCK, HOLLY, BABY, LINE, SEX

Did you detect any change in emotional level in yourself as you read them? Probably not. But a polygraph would reveal that certain words are more emotionally-loaded for some people than are others. Father, baby, and sex might mean much more to you than the other words because they obviously stand for things about which many people are emotional. But if you have a friend called Holly, or if you are a Christian, HOLLY and CROSS might also be emotionally-loaded words for you, and this would show on the polygraph reading. Thus the polygraph can give us more information about someone's emotions than they can themselves. Chapter 8 tells us more about this.

The study of human behaviour, thoughts and emotions over many years has enabled psychologists to see how certain psychological problems may arise, and how they may be treated; by charting human behaviour, patterns emerge which enable predictions to be made about the frequency with which one event may follow on another. Whilst there is also much to learn, there is already quite a lot that psychologists can predict about human behaviour and hence the measurement of personality and intelligence in part, if not in total, is a reality, as Chapters 2 and 10 will show.

Are psychologists devious experimenters?

Psychologists are sometimes charged with doing rather devious experiments. In the past this assertion was probably quite fair in relation to a small proportion of psychological studies and, later in this book (Chapter 4, for example), one or two such examples are given. However a certain degree of control over events under study is necessary in the initial stages of studying people, and there are good reasons for this. For example, if psychologists wish to study the effect of a substance on some aspect of human psychology or behaviour, then they must test it in such a way that the people taking part in the experiment do not know whether they are receiving the substance or not.

The psychological experiment

In order to illustrate the care which psychologists must take in planning experiments, an experiment carried out by Winifred Cutler and colleagues will be described. Research in some non-human mammals has indicated that female reproductive physiology can be affected by odours (chemical signals) from males. Cutler's research investigated this possibility in human females and this research explored the role of underarm (axillary) secretions and the menstrual cycle.

Having selected a particular sample of women to act as participants, and having decided what aspects of the menstrual cycle would be measured (in this case menstrual cycle length and regularity over a number of cycles), the aim was to compare individuals who received a given dose of chemical substance (male secretions) with those who received no dose. The problem was to ensure that the people did not know whether they were receiving the substance, despite the fact that participants had to consent to take part in the study and be aware that some substance might be used. (There are numerous regulations concerning these latter points which we need not consider here.)

Psychologists solve this problem by using a *placebo*, an inert substance which can be administered in exactly the same way as the substance under investigation. In this study, the placebo was ethanol which was given alone or with the chemical substance (the male secretions) mixed in to it without being detectable. Participants in the experiment were assigned at random to the experimental (male secretions) and control (placebo) condition, and each received identical treatment – both groups had the sub-stance or placebo placed on the upper lip and were told not to wash the area for six hours. This treatment was carried out three times a week for about 14 weeks. The pulse and blood pressure of each participant were also recorded at each treatment to dilute the focus of the study. Details of menstrual cycles during this peri-od were recorded.

As we have said, the participants were unaware of, or *blind*, to the nature of the study (the effect of male secretions on the men-strual cycle), and the technician administering the experimental substance/placebo was also blind to the purpose of the study. Thus we say that the study was double-blind.

Participants who know the nature of the study may be scepti-cal about the outcome, or indeed convinced that a particular out-come may occur and be concerned to demonstrate this outcome. Sometimes the very fact of taking part in the research can have effects on participants, even in the placebo group.

To return to the experiment, the researchers did find that male secretions had an effect. To find out the results, see Chapter 1.

What we expect affects what we see

Our beliefs about things can have quite a dramatic effect on us and everyday experience can confirm this. There are no scientifi-cally-proven aphrodisiacs, for instance, and yet many people firm-ly believe that they know of such substances. Providing that their belief is not disturbed, it is likely that the substance will 'work' for them. The psychologist must always be aware that if he or she seeks to investigate any aspect of humans, the expectations of those humans must be taken into account and, if necessary, *con-trolled for* in a study such as the drug study just described.

Perhaps all this control seems ludicrously contrived, but anoth-er example may serve to show how necessary such procedures are. Parents will often assert that they always treated their children in the same way, regardless of their sex. Yet, psychological research has shown that parents' treatment, or description, of babies varies greatly as a function of the sex of the infant.

In a study which we carried out, a nine-month-old baby was filmed with its mother. We showed the film to groups of people who were asked to make an assessment of the baby (its behaviour, appearance, healthiness and so on), but to some groups we said

'This baby is a little boy called John', and to others we said 'This baby is a little girl called Mary'. We found that on measures such as activity, fidgetiness, appearance and weight estimates, the 'boy' baby and 'girl' baby were consistently described differently. (Don't forget the baby was the same throughout.) For example, the 'boy' was seen as more active and more fidgety. Other studies show similar findings, and they reveal how easy it is for our judgements to be shaped by our pre-conceptions.

Experiments are not enough

The studies described indicate just one way in which psychologists can control events in order to study human behaviour, but there are many other methods which psychologists use. Perhaps you will have realized already that the experimental method cannot be applied to just *any* area which we want to investigate. Indeed, our discussion of the differences which parents report in boy and girl babies is a case in point. We cannot assign sex to one group and not another in order to investigate how 'sex' influences behaviour. We all have a biological sex – no one is truly neutral – and thus in exploring sex differences all we can do is *correlate* observed behaviour with one sex or the other. If we observe that males have shorter hair than females (that is, short hair and maleness are positively correlated), or that males cry less or fight more than females, we are not justified in saying that biological sex *per se* caused these differences.

Correlational studies provide much useful information for the psychologist, as we shall see, but these studies and experiments are only two of a number of techniques which psychologists have for investigating feelings, thoughts and emotions and all these methods are covered in the final chapter of this book.

Many people find methodology difficult to understand fully until they have more idea of the questions and problems which psychologists are seeking to understand. For this reason we have given you lots of examples of the psychologist's work first and then, with these examples in mind, you can look more closely at methodology at the end of the book.

What next?

The following chapters cover a range of topics which have been found to be of particular interest to those seeking to understand more about *behaviour, emotion* and *cognition*. The first chapter looks at a type of behaviour with which we are all very familiar – body language.

Answers to questions posed in *Psychology and common sense*, p.5

1.(**d,i**)   Score one point for realizing that a typical dream lasts many minutes (generally about 20 minutes), and take a bonus point for knowing that you dream several times every night (everyone does). You may think that you dream much less than this, because you probably only remember fragments of dreams that occur just before you wake up. Dream researchers made these discoveries whilst studying sleepers, recording their brain waves by sticking tiny electrodes onto their heads. The electrodes reveal characteristic patterns of electrical activity in the brain during dream sleep. Dreaming coincides with this brain activity (sleepers woken during the brain activity report dreaming), with rapid eye movements beneath closed eye lids (REM sleep), and, in men, with penile erection. Dream events appear to last about as long as the same events in waking life. Studies have demonstrated the universality of dreaming and these answers could not have been found by introspection alone.

2.(**c**)   Score one point. John is very likely to have thought that the bottle and the bowl contained the same amount of milk. This was a trick question, because a child a few years younger would probably have thought that the bottle contained more milk. But the child in question was nine years old, and the great majority of children have mastered the *conservation of substance*, as it is called, by that age. The famous experiment on which the question was based, and the underlying idea of conservation, comes from the work of the Swiss researcher Jean Piaget (discussed briefly in Chapters 6 and 9).

3.(**d**)   Score one point. People whose blindness is cured late in life are able to recognize familiar objects without touching them. This question has been debated since the seventeenth century, but it was not satisfactorily resolved until psychologists investigated it carefully in the 1960s and 1970s. Studies of a number of individuals who were born blind, but had their sight restored later in life, confirmed this finding.

4.**(b)** Score one point. The group decisions are likely to have been riskier than the average of the individual decisions. This is an example of the *group polarization phenomenon*. Although the phenomenon is strongly counter-intuitive, it is robust and easily exhibited in classroom demonstrations. A special case of group polarization (discussed in Chapter 4), called the *risky shift*, was discovered by two independent researchers in the late 1950s and early 1960s. Using quite different methods both researchers showed that group decisions tend, in general, to be riskier than individual decisions. Two hypotheses have been used to explain this. One states that during group discussions most group members are likely to discover that there are others present whose decisions, individually, are riskier than their own. Because people in general admire risk, the more cautious will then change their decision. The other debate suggests that the more risky arguments are more likely to be aired in a group discussion (again because riskiness is admired), and hence others will be persuaded by these arguments.

5.**(b)** Score one point. Exceptionally intelligent people are in general physically and mentally healthier than others. The evidence for this comes from various sources, including a continuing study of over fifteen hundred exceptionally intelligent children initiated by the American psychologist Lewis Terman in the early 1920s.

Terman's gifted sample – the 'termites' as they came to call themselves – were selected from the Californian school system in 1921. All had IQs above 135, which put them in the top one per cent of the population intellectually. Their ages at the beginning of the study ranged from 3 to 19 years. They were assessed on a variety of psychological tests and were also examined physically, and the sample was retested many times again until 1982. The researchers found that the physical and mental health of the 'termites', both male and female, remained 'good' to 'very good' compared with the rest of the population throughout this time.

Comment: How did you score? If you scored six points this is exceptionally good – but we cannot think how you did it, unless you have already read quite a lot of psychology. If you truly are a beginner in psychology, we predict a score of one or two because we think you could not possibly work out these answers purely on the basis of common sense. These questions are taken from Andrew Colman's book *What is Psychology?*, and if you are intrigued by them, we recommend that you read this book (see *Recommended Reading*) which is full of lots more questions of this type.

References

Cutler, W.B., Preti, G., Krieger, A., Huggins, G.R., Garcia, C.R. and Lawley, H.J. (1986). Human axillary secretions influence women's menstrual cycles: The role of donor extract from men. *Hormones and Behaviour*, *20*, 463–473. [The experiment using male axillary secretions.]

Recommended Reading

Colman, AM. (1981). *What is Psychology?* London: Routledge. [N.B. This book gives full details of all those people referred to in the five questions and answers posed in this chapter.]

1. *Body Language*

Humans have always viewed their ability to communicate via language as a very special and unique quality because highly complex and abstract ideas can be conveyed by this means. However, some emotions are often more accurately communicated by non-verbal signals; our bodies can indicate subtle changes in emotion that are often a better guide to our feelings than are words. Indeed, psychologists have found that where the listener feels there is a conflict between a person's words and their *body language*, they are five times more likely to rely on the latter. In evolutionary terms, many body language signals – facial expressions, postures, non-verbal sounds, odours and touch – evolved long before verbal language.

Of course, we may try to conceal our body language and perhaps put on a happy face, but because so many messages are given by different parts of the body at any one time, total deception of the perceptive observer is virtually impossible.

DOES BODY LANGUAGE COME NATURALLY?

There are both learned and innate elements in body language signals. For example, the nature of a smile is built into the human

15

species as a way of expressing pleasure and friendly non-aggression. Desmond Morris, the zoologist and author who is well known for his books and TV programmes on animal behaviour, suggests that it is derived from an appeasement gesture, and thus it can also include a fearful element, as in a nervous smile. Babies do not have to learn to smile. Deaf/blind babies smile in the same way as non-deaf/blind babies, and true smiles occur at about six weeks of age in all babies responding to social (rather than gastric) signals. Similarly, crying is an innate response and is shown by all babies, including those who are deaf/blind, in an instantly recognizable form. Nevertheless, we learn culturally acceptable ways of where and when to express these patterns. In Western society girls are permitted to cry more than boys. The extent to which the smile is used publicly also varies: Japanese people smile little in public, whereas Arabs do so much more freely.

'Involuntary' reactions are often real give-aways in the body language vocabulary. Turning pale, blushing, cold moist hands, prickling at the back of the neck (hairs standing on end), and a dry mouth all occur involuntarily and are controlled by the *sympathetic* part of the autonomic nervous system over which we have no conscious control. They are a result of the automatic *flight or fight* reaction of the body, in which blood is redirected to the muscles from the surface capillaries through the action of the hormone adrenaline.

Reddening of the face is a sign of anger, embarrassment or sexual awareness. In anger this occurs as a backlash to the white-faced stage when the *parasympathetic* part of the autonomic nervous system counteracts the effects of the sympathetic nervous system in order to restore equilibrium. At this stage we feel hot and uncomfortable and probably get a strong urge to go to the lavatory. Many an interviewee has entered the interview in the former state, and left it in the latter – the 'fight' for a job is won or lost and the body then restores its emotional and physical equilibrium in the second stage. Voluntary signals include those which we learn, without being aware of it, probably very early in life, together with those which we actively choose to display. An example of the first might be the use of touch in social interactions, and of the second our use of the head nod to say 'Yes'. Many of these signals are culturally specific – in Greece nodding the head means 'No' – and to understand other cultures fully we need to learn both their verbal and their body language.

Edward Hall compared the body language of Arabs, Japanese and Americans. He found that Arabs touch each other much more and stand closer to friends than Americans do, and that even when Americans were made aware of this difference they found it difficult to adapt to the style of interacting. These 'rules' of social interaction appear to be learned early in life and are very resistant to change.

Our first experience of cultural differences in body language is likely to be when we first meet someone from another country. Michael Argyle illustrates some of the differences in forms of greeting in his book *Bodily Communication*. On greeting, the Lapps smell each other's cheeks and rub noses, Polynesians stroke each other's faces, Arabs embrace, Japanese bow, and the British may just make a slight nod or jerk of the head. Without knowing these forms of greeting, it is clear that the scope for spoiling a potential friendship, or causing offence, is enormous.

The topic of body language is a very large and well-researched one and thus this chapter can only cover selected areas. In general, people tend to be most aware of their use of visual signals and for this reason we shall concentrate on these in most detail; touch and smell are discussed briefly, and signs of deception are also considered. The final part of the chapter explores ways in which psychologists' understanding of body language can be of use to us all.

THE FACE

In general, we view the face as the most important part of the body for conveying information about emotions – psychologists call this *facial primacy* – because the face is felt to be the primary source of information about feelings and attitudes. Studies of the face indicate that, despite the enormous number of possible facial expressions that we can display (for instance, one hundred different types of smile have been identified), there are only about six or seven facial expressions that we can identify reliably from the still face (see *Figure 1.3*).

Alan Fridland discusses an idea that goes back as far as Aristotle, that certain facial expressions in humans are universal. Many studies have shown that six facial expressions are readily recognized in tests where observers view a still face. These emotions are described

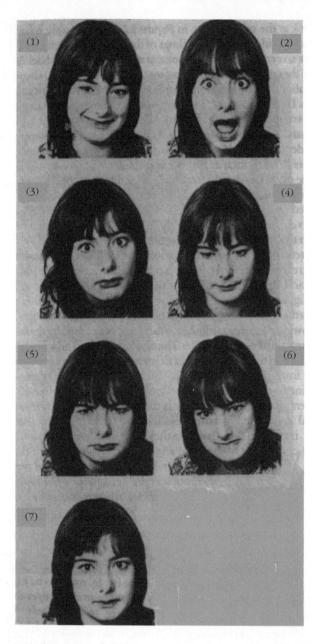

Figure 1.3: The seven facial expressions that are readily identified. Can you identify them? (Answers on p.40).

as: 'happy', 'fear', 'disgust', 'anger', 'surprise' and 'sadness'. Research in literate cultures generally finds these to be easily recognized but there is some research using people in Africa that shows rather lower recognition rates compared with Western cultures, and there is also data from Japan that suggests that the less positive emotions, such as 'fear', 'disgust' and 'anger', are not as easily identified. Research carried out in more isolated and nonliterate cultures produce rather different findings – the more contact such cultures have with Western cultures the more likely they are to recognize the so-called universal facial expressions. This latter finding suggests that other cultures may not conceptualize emotions and facial behaviour in the same way that we do in the West.

One problem in research on the meaning of facial expressions is the method used to carry out such work. Most studies used posed facial expressions rather than spontaneous ones, because the latter are hard to produce in the test situation. One early researcher in 1927 generated spontaneous or 'natural' facial expressions by getting people to do a variety of things that might generate the appropriate expressions. His work included getting a person to smell a tube containing a dead rat, and even hypnotizing a person and then telling them that members of their family had been killed. Such methods sound horrific and would be seen as highly unethical today. Even if they generated the desired result, and even if one could resolve the ethics of such work, it is obvious that as a means of furthering research on facial expressions they are very cumbersome. If posed expressions are used, people may be asked to say which emotion of a list of emotions is expressed in the face (*forced choice*), or they may be asked just to name the emotion that they think is shown (*free response*). It is the former method that generates, not surprisingly, higher agreement amongst participants.

If faces convey so little information that we can accurately identify, then why do we view the face as such an important source of information about emotions? Several factors need to be considered. Firstly, our interpretation of the face depends in part on the *context* in which the expression occurs. Often, without realizing it, we use this to help us decode the expression (see *Figures 1.4* and *1.5*). Can you guess what the people in *Figure 1.4* are feeling in the absence of a context, and in *Figure 1.5* would you be able to say what the child on the left was feeling if the snake was absent?

Figure 1.4: What are these people feeling? (See p.41 for answer.)

Display rules for facial expressions

Secondly, different societies have different 'display rules', that is, there are different rules about what should be expressed in different contexts. Paul Ekman and Wallace Friesen in 1969 described four types of display rules: those concerned with 'de-intensifying' the emotion; 'neutralising' the emotion, 'overintensification' of the emotion, and 'masking' the emotion. Thus boys or men may be expected to mask their distress if they want to cry having fallen over in the street, but in a football match they may show 'over-intensification' when experiencing the same level of distress. Another example might be that in some cultures the expression of grief at a funeral may be considered inappropriate, even though it is felt, whereas in other cultures this may be viewed as the appropriate place to display it. Hence, one can readily see why an observer from a culture with different 'display rules' might have difficulty in identifying which emotions are being experienced.

Facial expressions may change very rapidly so that the observer may not be able to identify an emotion even though they have

Figure 1.5: Would you be able to say what the child on the left was feeling if the snake was absent from the picture? *From Philip Jones-Griffiths (Magnum).*

observed the face change. Research shows that facial changes that last longer than two-fifths of a second can be *registered* by an observer, but cannot be *identified* unless they last about half a second or more. Video-tapes of faces show that in some cases many different emotions appear to be expressed in the face, some lasting as little as one-fifth of a second but these are not seen by the observer except on slow motion film. Psychologists call these 'micromomentary facial expressions'.

The left side of the face is sometimes said to be more expressive than the right side because it is controlled by the right, non-verbal, more intuitive, side of the brain. In posed facial expressions this does not seem to apply, and the face is equally expressive on both sides.

Facial expressions are not always of a pure or single emotion. The face can convey blends of emotions (*affect blends*) that also make interpretation more complex. One example might be a smile with the mouth that is not also conveyed by the eyes or other facial features. Evidence shows that genuine smiles involve the muscles at the corners of the eyes, making 'crow's feet'. Without these, the face does not convey the same feeling and the message given may be another emotion or a blend of several.

Despite the apparent complexity of the face, there is still evidence that we associate aspects of the face's *shape* with particular types of personality. There is evidence that a high forehead is viewed as a sign of intelligence, thin lips are seen as portraying conscientiousness, and full-lipped females are perceived as sexy. These attributes, however, are not linked reliably with such facial features, so the individuals possessing them may be quite unlike the stereotypes.

THE EYES

In general, most of us consider the eyes to be a very important part of the face for giving us information about a person:

> 'If looks could kill . . . '
> 'The evil eye . . . '
> 'He's giving her the eye'
> 'She looks right through you'

Eyes can give us away and reveal our innermost thoughts – we often distrust those who are shifty and won't look at us. 'Look at me when I'm talking to you,' must have been said by school teachers for decades. In many cultures, eye contact is a vital element in social interaction and we judge others according to how they use their eyes. Despite this we should not forget that there are clear cultural differences in how much eye contact is used.

Cultural differences in eye behaviour

In the West, eye contact is important when people talk to each other, but it is even more important to Arabs. According to Edward Hall, Arabs use more eye contact in conversation than Westerners and do not feel comfortable merely walking side by side and talking. Face-to-face contact (and even breath contact) is viewed as essential for a proper conversation. In contrast, the Japanese look at each other rather less than Westerners do, when in conversation. Once a brief eye contact has been made, they are more likely to allow their eyes to rest on the other person's neck than to continue to look at their eyes or mouth as we do in the West.

Use of the eyes has come to be associated with particular qualities. Modesty is revealed in downward glances, wonder and delight or amazement in wide eyes, craftiness in narrowed eyes, and staring is seen as an indication of aggression. But we must be careful not to impose our own culture's norms on others.

Eye expressions

The eye itself can only reveal a small number of emotions if we separate it from the rest of the face (including the eyebrows). Paul Ekman and Wallace Friesen studied eye expressions and reported the appearance of the eyes for six common emotions (see *Table 1.1*). If the eyebrows were to be added to the eyes, detection of some of these emotions would be easier. In particular, anger and disgust are revealed in eyebrow movements. Other studies suggest that only pleasure, anger and surprise (or combinations of these) are accurately identified by the eyes alone (see *Figure 1.6*).

Pupil size

In recent decades it has become widely known that we can give ourselves away, or reveal our emotions, via the change in size of

Table 1.1: Eye expressions (from Paul Ekman and Wallace Friesen, 1975)

1.	**Happiness**	Wrinkles are found below the lower eye lid and crow's feet at the corners of the eye.
2.	**Sadness**	The upper eyelids' corners may be raised due to the inner corners of the eyebrows being raised.
3.	**Surprise**	Upper eyelids raised, white showing above and possibly below the eye.
4.	**Fear**	Upper eyelid raised, white showing above the eye, lower eyelid drawing up and tense.
5.	**Disgust**	Upper eyelid lowered, lines show below lower eyelid which is pushed up but not tense.
6.	**Anger**	Eyes may appear bulging. Upper and lower eyelids are both tense, the upper lid may be lowered due to the brows being lowered and the lower lid may be raised. Eyelids may not show these patterns.

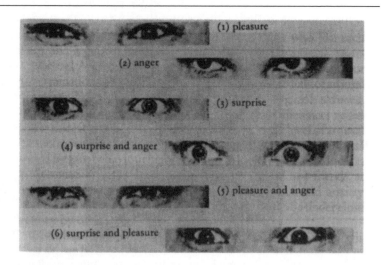

Figure 1.6: Emotions perceived from the eyes alone. (*From Argyle, 1975. After Nummenmaa*).

our pupils. Pupils can dilate by approximately 6mm, from as little as 2mm up to 8mm (see *Figure 1.7*).

Eckhard Hess was probably the first person to point out that pupil size reveals our emotional state and is not merely an

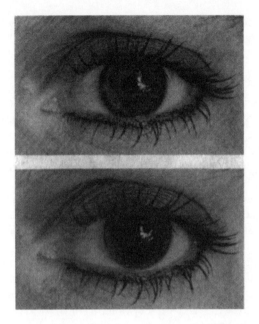

Figure 1.7: Pupil size variations. (*From Eric Crichton.*)

indication of the level of illumination. In general, dilated pupils are a sign of emotional arousal, interest and attraction, a sign that we like what we are looking at. Thus, males and females will 'dilate' when they find a member of the opposite sex attractive. Homosexual men and women will 'dilate' when viewing an attractive member of the same sex. However, sex isn't the only thing that makes us dilate; women's eyes usually dilate when they see a baby (men's do too, but only if they are fathers), and pupil dilation is also shown in response to things we like, such as food, pictures and so on.

At one time constriction of the pupils was also felt to be a sign of negative attitudes such as dislike or hatred. However, research studies have not been able to substantiate this. It seems that negative emotions are not revealed by pupil size, only the more positive emotions. The change in pupil size is only momentary, and most of us are not even aware that it is occurring, although it is said that Arabs seem to have been aware of this long before the research of Eckhard Hess in the 1960s. They screen their eyes when trading so as not to show too much interest in the goods they hope to purchase. Perhaps we should all keep this in mind when trying to strike a bargain!

Gaze and mutual gaze

Observe people in a cafe or restaurant, note who looks at whom, and for how long eye contact with another is maintained. Eye to eye contact, or *mutual gaze*, rarely lasts for long but it is continually made and broken by those who are talking or listening to each other. *Gaze* behaviour, the way we use our eyes, our 'looking behaviour', reveals much about the nature of the relationships between people. Returning to our cafe or restaurant, it is often said that married couples look at each other much less than those at an early stage in the 'pairing' process. Their lack of mutual gaze reveals their more established and settled status.

Psychologists suggest that gaze behaviour has four functions. The first is *regulating communication*: we show that we want communication to begin by trying to make visual contact, and, in the same way we avoid such contact to end, or avoid making, an interaction. Political candidates waiting hopefully at a polling station can tell whom of their usual voters are now voting for someone else because they avoid their eyes.

Monitoring feedback is also a key aspect of gaze behaviour – we find out how the other person is reacting by looking at them. *Cognitive* activity is also revealed by gaze. Gaze aversion often occurs when we are thinking or trying to work something out.

Intriguingly, there is some evidence that the direction in which we avert our gaze may reveal things about our interests and abilities. Paul Bakan researched this topic and found that males, more than females, tend to move their eyes consistently more in one direction than another – they tend to be 'right movers' or 'left movers'. The argument is that eye movements activate the opposite hemisphere of the brain, so 'left movers' activate the right hemisphere and vice versa. Left movers show more vivid imagery, are more likely to study the humanities or the classics, are more sociable, musical and religious; their right hemisphere seems to be more influential. Right movers activate the left hemisphere and are more likely to enjoy maths or science, sleep less and have more twitches and tics. This research is received with scepticism by some scientists but it has nevertheless led to the theory of *neurolinguistic programming* (NLP) which suggests that eye movements indicate the type of processing in the brain; that is, which hemisphere is involved in 'thinking'. Try *Exercise 1.1* (p.44) to test just how consistent people are in using eye movement when thinking. Before you read the exercise, find some right-handed male volunteers who are not familiar with the ideas just outlined.

Lastly, gaze behaviour is *expressive*; we reveal our feelings or emotions as we saw in the section on eye expressions and pupil size.

Gaze patterns

How does gaze behaviour reveal the regulatory and monitoring function described? If we observe how people use their eyes in interactions, what does it tell us about them as people?

In general, people who are talking spend less time looking at the listener, than the listener spends looking at the talker. The latter spends about 75 per cent of the time looking compared with about 40 per cent for the talker. Mutual gaze (simultaneous look-ing) will form only a small proportion of this time, and when it occurs this rarely lasts more than a second or so. These figures are based on the discussion of a neutral topic; gaze patterns change with more emotive topics, and with the status of individuals.

Topics which give rise to embarrassment, guilt or sorrow have the effect of reducing gaze, whereas in situations requiring co-operation, gaze appears to increase. Longer gazes indicate liking and trust in the person giving them, but they may also be used by those trying to simulate these feelings (see section on *Telling lies*).

One of the key aspects of an individual revealed through gaze is dominance: the power the person feels they have in a particu-lar context. A person who feels dominant uses less gaze, but someone who is trying to establish dominance is likely to use more gaze; people who feel themselves to be subordinate to those with whom they are interacting are likely to use more gaze in the interaction. It appears that the need to monitor the person is greater for the subordinate – the higher the status of an indi-vidual the less need they may feel to observe the behaviour of subordinates.

Psychologists measure gaze in the 'visual dominance ratio' (how much a person looks when speaking relative to how much they look at the other when listening). Less dominant people show much more looking than do more dominant people, who tend to show similar amounts in both situations. Nancy Henley points out that gaze behaviour differs noticeably in women and men. Women tend to display behaviour that is like that of the subordinate, and men show dominance in their use of gaze. She argues that:

nonverbal behaviour is a major avenue of social control on a large scale, and interpersonal dominance on a smaller scale.

It is clear that to the trained eye, or to the astute observer, our body language can reveal much about the way in which we see ourselves. Thus the need to understand the topic fully and to be aware of how we use our bodies in this way can be useful for us all (see the section on social skills training on p.40).

HAIR

We can express a great deal about ourselves with our hair because it is a part of our bodies over which we can have a high degree of control. Or most of us can – those who are bald cannot be creative to the same extent as those with hair, and if one looks at the research in the psychological literature on hair it is clear from the large number of studies that baldness causes a considerable amount of concern, anxiety and depression.

Hair colour has come to be associated with particular types of person and research supports this view. Susan Weir and Margaret Fine-Davies found evidence that we do apparently perceive blondes as less intelligent, hence the 'dumb blonde' stereotype, and see redheads as more temperamental and 'fiery'. However, other researchers found a more positive view of blondes than of redheads. In females, they were viewed as beautiful, pleasant and feminine, and in males as strong, active, pleasant, successful and good-looking. Redheaded women were seen as competent and professional but unattractive, whilst redheaded men came out very negatively. However, redheads should not be too downhearted, as research on responses to lonely hearts advertisements (by both males and females) found that redheads received more responses to their advertisements than blondes or brunettes did.

Hair *style* is so varied and also so greatly subject to fashion that we have not space to include it here, but it is obvious that what we choose to do, or not to do, with our hair can, as with clothes, convey a wide range of messages about the type of person we wish to project ourselves as.

GESTURE AND POSTURE

Our face is not the only part of the body to reveal emotions, other parts of the body also signal our emotions and attitudes. The term *emotional leakage* has been used to describe these signals which are found in the body below head level; as this term implies, emotions not revealed in the face may leak out elsewhere. Those in public life often have large lecterns or desks in front of them as much for protection and security as for their notes, since these barriers also conceal any 'leaked' signs of their public speaking nerves.

Showing your feelings

A number of gestures and postures have been found to accompany particular emotional states and these are summarized in *Table 1.2(a)*.

Maurice Krout, from the Chicago Psychological Institute, studied the meaning of signals which he felt were not intended as communication but were used *instead* of language, either when the person was prevented from speaking or when alone. He contrived experimentally to arouse strong emotions in his participants by putting them in rather awkward, uncomfortable or controversial situations. For example, in one of 15 contrived situations, Krout led each of his participants to believe that he or she was to receive a prize for an excellent performance, only then to discover 'accidentally' that through an error no prize was forthcoming. The person was at this point prevented from saying anything until given a signal to do so. This signal was given only after the participants's body language, including gestures of all kinds, had been noted. The results of this and many other studies of posture and gesture have shown the frequent occurrence of the following signals (see *Table 1.2(b)*).

In general, touching of the head or face by the hand indicates negative feelings about oneself and these signs are so common

Table 1.2: (a) Postures, gestures and their meaning

	Motivation	Posture or gesture
☐	FLIGHT	shoulder forward (one or both)
		chin in and hunch
		crouch (head to knees in seated person)
		rocking of head or body
		immobility
☐	AGGRESSION	'beating' postures
		fist clench
		hand to neck expand chest
☐	AMBIVALENCE	fumble
		head groom/scratch
		finger sucking

(b) Some common forms of emotional leakage

Posture or gesture	Motivation
Rubbing/stroking	self assurance
Rubbing arm of chair (when sitting)	emotional, restless
Making a fist	aggression
Foot flex and extend	aggressive/defensive
Hand to nose	fear
Fingers to lips	shame
Hand covering eyes	shame
Face picking/scratching	self blame or attack

that police and customs officers watch for them when questioning people. It should be noted however that feeling negative about oneself is not equivalent to having actually done something wrong or illegal. Indeed, there is some evidence that the more honest you are, the more uncomfortable you feel when under suspicion.

The orientation of our bodies toward those with whom we associate can reveal our attitudes and feelings towards them. If we like a person, we orient our bodies towards them for most of the time. We lean forward, stand closer, look more, touch more and show a relaxed posture. Mixed feelings about a person are revealed in ambivalent postures: for example, when sitting we might have our knees pointing away, whilst our trunk is oriented towards that person; tightly folded arms or high, tight leg crossing might reveal a withdrawal or protection of ourselves from the other. Postures of course change from moment to moment, so a snapshot glance will not necessarily reveal anything significant. It is the postures which we adopt *most* of the time which are important and revealing. Another sign of friendship is *posture mimicry* – the adoption, perhaps without realizing it, of a posture shown by someone we like or love (see *Figure 1.8*).

The close similarity that is frequently commented on in long and happily married couples, or between long-term friends, may well stem from posture mimicry because the long use of similar expressions, gestures and postures ultimately shapes or leaves marks on our bodies.

SMELLS AS PART OF THE BODY LANGUAGE

'What does she look like?'
'Is he attractive?'

When we describe a person we are most likely to describe their looks – few of us would give details of another person's smell, except, according to Edward Hall, those in Arab countries. In the West, comments on body smells cause embarrassment whereas the Arab appears to be comfortable with the variety of natural body smells and would not feel ill at ease commenting on a friend's bad breath or agreeable body odour. Indeed, in describing one person to another, body odour may be included just as they would remark on their looks.

As mammals, we might expect odours to have importance as signals because they seem to be so important in other mammals. Dogs are well known for their ability to distinguish individual humans by scent (except identical twins), but it is perhaps less well known that humans are quite good at making such distinctions too. Human babies show preferential responses to the smell of their own mother's milk compared to that of a strange mother within a few days after birth, and similarly mothers, fathers, aunts and grandmothers have been shown to be able to identify their 'family' baby by the odour of its vest when compared with an identical vest worn by another baby of the same age. These peoples' experiences of the baby ranged from as little as 0–8 hours. In some studies accuracy rates have been found to be over 90 per cent. This research has led to the idea that we have

Figure 1.8: Examples of posture mimicry. (*From Zefa Picture Library (UK) Ltd.*)

an 'olfactory signature' that has our own unique olfactory characteristics.

Another intriguing aspect of body odour is its capacity to have profound effects on the physiology of another's body. The synchrony of girls' and women's menstrual cycles can be achieved via such odours. Michael Russell showed that a human female exposed regularly for several months to the odour of a small amount of underarm secretion from another female (placed on the former's upper lip) will show synchrony of her menstrual cycle with that of the donor's cycle, even though the females have never met. Other research has shown that male odour applied in the same way to women having cycles that are longer or shorter than average developed cycles closer to the average length, relative to those in a control group. Of course most women are exposed to a daily bouquet of male and female body odours but the effects between females have been noted in girls and women living in close proximity, such as boarding schools or college dormitories.

Breath and face odour

Feeling another's breath on one's face is the stuff of romantic novels but is generally not something many of us allow to happen in day-to-day interactions. We avoid breath contact and view it as too close for comfort. Even social kissing in the West involves no mouth-to-mouth contact. However, Arabs do not avoid such contact. Just as they appear to enjoy body smells, they feel that withholding one's breath in conversation is being evasive or ashamed. Breath contact is as important to them as eye contact is to British people. Another culture that enjoys odour is the Eskimo culture. Rubbing noses is not just about physical contact – smelling the face of the one you greet is also an important part of this greeting.

Breath smells are also a source of information about diet. Eating spicy food, milk and milk products, garlic, onions and many other foods leave their signs on our breath. Dietary practices leave their own olfactory signatures and these may be a factor in cultural or racial prejudices. *They* smell different because their diet is unfamiliar to us.

Flatulence

It is hard to believe that breaking wind could be part of any signalling system but Günter Tembrock suggests that 'the noisy blowing of intestinal gases during defence (or flight) seems to have an acoustic signal effect . . . ' in the stallion. In humans, Louis Lippman suggests that it may be conspicuously performed with the intention of being insulting. It certainly appears to provide an endless source of amusement in the young and it was even developed into something of an art form by Le Petomane. Joseph Pujol (1857–1945), 'Le Petomane' (the Fartiste), was a Frenchman who had a most unusual talent. He discovered that he could take in, voluntarily, large quantities of water or air through his anus. He adapted this ability into a one-man show in which he could produce an extraordinary repertoire of sounds, and could even play tunes on a flute. The air flow was odourless because the air was drawn in and not generated in the gut (and thus this topic might more correctly be discussed in a section on acoustic communication). Flatulence often has two components, sound and odour, and both these aspects of body language were included in Lippman's research.

In Lippman's research study on flatulence, males and females indicated their attitudes to 'farting' in a range of situations (with or without noise/odours, in a group of acquaintances or group of strangers and so on). From this rather unlikely study the author concludes that in some respects females 'may be more tolerant of odiferous body processes', and their responses to this topic were more complex than males. However, the author suggests that the 'fart' might stand as a 'male weapon' and he argues that his study indicates that this behaviour pattern requires further study to elucidate its role in human interactions.

Perfumes as sexual attractants

In addition to natural odours from scent glands around the body – the feet, armpits, anal and genital region, chest and face – many adults add a variety of perfumes in the shape of soap, deodorant, creams, scents and so on. We wash off our natural smell and replace it with a socially acceptable one. Expensive perfumes, however, may include secretions used as sexual attractants for other mammals; the musk deer produces a substance which evidently adds potency to our perfumes. There is something rather ironic in replacing our own odours with those of other species. In nonhuman animals, certain odours have a potent effect in sexual behaviour. Odours from the male pig (boar) elicit the mating stance in females; this substance is now available in spray form and, in the absence of the boar, can induce the female pig to stand for artificial insemination. There is no known equivalent of this spray for humans. The closest we can find is cited by Iranaus Eibl-Eiberfeldt in his study of people in some Mediterranean areas. He observed villagers using odours to stimulate women in a courtship dance. A man carries a handkerchief in his armpit and during the dance removes it and waves it in front of the woman of his choice. The smelly cloth is then supposed to arouse the passions of the woman he has chosen.

Most of us would feel this use of axillary odours to be unpleasant, or even disgusting, but when we reflect that socially acceptable perfumes contain musk, then it may be that natural body smells are not really so different from the ones that we use in socially desirable perfumes.

TOUCHING

Being touched, or touching someone, can be a very potent form of social behaviour and can evoke reactions from warmth and friendship to revulsion. Perhaps because it can be so potent it is also under-researched.

. . . for some reason we have rarely touched on the way we touch. (Desmond Morris)

Being touched, or touching others, varies with our age, our sex, the context and the culture. To take the last first, some psychologists talk of 'contact' and 'non-contact' cultures and this is exemplified in a study by Marc Jourard in which the frequency of contact between couples per hour was counted in various cities worldwide. He found such contacts to be as high as 180 in San Juan, Puerto Rico, and 110 in Paris, France, to as low as 2 in Gainesville, Florida, and 0 in London, UK.

Our use of touch may in part be linked to our early experience of it. Before birth, touch is probably one of the first senses to become functional. A foetus aborted during the third month of gestation will respond reflexively to the touch of hair around its mouth. At birth, touch is a very important part of parental behaviour towards the new-born, and research shows that mothers are able to recognize babies by touch by feeling only the backs of their baby's hands. Evidently only a couple of hours experience interacting with the baby is necessary for this to occur. The extent to which touch is used by mothers varies in different cultures – Japanese babies are carried on their mother's backs and are physically closer to their mothers for longer periods than are babies in parts of the Western world where they are often wheeled around in pushchairs. In the latter situation, eye contact may be more important for mother and baby than it is in Japan, where, in adult life, eye contact is used less in social situations than it is in the West.

Ashley Montagu has suggested that tactile satisfaction is an essential element in the healthy development of children and without it they may not survive, as was found in orphaned American infants living in institutions in the earlier part of the nineteenth century. These children received virtually no touching, although their other basic physical needs were met. Young children however may show constitutional differences in their apparent need to be touched. Rudolf Schaffer identified children as 'cuddlers' or 'non-cuddlers' and his work suggested that there may be temperamental differences between children which are innate and which result in some children being disinclined to be touched. Non-cuddlers were found to be slightly less well adjusted as they got older, and slightly less competent in social situations.

Other research links personality characteristics with touching. Non-touchers, when compared with touchers, have been found to report more anxiety and tension in their lives, to be more withdrawn socially, and to have a number of other characteristics that are viewed less positively than those found in people who are 'touchers'.

In adulthood, being touched, whether or not the person is aware of it, appears to alter our perception of a situation. In America, a study was carried out at Purdue University in 1976, in which a woman at the library desk 'accidentally' touched students (male or female) when handing back their library cards. Later, they described her very differently from students who had not been 'accidentally' touched, but had otherwise been treated in the same way. The woman was described more positively – as warm, sensitive and trustful – by those who were touched (whether or not they recalled being touched) and as distant, formal and insensitive by those who had not been touched.

A number of other studies reveal the power of touching. Touching others may be useful in getting favours, getting signatures on petitions, getting bigger tips if you are a waitress, or greater compliance from your students if you are a psychology tutor.

Nancy Henley argued that touch is an indication of power. She observed that men are more likely to initiate touch with women, than women are with men, and suggested this is not merely a reflection of interest or affection. Observers viewing others who touch seem to regard the initiator of the touching as the person with the greater power if the touch is not reciprocated. Other studies indicate that the toucher is also seen as showing more assertiveness and warmth.

Touching is not always something that is done to us by others – Desmond Morris identifies a number of forms of self-touching which indicate aspects of our emotional state. Morris describes these 'self-intimacies' as comforting actions that are similar to those shown by others towards us. They include holding your own hand or arm folding, and may be used in situations where we feel anxious, depressed or lonely. Thus the language of touch is quite complex and we perceive it to indicate much about those who display it, or those that shun it.

TELLING LIES

We have seen that body language can give us away by revealing things that we may wish to conceal, but can our bodies actually convey to others that we are lying? Paul Ekman has carried out some fascinating research on this topic and he tells us that:

There are no signs of deceit itself . . . There are only clues that the person is poorly prepared and clues of emotions that don't fit the person's line.

Liars may prepare to lie, planning what they will say and how they will react, or they may be caught unprepared and lie on the spur of the moment without careful forethought. In the former case they will conceal and falsify what they *expect* others are going to watch most; in the latter they may have little opportunity to do this. Either way the key is that they have expectations about the signs that will give them away. Paul Ekman reports that everyone

thinks that liars will fidget and that restlessness is a clue to deception. Hence the liar is likely to control this aspect of his or her
behaviour. Carrying out research on lying has obvious ethical difficulties. However, one study which simulated a real-life situation
overcomes the problem to a great extent. American researchers
Paul Ekman and Wallace Friesen reasoned that nurses may sometimes find themselves in a situation where they must conceal from
their patients the true facts of their illness. They arranged for student nurses to see films of patients undergoing various treatments.
Subsequently the nurses were asked to describe what they had
seen, sometimes truthfully, and sometimes untruthfully (that is,
concealing the true seriousness of the problem), as if they were
actually telling the patient. Whilst doing this, their body language
was recorded on film so that truthful and untruthful explanations
could be compared.

When 'lying', nurses showed non-verbal give-aways. Hand-to-
face contacts increased relative to those shown in true reports
and, in lying, most hand gesticulations were reduced with the
exception of the shrug of the hand which was increased. Bodily
shifts also increased. The results showed that there were consistent differences in the use of gestures used in true and untrue
reports by the nurses. Paul Ekman points out that the student
nurses reduced their hand gesticulations when they were trying to
conceal their reactions (in line with what was said earlier about
people's expectations about signs of deception) but the hand-
shrug (an emblem, as it is called) has a direct translation into
words and means 'I'm helpless', 'I don't know', and leaked the
information that they were trying to conceal. He also notes
that this 'small rotation of the hands' may not be performed very
obviously as it might be performed in an honest encounter. He
often observed it while the student nurse's hands stayed in their
lap. He found that over half of the nursing students showed this
'emblematic' slip when they were lying, and Paul Ekman believes
that, 'The emblematic slip can be trusted as a genuine sign of a
message that the person does not want to reveal'.

Another interesting aspect of the experiment was the ability of
observers, viewing films of the nurses, to detect honesty or deceit.
Ekman found that those who saw just the face, or heard just the
words, rated the nurses as more honest when they were, in fact,
lying, but those who saw just the body did best at detecting deceit.

Thus, the nurses who had to lie were evidently able to control
their face and voice better than their bodies. Perhaps the lesson

here is to look for deception in places where one would not normally look for clues – the emotions are leaked via the body and perhaps through emblems.

People vary greatly in their ability to detect deception; many, without directions on what to look for, do no better than chance. However, with training we can learn to detect deceit, and the research of Paul Ekman and Wallace Friesen has gone some considerable way towards helping us identify the signs of deception.

APPLYING OUR KNOWLEDGE OF BODY LANGUAGE TO HELP PEOPLE

The study of non-verbal communication has led to a better understanding of how people interact socially and has helped psychologists identify what makes us more effective in dealing with others. To take an example already mentioned, the cultural differences in body language suggest that just as we need to learn a foreign language, we probably need to learn some of the uses of body language in other cultures to interact effectively.

Social skills training has become a very important application of our knowledge in this area and had its roots in assisting psychiatric patients to cope better. Edward Zigler and Leslie Phillips were part of a team which was able to show a clear link between recovery from schizophrenia and 'social competence' prior to the disorder. Their aim was to increase social competence as part of the process of rehabilitation of the schizophrenic.

Similarly, the clinician Joseph Wolpe wanted to assist excessively anxious and passive individuals to acquire skills that would enable them to stand up for themselves in situations where they would normally 'give in' to others. Using methods such as role-play, the anxious person enacts a situation which causes them difficulty and a therapist offers comments and advice. Gradually the anxiety caused by the difficult situation reduces as the patient recognizes that her or his ability to speak up works well in the role-play situation.

Michael Argyle and colleagues have become internationally known for their work on this topic and argue that social behaviour is acquired in the same way as any other behaviour: we have to learn it in the same way as we learn the skills of word processing, driving or swimming.

If you have never tried a role-play exercise, it is often hard to believe how effective the technique can be. Try *Exercise 1.2* (p.46) and you may begin to notice its uses yourself.

Social skills training (SST)

Courses on social skills training (SST) have become widely used. Although this field has its roots in clinical psychology, it has been widely used now in training for almost everyone from professional groups such as teachers, nurses, doctors, lawyers, police officers, customs officers and so on as well as the woman and man in the street. Courses on this topic can generally be found at Adult Education Centres. The technique has also been used to help children and adolescents with psychological disorders or just everyday problems.

The methods used in SST are those which would be used by an instructor teaching any new skill, and include modelling, practice and feedback. *Modelling* is the demonstration of the correct behaviour, for instance good eye contact, by someone proficient in the particular skill. The people being trained are able to observe the model and then practise the skills for themselves. The practice is carried out using role-play during training sessions, with additional 'homework' tasks between sessions. As the trainee practises the individual skill, or some more complex situation, such as starting a conversation, the trainer is able to give *feedback* on performance and then the trainee repeats the task as appropriate.

It is, of course, important that the newly learned skills transfer, or *generalize*, to real life. A way of encouraging generalization is to include as many 'real life' people as possible, such as parents or friends, in the actual training.

This application of psychology is probably one of the areas that most directly benefits all people. The techniques are surprisingly simple and easy to learn and for those who join Assertion Training or Social Skills Training courses they can be immense fun and provide enormous benefits.

Answers to *Figures 1.3* and *1.4*

Figure 1.3 (1) happiness (2) surprise (3) fear (4) sadness (5) anger
(p.18) (6) disgust (7) interest. (From Argyle, 1975.)

Figure 1.4
(p.20)
They are staff at the Fokker Space Company in the Netherlands looking at a television monitor as the unmanned Ariana 5 explodes 66 seconds after take-off from its launch pad. It seems likely that they are feeling surprise and shock.

References

Argyle, M. (1975). *Bodily Communication*. London: Methuen. [Body language figures taken from here.]

Argyle, M. (1990). *Bodily Communication, 2nd edn*. London: Routledge. [A detailed study of body language.]

Argyle, M. and Kendon, A. (1967). The experimental analysis of social performance. In L. Berkowitz (Ed.), *Advances in Experimental Social Psychology*, *3*, 55–98. [The study of performance in social situations.]

Bakan, P. (1971). The eyes have it. *Psychology Today*, *4*, 64–7, 96. [Eye movement and brain activity.]

Balogh, R.D. and Porter, R.H. (1986) Olfactory preferences resulting from mere exposure in human neonates. *Infant Behaviour and Development*, *9(4)*, 395–401. [Recognition of babies by odour.]

Cutler, W.B., Preti, G., Krieger, A., Higgins, G.R. Garcia, C.R. and Lawley, H.J. (1986). Human axillary secretions influence women's menstrual cycles: The role of donor extract from men. *Hormones and Behaviour*, *20*, 463–73. [Male secretions and the menstrual cycle.]

Davis, F. (1971). *Inside Intuition*. New York: McGraw Hill. [Olfactory characteristics of twins.]

Dunlap, K. (1927) The role of eye-muscles and mouth muscles in the expression of the emotions. *Genetic Psychology Monographs*, *2*, 199–233. [The generation of spontaneous or natural facial expressions.]

Eibl-Eibesfeldt, I. (1970). *Ethology: The Biology of Behaviour*. New York: Holt, Rinehart and Winston. [Facial expressions of deaf–blind children; odours and Mediterranean people.]

Ekman, P. (1992). *Telling Lies: Clues to Deceit in the Market Place, Politics and Marriage*. London: W.W. Norton & Co. [All about lies, quotation on page 80.]

Ekman, P. and Friesen, W.V. (1969). The repetoire of nonverbal behaviour: Catergories, origins, usage and coding. *Semiotica*, *1*, 49–98. (Four types of display rules for facial expressions.)

Ekman. P. and Friesen, W.V. (1974). Detecting deception from the body or face. *Journal of Personality and Social Psychology*, *29*, 288–294. [Experiment on deception.]

Ekman. P. and Friesen, W.V. (1975). *Unmasking the Face*. Englewood Cliffs, N.J.: Prentice Hall. [Facial expressions.]

Fisher, J.D., Rytting, M., and Heslin, R. (1976). Hands touching hands: Affective and evaluative effects of an interpersonal touch. *Sociometry*, *39*, 416–421. [Purdue University study.]

Fridlund, A.J. (1994). *Human Facial Expression: An evolutionary perspective*. San Diego: Academic Press. [Emotions expressed in the face.]

Hall, E.T. (1969). *The Hidden Dimension*. New York: Anchor Books. [Body language in Arabs, Japanese and Americans.]

Henley, N.M. (1977). *Body Politics: Power, sex and nonverbal communication.* Eaglewood Cliffs, N.J: Prentice Hall. [Gaze behaviour quotation on page 179.]

Hess, E.H. (1965). Attitudes and pupil size. *Scientific American, 212,* 46–54. [Pupil size.]

Jourard, S.M. (1966) An exploratory study of body accessibility. *British Journal of Social and Clinical Psychology, 26,* 235–242. [Contact between couples.]

Kaitz, M., Lapidot, P., Bronner, R., and Eidelman, A. (1992). Parturient women can recognize their infants by touch. *Developmental Psychology, 28,* 35–39. [Recognition by touch of an infant's hands.]

Kendon, A. (1967). Some functions of gaze-direction in social interaction. *Acta Psychologica, 26,* 22–63. [Four functions of gaze behaviour.]

Knapp, M.L. (1992). *Non-verbal Communication in Human Interaction.* New York: Harcourt Brace Jovanovich College Publishers. [Relevant to many topics and includes Morris and Montagu references to touch and foetal responses to touch.]

Krout, M.H. (1954). An experimental attempt to determine the significance of unconscious manual symbolic movements. *Journal of General Psychology, 51,* 121–152 [A study of blocked emotions.]

Lippman, L.G. (1980). Toward a social psychology of flatulence: The interpersonal regulation of natural gas. *Psychology: A Quarterly Journal of Human Behaviour, 17,* 41–50. [Flatulence.]

Lynn, M. and Shurgot B.A. (1984). Responses to lonely hearts advertisements: Effects of reported physical attractiveness, physique and coloration. *Personality and Social Psychology Bulletin, 10(3),* 349–357. [Hair colour research.]

Macfarlane, A. (1975). Olfaction in the development of social preferences in the human neonate. In *Parent–Infant Interaction Ciba Foundation Symposium, 33.* New York: Elsevier [Studies of smell recognition.]

Montagu, A. (1978), *Touching: The human significance of the skin.* New York: Columbia University Press. [Studies of the importance of touch.]

Morris, D. (1977). *Manwatching: A field guide to human behaviour.* London: Jonathan Cape. [Many aspects of body language; eyes, gestures and touching.]

Russell, M.J., Switz, G.M. and Thompson, K. (1980). Olfactory influence on the human menstrual cycle. *Pharmacology, Biochemistry & Behaviour, 13,* 737–738. [Odours and the human menstrual cycle.]

Schaffer, R. (1977). *Mothering.* London: Fontana. [Cuddlers and non-cuddlers.]

Secord, P.F., Dukes, W.F., and Bevan, W. (1959). Personalities in faces, I: An experiment in social perceiving. *Genetic Psychology Monographs, 49,* 231–279. [Face and personality types.]

Spinrad, P. (1994). *The RE/Search Guide to Bodily Fluids.* New York: Juno Books, LLC. [Le Petomane.]

Tembrock, G. (1968). Communication in land mammals. In T.A. Seboek, (Ed.), *Animal Communication: Techniques of study and results of research.* Bloomington: Indiana University Press. [Quotation on stallions on page 380.]

Trower, P., Bryant, B. and Argyle, M. (1978). *Social Skills and Mental Health.* London: Methuen. [Gives an introduction to theory and practice in social skills.]

Weir, S. And Fine-Davis, M. (1989). 'Dumb blonde' and 'temperamental redhead': the effect of hair colour on some attributed personality characteristics of women. *Irish Journal of Psychology, 10(1),* 11–19. [Hair colour in personal advertisements.]

Wolpe, J. (1958). *Psychotherapy by Reciprocal Inhibition*. Stanford, California: Stanford University Press. [The beginnings of assertion training.]

Zigler, E. and Phillips, L. (1961). Social competence and outcome in psychiatric disorder. *Journal of Abnormal and Social Psychology, 63,* 264–271. [Schizophrenia and social competence.]

Recommended Reading

Argyle, M. (1990). *Bodily Communications*. London: Routledge.

Hollin, C.R. and Trower, P. (Eds)(1986). *Handbook of Social Skills Training, Volume 2: Clinical Applications and New Directions*. Oxford: Pergamon Books.

Knapp, M.L. (1992). *Non-verbal Communication in Human Interaction*. New York: Harcourt Brace Jovanovich College Publishers.

LATERAL EYE MOVEMENTS AND PERSONALITY

This experiment examines Paul Bakan and Floyd Strayer's research on lateral eye movements, thinking and personality. These researchers believe that there is evidence that people, and in particular men, are consistent in the direction in which they move their eyes when asked questions by a person facing them. On average, 75 per cent of eye movements of an individual are to either the right or left. To do this exercise you will need to find a number of right-handed male volunteers – be sure *not* to tell them that you are studying lateral eye movements. Just say you want them to think about some proverbs and answer a few questions. You will want to do this exercise one person at a time, and make sure you read all the instructions through first.

INSTRUCTIONS: Ask your participant to sit at a table facing you. There should be no one else present to distract them. Tell him that he will be presented with a series of proverbs to think about and interpret in his own words. You, the interviewer, must tell the participant that he cannot give his interpretation of the proverb until you give the signal 'Now'. To start, establish eye contact with the participant, state the proverb and then *note the direction of the first lateral eye movement* as the participant begins to reflect on his interpretation of the proverb. Then say 'Now' and let him give his response. After each proverb, say 'That's fine', or 'Good' (do not discuss what is said), and go on to the next proverb. The twelve proverbs are as follow.

PROVERBS
1. A rolling stone gathers no moss.
2. The hardest work is to go idle.
3. In the mirror, everyone sees his best friend.
4. A watched pot never boils.
5. Better a good enemy than a bad friend.
6. If you can't bite, don't show your teeth.
7. A poor worker blames his tools.

continued

continued ---

LATERAL EYE MOVEMENTS AND PERSONALITY

8. He that lies on the ground cannot fall.
9. Better a bad peace than a good war.
10. What saddens a wise man saddens a fool.
11. They that are mute want to talk most.
12. Words should be weighed and not counted.

FINDINGS

On completion of the exercise you will have 12 scores of left or right. Make sure you recorded responses to your subjects' left or right (and not yours). It may be useful to write on your score paper 'Left' on your right and 'Right' on your left to remind you. Was there a consistent pattern of around 9/12 or more responses in one direction? If so, the qualities of each participant may correspond with those set out in the chapter section entitled *Gaze and mutual gaze*.

If you find a consistent pattern in males, why not go on to try this exercise with female volunteers. Bakan and Strayer found that they were less likely to show a consistent lateral eye movement pattern. What do you find?

ASSERTIVENESS – 'REFLECTING BACK'

Recall an incident in which you were faced with an emotional outburst from someone – perhaps an argument, or a situation in which someone was angry or upset with you, or was putting pressure on you. The first step is to analyse what happened. Consider both *what* was said and *how* it was said to you.

ANALYSING THE SITUATION
1. Identify the EMOTIONS of the other person. (What did their body language reveal?)
2. Note the FACTS being stated. (What did they actually say?)
3. Identify the NEEDS of the other person. (Note: facts and needs may be different; needs may not be expressed directly – consider their body language.)
4. What response did you make, and what response would you like to have made?

ASSERTIVE HANDLING OF THE SITUATION
Let us take as an example, a situation where someone has angrily demanded that you do 'X', which you think is unreasonable. First, analyse the situation, going through points 1 to 3 listed above. Role play this situation with a friend, with your friend taking the role of the other person. You should try to respond with planned assertive answers by first 'reflecting back' your reading of what has happened:

1. 'I can see that you are angry . . . ' (Emotion)
2. 'Because I will not do X on my day off . . . ' (Fact)
3. 'And you cannot get anyone else to do it' (Need)

By making responses 1–3 you have clarified the situation, gained time in planning your final response, and, by recognizing the other person's emotion, defused it somewhat. You are now ready to give your reply:

4. ' . . . but I am not prepared to do X.'
   [Don't make *any* excuses here, or you give the other person room to negotiate.]

continued

continued --

ASSERTIVENESS – 'REFLECTING BACK'

WHY IT WORKS

By sorting out the emotions first you can often defuse the situation. For example, you may find that the other person gives a reason for his or her emotion (for example, the train was late this morning). This often calms the situation down, and takes the pressure off you. Role play other examples from your own experience with a friend and try to sort out the three important elements – EMOTIONS, FACTS and NEEDS. Then act out the situation as shown in the example. Did your response sound reasonable to your friend? Many people are surprised to find that the responses outlined do not sound impertinent; indeed, they often sound firm and fair, whereas making poor excuses simply makes the other person more angry at your refusal.

2. *Your Personality*

YOUR PERSONALITY

Many of us first take an interest in psychology because we have become intrigued by some characteristic or behaviour of our own or of another person and become curious to know more about it. A colleague at work, for instance, may often act in an aggressive way, whilst another is quiet and withdrawn, and a third is sociable, friendly and outgoing.

Curiosity is increased when two people differ markedly despite the fact that they have been exposed to apparently similar circumstances. Brian and Danny have both been exposed to the stress and turmoil of suddenly being made redundant. Their financial, domestic and general life circumstances are much the same and yet they react in different ways. Brian becomes increasingly anxious, dejected and apathetic while Danny recovers quickly from his initial disappointment and remains undaunted by the blow, maintaining a steadfast, if unrealistic, cheerfulness. In trying to understand these differences between people we are concerned with the study of *personality*.

EVERYONE HAS PERSONALITY

Beyond the assertion that personality concerns individual differences it is very difficult to give a more detailed definition of personality with which psychologists of different persuasions will agree. In general, psychologists see personality as concerned with the stable, consistent *internal* aspects of the person's functioning. It must also be borne in mind that the man or woman in the street may use the term 'personality' in a different way. They might, for example, refer to someone as having 'lots of personality' or 'not much personality'. Personality, here, refers to the possession of attractive or salient social qualities. For the psychologist, everyone has a personality and the person of low social attractiveness is of as much interest, as much in need of explanation, as the opposite type.

IT DEPENDS ON YOUR POINT OF VIEW

Personality is one of the most perplexing fields of study to the reader new to psychology. This perplexity may be shared by students and psychologists themselves. One of the authors of this book who has taught psychology to medical students understands well why personality theories cause problems. Medical training involves the learning of many (apparent) *facts*. Medical students starting to learn about the psychology of personality are alarmed to discover that what appear to be simple human behaviours can be viewed in radically different ways, depending on the theoretical orientation of the person studying the behaviour. For example, in discussing 'difficult', uncontrollable behaviour in a child (such as refusal to comply with parents' requests, tantrums, aggression), they would be startled to find that the typical psychology textbook might give four or five different explanations. One might emphasize the child's general temperament and its biological foundations; another might suggest that difficult behaviour is learned or conditioned because the parents rewarded (reinforced) the child's problem behaviour by giving in to his or her wishes;

yet another that the unacceptable behaviour is merely a symptom of underlying unconscious conflict stemming from relationships in infancy ... and more.

Not only is there a multiplicity of explanatory theories, but they suggest radically different ways in which the child and family should be assessed and treated, ranging from treating the child with drugs to behaviour modification and family therapy. A common reaction to this quandary is to ask 'Which theory is correct?', but this proves to be a question without a clear-cut answer. In this chapter we sketch a few contemporary approaches to personality and personality problems and consider some of their strengths and limitations.

THE TRAIT APPROACH

We are all trait theorists to some degree. In describing the 'nature' or behaviour of a person we like, we might say they are 'friendly', 'interested in people', 'intelligent', or 'perceptive'; and conversely, the villains in our lives are 'distant', 'uninterested in people', 'stupid' and 'unperceptive'. Individuals may be idiosyncratic in terms of the relative importance of particular traits in their judgements of themselves and others, as we shall see when we discuss *Personal Construct Theory*, but we all have a vast number of terms available to us to describe the attributes and dispositions of people. It has been estimated that there are 18,000 or more 'trait' descriptions of this sort in the dictionary.

Naming is not the same as explaining

A trait description is no more than a summary of some consistencies in the behaviour of the person we are judging but it is easy for people to believe that, in attributing a trait to someone, we have somehow *explained* their behaviour. Thus they act in an unfriendly way because they are unfriendly people. The evidence for their being unfriendly is that they act in an unfriendly way! This is, of course, entirely circular. It is important to bear in mind, therefore, that traits are no more than summary descriptions of people.

It's all a matter of degree

There have been many studies of single traits in psychology. The most common approach is to view a trait as a *dimension* in terms of which people vary. Thus, on a dimension of 'dominance', there will be individuals who obtain extremely high scores, others who obtain very low scores because of their submissive behaviour, with the majority of the population near the middle of the range.

Most trait researchers attempt to create reliable, objective tests of the particular dimension they are interested in and then use such tests to discover how other aspects of behaviour can be predicted from test scores. For example, the researcher might speculate that 'dominance' is an important requirement for being an effective leader, and go on to compare successful and unsuccessful leaders on a measure of dominance to see if this particular prediction is upheld. A vast number of single trait tests of this sort now exist and are widely used in work, educational and medical settings.

Just how many traits are required to account for differences between people is a matter of some debate. Some of the best known and most influential personality theorists have brought a particular statistical technique, factor analysis, to bear on this question. Perhaps the most famous and enthusiastic exponent of the factor analytic approach has been the British psychologist, Hans Eysenck (1916–).

EYSENCK'S THEORY:
THREE CRITICAL DIMENSIONS

Factor analysis is a mathematical method for investigating the degree of association ('correlation') between different behaviours or between different traits. It reduces the complex patterns of association found to a small number of underlying clusters or 'factors'. It is a way, then, of revealing the underlying structure; a structure not likely to be easily visible to anyone who simply scans the scores of a large number of people on a whole range of tests or observations.

Eysenck has used and advocated the factor analytic method for more than 40 years, studying very diverse groups of people and using a wide range of measures – scores from questionnaires, ratings of the person by others, scores on psychological tests or even biographical information (for example, whether or not the person ever received psychiatric treatment). He claims that throughout this work three underlying factors have been revealed with considerable consistency. The two long-standing factors he has described are *Extraversion–Introversion* and *Neuroticism–Stability*. To these he added a third in the 1970s, the dimension of *Psychoticism–Impulse control*. Eysenck calls these 'types', each type being composed of a cluster of traits which together define the type.

Extraversion–Introversion The associated traits which make up Extraversion include sociability, liveliness, activity, assertiveness, the tendency to be sensation-seeking, carefreeness and dominance. The implication is that individuals high on any one of these traits will tend to be high on the others.

Neuroticism–Stability Neuroticism, on the other hand, comprises traits of anxiety-proneness, depression-proneness, guilt feelings, low self-esteem, tension, moodiness and emotionality.

Psychoticism–Impulse Control Psychoticism, in turn, includes aggressiveness, coldness, lack of empathy and a divergent kind of creativity.

The distribution of each of Eysenck's types in the population is a 'normal' one, meaning that both extremes of each dimension are relatively rare, with most people scoring near the mid-point of the continuum, showing, for example, a balance of introverted and extraverted tendencies.

FROM DESCRIPTION TO EXPLANATION

What distinguishes Eysenck from a number of other trait and factor analysis researchers is his attempt to move beyond descriptions of how traits and behaviours cluster together (the *taxonomy* of behaviour) to the *dynamics* of behaviour: the attempt to explain *why* humans differ on these three dimensions. The specifics of his explanatory theory have changed over the years as it has been reformulated to accommodate new findings. We shall look here, however, at some of the more enduring aspects of the theory, concentrating particularly on the Extraversion–Introversion dimension.

It's mainly in the genes

Eysenck sees individual differences as firmly rooted in biology. For him, the cause of extraverted patterns of behaviour is firmly located within differences in the nervous system, and the type of nervous system a person has is genetically determined. This is not to say that Eysenck rules out environmental factors. Social factors also contribute to whether a person is extraverted or introverted in behaviour, but Eysenck clearly sees himself as a crusader against over-enthusiastic environmentalists who have entirely ruled out biological predispositions.

The extravert is inhibited?

The Extraversion–Introversion dimension is identified with differences in the level of *arousal* in the cerebral cortex. The level of arousal is, in turn, a product of the activity of a *cortico-reticular loop*, involving a part of the mid-brain called the *ascending reticular activation system*, one of whose functions is to alert and activate the parts of the brain responsible for 'higher' psychological functions. In simple terms, the introvert's cortex is more aroused, and more arousable, than the cortex of the extravert, which is more prone to 'inhibition'. The cortex is responsible for many of the higher level 'control' functions of the brain and thus, paradoxically, a high level of arousal in this structure is associated with controlled, rather than excited, behaviour. Similarly, alcohol, which generally has an inhibiting effect on brain functions, will reduce arousal in the cortex and produce less controlled, more extraverted, social behaviour.

From explanation to practical prediction

Eysenck suggests that these individual differences in arousal affect a range of basic psychological processes which produce the extraverted or introverted pattern of behaviour that we actually observe, and he made predictions about how extraverts and introverts would differ on a wide range of tasks. Attempts to verify or refute these predictions have generated an enormous number of studies and experiments over many years. Hans and his son, Michael Eysenck, have attempted to draw conclusions from such work and to defend the theory against the criticisms that have been made of it.

Amongst the predictions of the theory are that extraverts (Es) and Introverts (Is) will differ in their 'vigilance'. 'Vigilance' refers to a state of readiness to detect and respond to small or infrequent changes occurring in the environment, as in scanning a radar screen to detect a 'blip'. The Eysencks predict poor vigilance in extraverts because, in everyday language, they have poor concentration and become easily bored.

Another important prediction was that Es and Is differ in their *conditionability*, Is being more easily conditioned and hence more likely to be socially conforming. In his early work, Hans Eysenck made this idea the basis of a theory of criminality and it has, therefore, attracted much attention. In general, there has been little evidence to support the idea that a general factor of conditionability exists. There may also be important differences between 'aversive' conditioning (for example, learning to associate fear with a neutral stimulus) and 'appetitive' conditioning (learning to associate gratification or pleasure with a neutral stimulus). More recently the theory has been reformulated to suggest that it is the impulsivity component of extraversion, rather than the sociability aspect, which is related to low conditionability. It remains to be seen how this prediction will fare.

Are introverts more sensitive?

One of the many interesting predictions from the theory is that Es and Is differ in the *sensory thresholds*; the introvert's aroused cortex is more alert and hence more efficient at detecting low levels of stimulation. As introverts are more aroused by stimulation so they will react more to stimuli.

It is not difficult to see how differences in sensitivity to stimulation might have consequences for medicine and related areas. One of the authors recalls having some painful dental treatment, in the middle of which the dentist asked why individuals vary in their pain sensitivity. He was able to suggest that 'Git gall gepends gone gehter gou gare gan gintrovert gor gextravert'. At least, according to Hans Eysenck's theory, if introverts are more sensitive to stimulation we would expect them to feel pain more acutely. Eysenck sees pain as part of a continuum of sensory stimulation. Both very low levels (such as sitting in the dark in a quiet house) and high levels of stimulation (for example, a crowded, noisy party) may be perceived as unpleasant, while stimulation in the intermediate range is pleasant or neutral. If introverts generally 'amplify' stimulation because of the nature of their nervous system, we would expect them to be *less* troubled by low levels of stimulation, but to be made uncomfortable by high levels of stimulation *sooner* (at a lower point on the continuum). Extraverts, conversely, will find low levels of stimulation more unpleasant but will be more tolerant of high levels of stimulation. Eysenck labels the introvert as *stimulus–aversive* and the extravert as *stimulus–hungry*. So at a noisy party we might expect the introverts to be the first to complain about the music being played too loudly, though this assumes that they would be bold enough to voice their irritation, and also that they would have attended the party in the first place! For a discussion of developments and findings for this aspect of Eysenck's theory, the reader should consult the relevant sections of Hans and Michael Eysenck's book on personality and individual differences.

Criticisms of the factor-analytic approach

The factor-analytic method has not been without its critics, some saying that the apparent objectivity of these statistical methods is illusory. There is certainly a subjective element, in that what is derived from factor analysis depends in part on the nature of the items included in the first place, and the mathematical patterns derived need to be labelled and interpreted by the researcher. Moreover, a number of different factor analytic methods exist, making it possible to derive quite different factors from the same test results.

CATTELL'S 16 DIMENSIONS

One check, therefore, on the validity of any assertion that core personality dimensions have been isolated (as claimed by Hans Eysenck) is to compare the findings with those of other researchers using different methods. One researcher, Raymond Cattell, concluded that there are 16 major personality factors, rather than Eysenck's three. Closer inspection of Cattell's work, however, reveals many similarities with Eysenck's conclusions. Cattell was not concerned to establish *independent* factors and his 16 dimensions are correlated with each other. If an attempt is made to derive 'second order', or more general, factors from Cattell's work, the two major factors produced are strikingly similar to Eysenck's Extraversion–Introversion and Neuroticism–Stability. There does indeed seem to be an emerging consistency of findings.

THE BIG 5

There have been many subsequent re-analyses of Cattell's data which have suggested that the correlations can be reduced to five underlying factors. In recent years, a degree of consensus has emerged that these five factors recur again and again: *extraversion, warmth, conscientiousness, stability* and *openness*. Some of the typical characteristics making up the 'Big 5' are shown in *Table 2.1*.

Again, it can be seen that a substantial degree of overlap exists with Eysenck's dimensions.

It would appear that some progress has been made in mapping the broad temperamental dimensions on which individuals vary.

Table 2.1: THE BIG 5: Examples of traits

---

(1) EXTRAVERSION	*High:*	talkative, assertive, outgoing
	Low:	quiet, retiring, withdrawn
(2) WARMTH	*High:*	kind, affectionate, warm
	Low:	cruel, cold, unfriendly
(3) CONSCIENTIOUSNESS	*High:*	organized, efficient, reliable
	Low:	disorderly, careless, irresponsible
(4) STABILITY	*High:*	calm, unemotional, stable
	Low:	tense, emotional, anxious
(5) OPENNESS	*High:*	wide interests, imaginative, original
	Low:	narrow interests, restricted views, conventional

Few would claim that knowledge of a person's position on two or three dimensions would tell the complete story about their personality. But controversial though Eysenck's theory may be, few theories can have generated so many testable hypotheses across so many areas of psychological enquiry.

'AM I ME OR AM I THE SITUATION?': THE PROBLEM OF CONSISTENCY

The American psychologist, Lawrence Pervin, has encapsulated in this question a debate which has rumbled on for well over 20 years amongst personality researchers. What is at issue is easily demonstrated. Ask a person who knows you well to name one of your most undesirable personality traits.

One of the authors of this book was bold enough to try this experiment and was told that he was 'obsessively tidy' by a colleague who had clearly found this characteristic to be rather tiresome. The immediate response to this label was to become aware of how unfair and over-generalized it was. Admittedly he kept his office very tidy and was fussy about clearing his desk before leaving, but, on the other hand, his wife complained he was appallingly messy when working in the kitchen and his daughter had opined that he was the scruffiest dad in the playground on the days when he picked her up from school. Anyway, his pattern of tidiness in the office had not been present in his previous job. Was this because the amount of paper work in his current job meant that he had to be tidy to prevent being overwhelmed?

It all depends?

How can we maintain the notion of a trait of tidiness, with the implications of consistency over time and across situation, in the light of such apparent inconsistencies? Does the concept of a fixed personality not collapse and need to be replaced by the notion that particular responses have been learned to particular situations?

These questions and a range of related ones were raised by Walter Mischel in 1968 in a book which burst like a bombshell at the heart of personality theory; until that time it had emphasized the importance of the stable characteristics of individuals. Mischel produced evidence which, he suggested, demonstrated that intellectual skills apart, traits and dispositions showed little evidence of stability over time or across situations. Where consistency was present, he argued, it was because of similarities in the situation. According to Mischel, although the attribution of trait characteristics such as 'sociability', 'aggression', 'shyness' appears to be a useful way of organizing our perceptions of other people, traits do not reflect the actual patterning of behaviour in the real world. Perceived consistency may be simply a matter of the 'halo' or stereotyping effect, whereby the perception of a characteristic in one setting leads one to expect and perceive it in other settings.

Mischel's criticisms had some major implications for the assessment of personality. The vast majority of personality tests assume consistency of personality, and at the time Mischel's book appeared, personality testing was a major industry in the United States. Established tests such at the *Thematic Apperception Test* (TAT), the *Cattell Sixteen Personality Factor Inventory* (16PF) and the *California Psychological Inventory* (CPI) all assume consistency. If Mischel was correct, it would be expected that any test of a trait or disposition would be poor at predicting actual behaviour in a specific real-life setting. To return to the earlier example, our author's score on a test of 'obsessive tidiness' would not be very useful in predicting how neat and clipped he kept the edge of his garden lawn. Mischel found that correlations between trait scores and actual behaviour were indeed very low. Given that the whole purpose of personality testing is often to make *specific* predictions (for example, using personality tests to predict who will not be a good salesperson, who will or will not be readmitted after discharge from a psychiatric hospital), Mischel's conclusions were of considerable practical importance.

Mischel's critique was particularly influential because it also suggested an alternative approach to personality and its assessment. This was to focus on external factors, the environmental situation itself, as a cause of behaviour. Such a focus was consistent with the behavioural, or 'social learning', approach to problems which was becoming well-established in clinical and other areas of applied psychology in the 1960s and 1970s. From this viewpoint, the best predictions about a person's future behaviour in a particular situation can be made by assessing how he or she has behaved in similar situations in the past.

Assessing the person or the situation

It is not difficult to see how 'situationism' of this sort suggests very different techniques for assessing a person's suitability for a job, for instance, or for assessing the problems of a patient on discharge from a psychiatric hospital. The situationist would try to define the specific tasks the person might meet in the job, or in living outside the hospital, and then assess how the person would behave or has behaved in situations of this sort. It might even be desirable to devise a similar situation for the person to respond to at interview. The traditional trait approach to assessment would be to assess dispositions of a very general sort through personality tests or interview assessment. As we shall see, there is something to be said for combining both person and situation factors in assessment.

As might be expected, Mischel's book stimulated some forceful and cogent defences of trait theory and attacks on the new situationism. The counter-attack has been of two kinds: first,criticisms of the kinds of methodology used in the studies quoted by Mischel, and, second, theoretical criticisms. Kenneth Bowers and Jack Block in the United States are amongst those who have written in defence of the trait approach. Bowers has concentrated on some of the logical inconsistencies of the extreme situationist position, while Block argues that many of the studies reported by Mischel were badly carried out, and that many were done with children, who would be expected to be less consistent than adults. Block's own work, studying individuals long-term over a period of 20 years, found evidence of considerable consistency over time in personality ratings. Individuals rated as 'dependable' and 'responsible' at school tended to be rated in the same way some 20 years later. A similar consistency over time has been reported for aggressive boys by the Norwegian psychologist Dan Olweus.

THE PERSON AND THE SITUATION: THE INTERACTION

Mischel perhaps overstated the case against trait consistency. It was a necessary corrective at the time and it has been productive in bringing traditional personality theory back to a consideration of the effects of settings and situations. Lawrence Pervin suggests that psychology in general undergoes periods of shifts of emphasis. There are periods when theories emphasize *internal* determinants of behaviour and periods when *external* factors are stronger. The effect of Mischel's early work was to produce some shift towards an appreciation of the external situation. Contemporary thinking about personality tends to be increasingly *interactionist*, accommodating both internal and external factors.

Mischel now acknowledges some stability of personality over time and setting, while at the same time recognizing that people show what he calls 'a great discriminativeness' in their behaviour, depending on the situation they are in:

Complex behaviour is regulated by interactions that depend ultimately on situational variables, as well as on dispositions. Humans are capable of extraordinary adaptiveness and discrimination as they cope with a continuously changing environment. (1981, pages 517–18).

Consistency may be more evident for some individuals than for others and more evident for some traits than for others.

The world is largely what we make it

The word 'interaction' used in the heading to this section signifies not only that *both* person and situation are important, but also that the effect of situations will vary with the nature of the persons exposed to them, and, conversely, that the effect of personality traits will vary with the situation. Major life changes, such as changing job, getting married or moving house, may overall be associated with stress and anxiety, but there will be some individuals who thrive on such changes while others suffer. It might not be possible to separate personality and situation. Particular personalities may *create* life changes while others minimize them. In this sense, the environments to which we are exposed are, in part, an expression of our personality.

PREDICTING DANGEROUSNESS: THEORIES IN ACTION

Perhaps the person/situation debate may seem largely academic and of little real social importance to most of us, but this is far from being the case. Many important decisions are made on the basis of predictions about future behaviour and attempts to make such predictions inevitably involve consideration of the relative importance of person and situation.

One of the most difficult areas of social decision-making is that of whether or not to detain offenders who have been extremely violent. Is the person still 'dangerous' and likely to act in a violent way in the future? Judges, doctors, psychologists, social workers and others are called upon to make such assessments. The traditional approach has been to investigate internal characteristics of the person. Does he or she have an aggressive personality? Is he or she lacking in impulse control? Or is the person suffering from mental illness?

Attempts to predict future dangerous behaviour in this way have been largely unsuccessful, few tests or interview methods being able to predict who will or will not reoffend violently should they be discharged. Ronald Blackburn, a clinical psychologist involved in such decisions, has reviewed the problems of making predictions in this way. The situationist argument would be that violence is highly specific to particular environmental conditions. To predict violence we need to know the situations and confrontations to which the person will be exposed. Estimates of present aggressiveness will, at best, have only very weak associations with future violence. From this point of view, attempts to predict violence are doomed to failure because we have little information about the situations to which the person will be exposed.

Blackburn himself concludes that violent behaviour *does* show some consistency across situations and over time and that aggressive dispositions are therefore worth assessing. Once again, the interactionist account would suggest that both situational and dispositional factors need consideration. We need to know whether the person has an aggressive personality and also the particular situations to which he or she is likely to respond with violence. These situations, of course, may be very idiosyncratic. There will be violence-prone people who respond violently only in reaction to domestic disputes (arguments with a spouse), while others react mainly to abuse in a work setting, and others again only to pressures in violent gangs.

COGNITIVE PERSPECTIVES: IT DEPENDS ON HOW YOU LOOK AT IT

Views about personality have always, inevitably, reflected accepted general psychological theories and methods of the time. One of the striking features of much of psychology in the 1980s and 1990s has been its 'cognitive' flavour, and this has permeated thinking about personality and personality problems. The meanings of 'cognitive' and 'cognition' are various, but the terms usually refer to mental representations of events: to the processes of interpreting, predicting and evaluating the environment, as well as to beliefs, thoughts and expectations. What the cognitive theorist brings to the study of individual difference in behaviour is summed up in the oft-quoted maxim of the philosopher Epictetus, that *'Men are not moved by things, but the views which they take of them'*. Cognitive theory, then, leads us to try to understand, assess and, in a clinical context, change, mental representations of the world including the self and the external environment.

There is no one cognitive approach to personality. We describe here two areas of research which share a cognitive perspective.

PERSONAL CONSTRUCT THEORY

The American psychologist George Kelly proposed an elaborate theory of personal constructs in the 1950s which was some 20 years or more ahead of its time, anticipating many later developments in cognitive theorizing, though Kelly himself would reject the term 'cognitive' as being too narrow to characterize the theory. Kelly's starting point is a view of the person as a scientist engaged in the task of interpreting and theorizing about the world and using these theories to predict the future. This theory is rooted in the philosophical position of constructive alternativism, which states that the world can be construed in infinitely varied ways. Individuals construe the world in terms of *personal constructs* which are bi-polar descriptions, these personal constructs being organized into systems. Thus a person may view his or her relationships with other people in terms of the bi-polar construct 'a relationship in which I am dominant' versus 'a relationship in which I am submissive'. Any one important construct will have implications for other constructs in the system. A relationship in which 'I am submissive', for example, might imply for that person 'an uncomfortable relationship'. The importance of constructs will vary for different individuals (constructs are *personal*) as will the implications of the construct within the system: thus, for some people submissiveness may be associated with comfort and relaxation.

The nature of the personal construct approach to personality is best shown by exploring your own construct system. Kelly devised a method for doing this – the *Repertory Grid* – which has been widely used in a range of applied settings including hospitals, prisons and education. Instructions for completing a grid on yourself are given in *Exercise 2.1*. You might wish to try this exercise before reading the next section which describes the use of the repertory grid with a psychiatric patient seen by one of the authors.

James was a man in his early 30s who worked for an insurance company doing what most people would consider 'a good job'. He had applied for promotion some months before he sought help from a psychologist, but had been unsuccessful. He was upset by this for a few weeks but eventually regained his equilibrium. Shortly afterwards an important relationship with a girlfriend broke up. He reported good relationships with his parents and his two brothers. In the period before coming to see a psychologist he had been moody, irritable and prone to bouts of depression. He was pessimistic about his future and about the world in general.

The repertory grid technique was used to explore his view of significant people in his life and of himself and to elicit the constructs actually important to him. An interview established that the major people in his life at the time were his father, his mother, a brother whom he saw frequently, a friend at work, his boss at work and his ex-girlfriend. Constructs elicited from James are shown in *Table 2.2*. James was asked to think about each of his important people and to decide where he would place them on each construct.

There are a number of mathematical methods for assessing which constructs were the most important for James. These suggested, and he was able to confirm this himself, that the construct relating to 'respect' (1) was a vital one. There was an association between this construct and constructs (2) 'educated' and (6) 'successful'. A second important construct was that relating to 'confidence' (7) which was also associated with constructs (3) and (5).

Table 2.2: James' personal constructs

1. 'respected by others'	versus	'looked down on by others'
2. 'educated'	versus	'poor education'
3. 'warm, open people'	versus	'cold'
4. 'over-emotional'	versus	'stable'
5. 'relates easily to others'	versus	'has difficulties in relating'
6. 'successful at work'	versus	'a failure'
7. 'confident with other people'	versus	'unsure of themselves'
8. 'did well at school'	versus	'did poorly at school'

These two groups of constructs cluster together then, suggesting they reflect two important dimensions for James in judging himself and others. Another way to demonstrate this is to plot the location of significant people on important dimensions. This is illustrated in *Figure 2.1.*

Perhaps the most striking thing about this map of James' world is the great distance between himself as he is and how he would like to be. He falls short on both the 'respect' and 'confidence' dimensions. Despite his good job, he clearly has major doubts about his achievements and his status in relation to other people. The other males in his family, his father and brother, approximate to his ideal. It is not difficult to see how many lines of further enquiry a repertory grid of this sort opens up and we shall leave it to you to think further about what sort of help James might need, given his view of the world.

If you are interested in a further use of the repertory grid, see Chapter 11.

ATTRIBUTION: ANSWERING THE QUESTION 'WHY?'

George Kelly has not been the only psychologist to stress that people create theories about themselves, others and the world in general, and that understanding personal theories is crucial to understanding their behaviour. Over the same period that Kelly's theory was beginning to influence the thinking of many clinical psychologists, a line of research was gathering pace within experimental social psychology, and has become known as *Attribution Theory.* Attribution theory concerns itself with one particular form

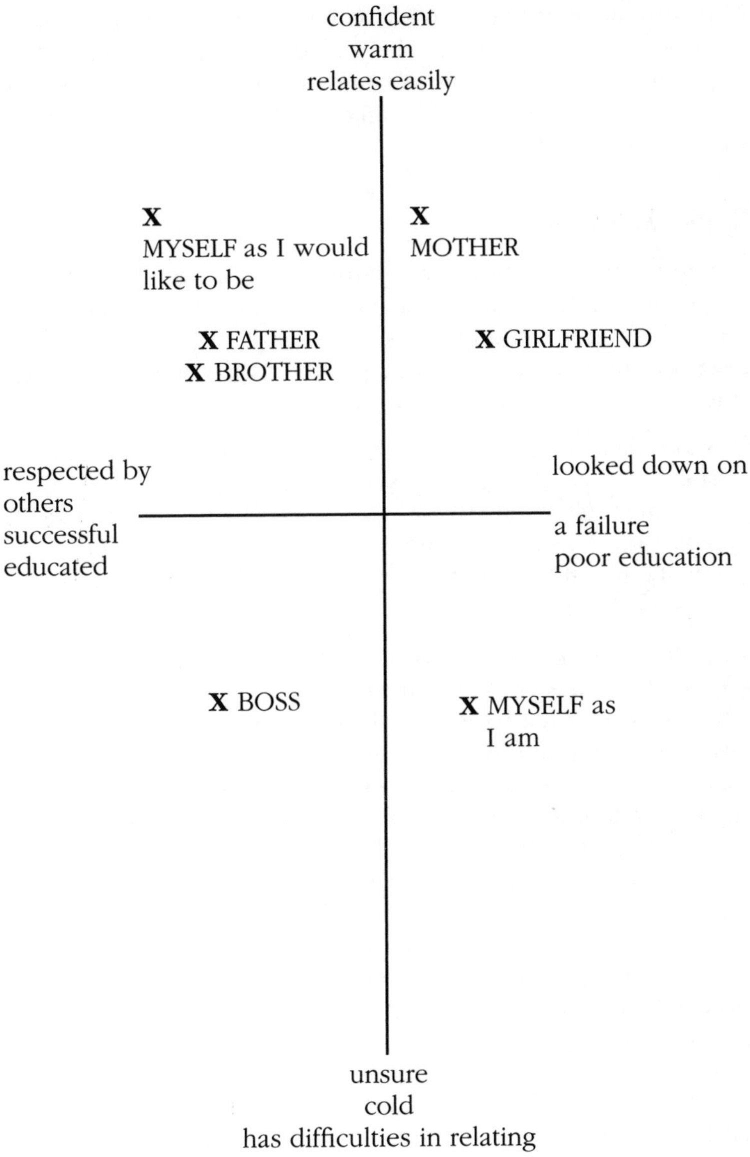

```
                        confident
                         warm
                    relates easily
                          │
                          │
                          │
     X                    │  X
     MYSELF as I would    │  MOTHER
     like to be           │
                          │
          X FATHER        │      X GIRLFRIEND
          X BROTHER       │
                          │
  respected by            │        looked down on
  others        _____│_____
  successful              │       a failure
  educated                │       poor education
                          │
                          │
          X BOSS          │    X MYSELF as
                          │      I am
                          │
                          │
                          │
                          │
                          │
                          │
                       unsure
                        cold
                 has difficulties in relating
```

Figure 2.1: James' view of important people.

of construing the world, namely with the perception of *causality*. 'Causality' refers to the person's perception of the cause of an event, that is, '*Why* did this occur?'. From an attributional perspective, people are viewed as engaged in the task of explaining *why* events happen.

Laying the blame

Arriving at an attribution for a particular action involves the use of complex information about the *context* of the action. If you see, for example, a stranger (*A*) assault another person (*B*) in the street, in order to arrive at an attribution for why this has happened, you would need to consider:

- Is *A* violent in general or is his or her violence specific to *B*? This is called 'distinctiveness' information.
- You might also need to consider whether *B* is often the victim of assaults by other people ('consensus' information).
- Finally, has *A* hit *B* before or is this the only occasion? ('consistency' information).

Contextual information of this sort will play a part in determining whether we isolate *A*, *B*, or some temporary factor in the situation as the *cause* of what happened. It is obvious that on many occasions in everyday life we fail to make rational use of such information. If a stranger acts in an unfriendly way towards you, you might assume that you have offended her or him in some way without attempting to find out whether she or he acts in this way towards everyone (failing to use 'distinctiveness' information). Similarly, you might explain some problems you have in terms of your 'inadequacy', without stopping to consider that many other people have an identical problem ('consensus' information). If you would like to find out a bit more about your own attributional style, try out *Exercise 2.2*.

Psychologists have asked whether, when we try to explain behaviour, we evaluate the situation rationally or whether we are biased towards arriving at particular sorts of attribution. One particular form of bias has been suggested in studies. People in general often show a 'positivity' bias, that is, a tendency to explain things in such a way as to maintain self-esteem. Many of us tend to explain successes in terms of our own qualities and failures in terms of factors outside ourselves. As we shall see later, people vary markedly in this. People with psychological difficulties often show a reversed positivity bias, habitually explaining bad events in ways that are highly damaging to their self-esteem.

ATTRIBUTIONS AND PSYCHOLOGICAL DISTRESS

Bias in the attribution process has been reported in a number of groups who present with psychological problems. Distress may be generated, for example, by the tendency to attribute some difficulty or problem behaviour to a *negative internal disposition*. Suppose, for example, that Michael is gauche in social situations. He attributes this gaucheness to his 'social inadequacy', which, in turn, makes him even more anxious and gauche in subsequent situations. A sexual failure with a member of the opposite sex may be attributed, quite falsely, as indicating that 'I must be homosexual' and the effect of this is to further impair confidence in heterosexual situations. 'Exacerbation cycles', as they have been called, have been reported in relation to a range of neurotic problems.

One of the most important applications of attributional ideas has been to depression. Christopher Peterson and Martin Seligman have argued, and amassed much evidence to support their view, that there is an habitual way of construing causality – an *attributional style* – which predisposes people to become depressed, should they experience unpleasant and stressful life events. The person prone to depression explains 'bad' events that happen in particular ways. First, they attribute the event 'internally' rather than 'externally'; and second, the internal case is 'stable' rather than 'unstable'. Finally the internal cause is 'global' rather than 'specific'. Let us illustrate this by an example quoted by Seligman himself.

If the event which you are trying to explain is a rejection by a girlfriend, and you are predisposed to depression, you explain this occurrence in terms of something about you rather than something about her ('I am unattractive', rather than, 'She was cruel'). You may make depression even more likely if your explanation is stable and unlikely to change ('I am unattractive', rather than, 'I had been acting strangely'). Finally, you may explain the rejection in terms of a very general quality of yourself which extends beyond the particular situation ('I am useless as a person,' rather than, 'I have difficulty in sexual relationships').

Depressed people have been shown in some studies to think in this way, but the question must then be asked whether the attributional style is a consequence of the depression rather than a cause of it. Ideally, to prove Seligman's theory, it needs to be demonstrated that bad attributional styles *precede* depression. To assess people's attributional style prior to them meeting stressful life events and becoming depressed is no easy task.

Attributions in relationships

Biased attributions may be associated not only with personal distress but also with relationship problems. The research suggests that how we attribute causes for the 'negative' behaviours of our partners has an impact on our relationship and, in a marital relationship, on our degree of marital dissatisfaction. Men in unhappy relationships and in violent relationships have been shown to attribute their partners' negative behaviours to a negative intent and to selfish motives on the part of their partner. The tendency to blame others, as well as to blame the self, can be damaging when it becomes an inflexible way of viewing the world.

As we suggested earlier, the cognitive approach to personality and personality problems is currently still in the ascendant, reflecting the general influence of the cognitive perspective within psychology. Some of the weaknesses of cognitive theories will undoubtedly have occurred to the reader. The reading suggested for this chapter at the end of the book will provide the opportunity to explore this and other matters in greater depth.

References

Blackburn, R. (1983). Psychometrics and personality theory in relation to danger-ousness. In J. Hinton (Ed.), *Dangerousness: Problems of assessment and pre-diction*. London: George Allen and Unwin. [This chapter illustrates the relevance of theoretical disputes to a real-world social problem.]

Brewin, C. (1985). Depression and casual attributions: what is their relation? *Psychological Bulletin, 98*, 297–309. [Analyses critically the evidence relating depression to abnormal attributions as suggested by Peterson and Seligman and others.]

Block, J. (1995). A contrarian view of the five-factor approach to personality description. *Psychological Bulletin, 117*, 187–215. [Gives you a summary of the Big 5 approach, plus a detailed critique of it.]

Block, J. (1971). *Lives Through Time*. Berkeley, California: Barcroft Books. [A lon-gitudinal study of stability of personality over time.]

Bowers, K. (1973). Situationism in psychology: an analysis and critique. *Psychological Review, 80*, 307–336. [An influential critique of the extreme situ-ationist position.]

Eysenck, H.J. and Eysenck, M.W. (1981). *Personality and Individual Differences: A natural science approach*. New York: Plenum. [Explains Eysenck's theory and also his attempt to update his thinking in the light of research.]

Hewstone, M. (1989). *Causal Attribution: From cognitive processes to collective beliefs*. Cambridge: Blackwell. [An excellent overview of attribution theory.]

Kelly, G. (1955). *The Psychology of Personal Constructs, Vols. 1 and 2*. New York: W. W. Norton. [The 'classic' and original book on personal construct theory.]

Mischel, W. (1968). *Personality Assessment*. New York: Wiley. [A classic in per-sonality theory.]

Mischel, W. (1981). *Introduction to Personality, 3rd edn*. New York: Holt, Rinehart & Winston. [Deals with personality theory.]

Olweus, D. (1979). Stability of aggressive reaction patterns in males: a review. *Psychological Bulletin, 86*, 852–875. [Consistency over time in aggressive boys.]

Pervin, L.A. (Ed.) (1990). *Handbook of Personality Theory and Research*. New York: Guilford. [The problem of consistency.]

Peterson, C. and Seligman, M.E.P. (1985). Casual explanations as a risk factor for depression: theory and evidence. *Psychological Review, 91*, 347–374. [Argues that there is an habitual way of construing causality.]

Zuckerman, M. (1991). *Psychobiology of Personality*. Cambridge: Cambridge University Press. [An exhaustive and critical review of biological bases.]

Recommended Reading

Cook, M. (1993). *Levels of Personality*. New York: Cassell.

Pervin, L.A. (Ed.) (1990). *Handbook of Personality Theory and Research*. New York: Guilford Press.

EXPLORE YOUR OWN CONSTRUCT SYSTEM

In recent years, some very complex ways of analysing reperto-ry grids have been developed, most of them requiring the assis-tance of a computer. Nevertheless, it is not difficult to evaluate your own grid in a very simple way. You will need to allow about one hour to complete this exercise.

1. Prepare 10 pieces of blank card, each about the size of a filing card. Mark each card in the top left-hand corner from '*a*' to '*j*'.

2. On card '*a*' write 'Mother', on '*b*' 'Father', on '*c*' the name of your spouse/girlfriend/boyfriend, on '*d*' the name of someone you dislike, on '*e*' the name of someone you consider successful, on '*f*' the name of a friend, on '*g*' the name of your immediate 'boss' or employer, on '*h*' the name of any other family member. On '*i*' write 'Myself as I am', on '*j*' write 'Myself as I would like to be'.

3. Put card '*i*' on the table in front of you. Shuffle the other cards and randomly select two cards from the pack and put them on the table with '*i*'.

4. Think about the three people whose cards are in front of you. Try to identify some important way in which two of these people are similar and different from the third. For example, both my father and myself are 'sym-pathetic', while my boss is 'unsympathetic'. Record this 'construct' on a separate sheet of paper.

5. Keep card '*i*' on the table. Put the other two cards back in the pack and shuffle. Randomly select two others.

6. Repeat *4* above.

7. Continue doing this until you have a list of 8 constructs.

8. On a separate sheet of paper construct a Repertory Grid like that shown on the other page, using your own eight constructs across the top. The 'people' whom we have used are termed 'elements' in the repertory grid.

9. Think about Construct 1. Think about each person from '*a*' to '*j*' in turn, and apply the construct to them. If they are like the first end of the construct ('sympathetic'), put

----- *continued* -----

EXPLORE YOUR OWN CONSTRUCT SYSTEM

a '1' opposite their name. If they are like the other end
of the construct ('unsympathetic'), put a '0'.

10. Repeat 9 for constructs 2 to 8.

LAY-OUT FOR YOUR GRID

People (Elements)	Personal constructs			
	1. Sympathetic – Unsympathetic	2. Clever– Stupid	3. Assertive – Shy	4. Etc.
a	1	1	1	
b	1	0	1	
c	0	1	0	
d	0	0	0	
e	1	1	0	
f	0	0	1	
g	1	0	1	
h	0	0	0	
i	0	1	0	
j	0	0	0	

Things to ponder

☐ Reflect on the fact these are your personal constructs.
Another individual would provide a very different list.
Are/were you aware that these are the dimensions you
used to structure your world?

☐ How do your constructs associate with each other?
Check this by comparing any column of '1's and '0's
with any other columns. If the pattern of vertical '1's and
'0's in any pair of vertical columns match (or nearly
match) this suggests overlapping meaning between the
two constructs. Does it surprise you that any particular
constructs match? What does a match reveal about your
way of thinking? Remember that a reversed match (all
'1's match with '0's) is equally significant.

--- *continued* ─

continued ---

EXPLORE YOUR OWN CONSTRUCT SYSTEM

☐ How do the people compare with each other? Do any people have identical or similar patterns of '1's and '0's in the horizontal rows? Are the similarities surprising? What do they suggest?

☐ Who is most like 'Myself as I am'? Would you have guessed this?

☐ How similar is 'Myself as I am' to 'Myself as I would like to be'? On which constructs is there a gap between your actual and ideal self?

EXERCISE 2.2

YOUR ATTRIBUTIONAL STYLE

1. Think about the two worst things that have happened to you in the past year. Write 200–300 words describing each event.

2. Consider the two events again. For each event write a few sentences explaining *why* the event happened.

3. Complete *1* and *2* before turning to p.73.

Seeing the point of the exercise might bias how you carry it out

--- *continued*

continued -

YOUR ATTRIBUTIONAL STYLE

4. Attribution theory would suggest that you would sponta-
neously try to *explain* the two events. Look through your
two original accounts. Are there any phrases that suggest
an explanation ('because', 'therefore', 'as a result', 'since',
etc.)?

5. Look through both your spontaneous accounts and the
explanations asked for in item 2, and try to classify your
explanations in terms of Peterson and Seligman's depressive attributional style (*see text*).

6. How similar were the explanations for the two events in
terms of (a) internal (b) stable (c) global factors?

7. What might your own attributional style be for bad events?

3. Your Sex: On Being Male or Female

'Are men physically bigger, and therefore stronger than women?'
'Is it more natural for women to look after babies than for men?'
'Do boys fight more than girls in the school playground?'

There are no simple answers to any of these three questions. The first one refers to *sex*, which is biological; we all come into the world with a certain genetic make-up, internal physiology and body structure, and these typically (though not always) remain unchanged throughout our lives. Sex differences may well affect behaviour involving physical characteristics such as strength.

However, the second and the third questions refer to different *patterns of behaviour*: these are much more varied and susceptible to change, and they involve cultural beliefs about what is and is not appropriate for males and females. The terms 'masculine' and 'feminine' refer to *gender*; the stereotype of the 'masculine' person is someone who is tough, ambitious and dominant, while the 'feminine' person is seen as gentle, non-assertive, and concerned for the welfare of others. But this leads to an important question: are these stereotypes true in real life? In other words, how are sex and gender related to one another?

Figure 3.1: Oscar Wilde (1854–1900).

It is quite easy to think of examples of males who could be described as feminine. Oscar Wilde (1854–1900) and Frederic Chopin (1810–1849) are two good historical examples, and it is interesting to note that both were well known in the world of the arts. It is also possible to think of females who act in a typically 'masculine' way: Britain's ex-prime minister Margaret Thatcher is an obvious example, reputedly and jokingly described (by her male colleagues) as 'the strongest man in the Cabinet'. However, these figures may well have been 'the exception that proves the rule', and were active at a time when gender stereotypes were more powerful than they are now. We need to ask whether equivalent contemporary figures – America's Hillary Clinton or Britain's Tony Blair, for example – conform to stereotypes which are subject to a good deal more scrutiny and criticism in the 1990s. Indeed, the lifestyles and behaviour of popular entertainers such as Julian Clary and Michael Jackson deliberately exploit the ambiguity of these stereotypes. It may well be that people can 'slip into' stereotypes when it suits them and then slip out of them again just as easily: these days our behaviour can be much more flexible.

SEX OR GENDER?

In other words, sex and gender are not related to one another in a simple, direct manner. It seems very plausible that gender differences have their origins in biological sex differences, but the fact that masculinity and femininity are defined by society, and subject to changes in fashion, means that the link is by no means clear-cut. This issue is actually just another version of one of the oldest debates in psychology, the so-called 'nature–nurture' issue. Psychologists have been debating the question of whether our behaviour is determined by our biological make-up (our 'nature'), or by what we learn (our 'nurture'), for as long as the subject has been in existence.

One development which arose when this debate was at its height in the 1960s and 1970s was the rediscovery of the concept of *androgyny*: this derives from the Greek words *andro* and *gyne* meaning 'man' and 'woman'. The idea was that males should not be confined to masculine behaviour, nor females to feminine behaviour, because this effectively means stifling half of one's personality. Instead, the suggestion was that both sexes should endeavour to be *androgynous*: to be able to act in either a masculine or a feminine manner when the situation demands it. Men should not have to keep a 'stiff upper lip' in emotional situations where the natural thing to do is to cry, for example, and women should not have to hold back the desire to win in competitive situations, such as in sports or in career advancement.

The concept of androgyny was very much in tune with the ideals of feminism at the time, and became the subject of a good deal of research and investigation. The main pioneer in this field was Sandra Bem of Cornell University. She proposed that androgyny is a 'psychologically healthy' state of mind and behaviour, and that it might be correspondingly *un*healthy to be too traditionally feminine a female, or too masculine a male.

To investigate this proposal, Bem worked out a psychological test to measure people's masculinity and femininity, called the *Bem Sex Role Inventory* (BSRI). This test, which has subsequently been adapted and developed in a great deal of further work, consists of a list of 60 adjectives, such as 'forceful', 'competitive', 'affectionate', 'gentle', 'adaptable' and 'truthful'. When you take the test you are asked to say how well each of the 60 adjectives describes you by giving it a score on a scale ranging from 1 ('never or almost never true of me') to 7 ('always or almost always true of me'). Twenty of the adjectives describe 'masculine' characteristics, 20 describe 'feminine' ones, and 20 are neutral. By adding up people's scores on each, Bem was able to work out how people assessed their own 'masculinity' and 'femininity'.

Many researchers have made use of Bem's test since she first devised it, and it has been adapted for groups of different ages and nationalities, as well as being scored and analysed in different ways. One of the most common methods has been to use people's scores on the masculinity (M) and femininity (F) scales to classify them into one of four distinct types:

1. 'Androgynous' people are those who score above average on both masculinity and femininity; they are men and women who report being able to display both types of behaviour in appropriate situations.

2. 'Feminine' people are those who score above average on femininity but below average on masculinity, and vice versa for those who are 'masculine' on the test. Not many males come out as 'feminine', and not many females as 'masculine', although there may be more of the latter than the former.

3. By far the largest groups of people are of course 'masculine' males and 'feminine' females; these are the people who do indeed display the stereotypical self-image of their sex.

4. People who score low on both scales are described as 'undifferentiated', neither masculine nor feminine.

How do these four groups fare in various aspects of life? A lot of research conducted at the time suggested that 'androgynous' people were better off in a variety of ways. Different studies suggested that they were more effective as parents; more mature when making moral judgements and decisions; that they had better emotional feelings about themselves; that they were more adaptable to new situations; and so on. However, later research cast some doubt on this, some of it even suggesting that masculinity was strongly linked with well-being in both males and females.

The debate has moved on since then. As we saw earlier, people in the 1990s seem to be much less bound by gender stereotypes, and can cast them on or off as the situation demands. This is reflected in the more recent developments of Sandra Bem's work, which she calls *gender schema theory*. The central idea of this is that gender-typing stems as much from the way we interpret new information in terms of male and female as it does from whether we ourselves behave in gender-stereotyped ways.

Our self-concepts can be thought of as a complex network of concepts and associations which we use when we encounter a new person, group, or situation, and Bem suggests that in some people, the *gender schema* can form the basis of this. Sex-typed people are those who tend to organize their perceptions of self and others in terms of male and female, masculine and feminine, whereas less sex-typed people do not. The important point is that this is not the same thing as arguing that males should be more feminine and females more masculine. The message for the future is that we should try to weaken the grip that gender-based distinctions have on many of of our ways of thinking and behaving.

BIOLOGICAL INFLUENCES

When a baby is born one of the first things we are likely to be told is, 'It's a girl', or 'It's a boy'. Apart from the health of the newborn, the sex of the child is a vital question for most parents and it's an easy one to answer – as a rule. The possession of male or female genitals determines the label that we are given (our assigned sex) and the genitals develop as a result of the influence of our sex chromosomes. The female possesses two X chromosomes and the male possesses an X and a Y; these are represented as XX and XY respectively.

Most of us take our sex for granted. If we are females we look female, feel female, act like a female and have all the appropriate physical attributes of females both externally and internally, and the same applies to males. Imagining ourselves without a sex, as some sort of neuter, is impossible – our sex is central to our lives, even though of course we are all aware of slight variations between individuals: in physical attributes such as the size of a woman's breasts or a man's penis. Our feelings and behaviour can be more or less typical of our assigned sex, but, in general, we have no difficulty in recognizing an individual as either male or female.

Maleness is determined by the presence of the Y chromosome and thus by definition a male's sex is determined by his father.

King Henry VIII was quite wrong to blame his wives for not having sons – it was his fault if it was anybody's – but of course it was not under his control.

In the absence of the Y chromosome, an individual develops as a female, and even if only one X chromosome is present (as in Turner's syndrome) the resulting individual is female (although she shows some abnormalities). Having two XX chromosomes is not enough to make an individual female if a Y is also present (as in Klinefelter's syndrome); the individual will develop as a male (although again there are some abnormalities present). These genetic abnormalities are very uncommon but they reveal something about the nature of sex. A neutral individual never develops; it is female unless a Y is present (contrary to the Biblical view that woman was formed from man's spare rib, it is the male that is made out of a form that is essentially female) but the possession of the appropriate sex chromosomes is not sufficient for ensuring that the individual develops into a male or female, as we shall see.

The presence of the Y chromosome speeds up the growth and division of cells which form the male gonads (or testes) and by about 16 weeks after conception the male is fully differentiated, sexually. The differentiation of the gonads (ovaries) in the female starts and ends later and is achieved by about 20 weeks' gestation. Once formed, the testes and ovaries begin to secrete sex hormones and the rest of the process of sexual differentiation is under hormonal control. If hormonal secretions are interfered with in some way, development may proceed along different lines and a genetic male may be feminized, or a female masculinized. In other words, the possession of particular sex chromosomes does not in itself mean that a person will develop fully as a male or female. Genetic sex guarantees us neither a male nor a female body, nor a gender identity which makes us feel appropriately masculine or feminine. As we shall see in the next section, various genetic and hormonal abnormalities have helped us to understand more about relationships between sex and gender.

HORMONES AND BEHAVIOUR

Male hormones are collectively called *androgens* and the chief one of these is *testosterone*. Androgens have a masculinizing action on the developing body and are responsible for the growth of the extra muscle and bone which characterize the body of the adult male.

The female is hormonally more complicated than the male. She has *oestrogens*, which, in early development, are concerned with sexual differentiation, and later are concerned with the growth of the eggs (or ova) in the ovaries, with the maturation of her genitals and breasts, and with the increased deposition of fat during adolescence. Also present in the female is *progesterone* and its role is to prepare the womb (or *uterus*) for pregnancy, maintaining the pregnancy after conception, and nourishing the developing embryo. In adult females, the secretion of oestrogens and progesterone is cyclic, and, on average, the cycle, known as the menstrual cycle, is repeated every 28 days.

In both sexes the appropriate sex hormones are produced by the gonads (the testes and the ovaries), but the gonads are controlled by the *pituitary gland* and the *hypothalamus* in the brain. It should be noted however that apart from the gonads, small quantities of sex hormones may be produced at other sites in the body, for example in the *adrenal glands*; and in both sexes, hormones more usually associated with the *opposite* sex are to be found.

The expression of various types of sexual and non-sexual behaviour is affected by sex hormones. Indeed, almost all forms of behaviour can be displayed by both males and females. Examples from non-human animals illustrate this point, although of course we cannot assume that humans function in exactly the same way. Mounting in mammals is a pattern of behaviour which we associate with male sexual behaviour – because it is a typical pattern in copulation. However, a female may also show this response around ovulation. Indeed a cow, when ready for the bull, will often mount other cows, and the farmer observing this knows she is ready to mate (or ready for artificial insemination). Thus 'male' sexual behaviour of this type is shown by both sexes and is not uniquely male. Aggressive behaviour in many animals, including humans, is often viewed as more typical of the male but females can be highly aggressive in some situations, such as when protecting their offspring.

Physiological studies of rodents have shown the impact of sex hormones on development and behaviour. If a male rat is castrated at birth before full sexual differentiation has occurred, and then primed with female hormones, in adulthood, its behaviour is like that of a female, although it cannot reproduce. Similarly, the removal of ovaries from the infant female rat makes her behaviour more masculine in adulthood and she behaves as a male in the presence of a receptive female. In both these cases, genetic sex does not determine the behaviour; it is the presence or absence of hormones that plays the crucial role.

SEX AND GENDER IDENTITY

Does having male hormones, and developing physically along male lines make an individual feel like a male? *Gender identity* is the individual's private experience of himself/herself as male or female and psychologists do not, as yet, have a full understanding of how gender identity develops. There are several approaches or theories concerning how it might develop. The first approach that we shall look at is the biological one.

Biology and gender identity

Parents often express concern when their children show an excessive interest in the toys of children of the opposite sex. They feel that it is not 'right' and may actually lead them to express behaviour and feelings inappropriate to their sex. All cultures have views about what characteristics, behaviour patterns, dress and occupations are appropriate for a given sex, and the acquisition of these is called *sex-typing*. A concern over a deviation from sex-appropriate patterns suggests that, deep down, we believe this might lead to something undesirable.

If biology determines gender identity, then presumably 'boys will be boys' and 'girls will be girls', whatever happens to them. What evidence have we that this might be so?

One research study that has been used to advance this argument is that by Julianne Imperato-McGinley and colleagues in 1979. These researchers studied a community from the city of Santa Domingo in the Dominican Republic. Amongst the people in this community is a rare genetic disorder (5 α-reductase deficiency) which results in what appears to be a sex and gender change in some individuals at puberty. The researchers identified 37 boys who had this disorder where disruption of testosterone metabolism led to the male genitals not being properly formed before birth. Eighteen of these boys had been thought to be girls at birth and had been raised as such; the remainder of the sample had been brought up as boys. At puberty, activation of male hormones in the children caused masculinization of the genitals and the development of secondary sexual characteristics – it appeared that girls were turning into boys.

In studying these young people, Imperato-McGinley reported that these individuals were able to change their gender identity – they shifted from a female to a male gender identity after puberty, in all but one case (one other case changed gender identity but did not adopt the male gender role). It was argued that the hormone surge of puberty enabled these 'girls' to become boys in psychological terms. Their biology, in terms of hormones, was the essential factor in influencing the gender identity that was subsequently established.

This research was used to counter the ideas of John and Joan Hampson who argued that at birth the infant is psychosexually neutral, and that gender identity is learned as a result of the way in which the child is reared (that is, as a boy or a girl). The Hampsons' work was based on the study of over a hundred pseudohermaphrodite individuals. In these people there exists a contradiction between their external genitals and various internal structures such as gonads, chromosomes and hormones. They are not true hermaphrodites – they do not possess fully functional male *and* female parts as do some other creatures (for example, the earthworm). The Hampsons' sample had all been reared as the sex which, later medical investigation showed, was wrong. Almost all the people studied were reported to be fully adjusted to their assigned sex (the wrong sex biologically); they felt themselves to be the sex that they had been brought up to believe they were, even in the face of later contradictory evidence. Thus the Hampsons argued that biology did *not* determine gender identity; it develops gradually over the first few years of life.

The Hampsons' findings can easily explain why the pre-pubescent boys in the Imperato-McGinley studies who were reared as girls were able to establish a female gender identity (presumably through learning). But after the changes at puberty (brought about by their true biological sex and hormonal secretions), it is less easy to explain why they then took on the male gender identity, except on the basis that they were then treated as boys.

What can we conclude from these research findings? Julianne Imperato-McGinley and colleagues believe that androgens play a greater role in determining gender identity than does the sex one is reared as. They suggest ' . . . *that gender identity is not unalterably fixed in early childhood but is continually evolving, becoming fixed with the events of puberty.'*

Thus, can we conclude that biology can override environmental influences? We think not. We cannot overlook the fact that both studies are concerned with individuals who are quite different from the norm; in such people the pressures to be normal are presumably greater than they are for most individuals. The Santa Domingo study would seem to indicate that, in males with this particular disorder, gender identity can be shaped by rearing but hormonal influences may play a role in changing the initial gender identity. However, it could also be said that as their bodies became masculinized this served as a pressure for them to adapt. It was noted that as bodies changed they showed 'self-concern over their true gender' and they eventually became convinced that they were men. Perhaps our only conclusion can be that there is no single answer to the establishment of gender identity and the relative contribution of nature or nurture, and the interaction between the two varies depending on the circumstances of a given individual's biology and rearing. However, we do know that another condition – transsexualism – adds further to this debate and we shall now look at this.

Transsexualism: being trapped in the wrong body

There are some individuals whose biology indicates that they are clearly one sex but they themselves believe that they are another. Thus, a male may believe he is a female trapped in a male body, or vice versa. Transsexuality has not been linked with a physical cause, although research has been carried out to see if there are any differences in, for example, hormone levels, but no clear differences have been identified. There does seem to be evidence that the parents of transsexuals have permitted them, or even encouraged them, to dress as the opposite sex in childhood, suggesting that early learning experiences may play a role in this condition. Whatever the cause, this gender identity problem causes enormous amounts of anxiety and depression and many such individuals seek sex-reassignment surgery as a solution to their problem. In this surgery, the existing genitalia of a transsexual are removed and a substitute for the genitals of the opposite sex is constructed. Such surgery may be complex and the whole procedure takes a long time to complete. James Morris, a journalist and travel writer, had sex change surgery in middle age and became Jan Morris. Her experiences are recorded in a book entitled *Conundrum* which gives an insight into this condition.

Transsexualism lends some support to the notion that early life experiences, or learning, may play a role in gender identity development but there are other theories about gender identity development which we should also consider.

Psychoanalytic theory: anatomy is destiny

Sigmund Freud's views of the development of gender identity centres around his theory of psychosexual development. Freud argued that for both boys and girls the primary love object is the mother but during what he called the *phallic* stage of children's psychosexual development, at around the age of 3–5 years, their interest focuses on the genitals as a source of pleasure. At this time he suggested that children become aware that boys' and girls' genitals differ and in particular they become aware that boys have a penis. At this stage, children, he argued, have sexual feelings towards the parent of the opposite sex and feel jealous of the same sex parent. Freud called this the *Oedipus complex* for boys, and the *Electra complex* for girls. In brief, a boy fears castration by the father since he has now become a rival for his mother's affections. The solution to this problem is for the boy to identify with the father (to become like him) and thus he will also appeal to his mother. So he gives up his initial love for his mother and identifies with the father who is seen as the aggressor. For the girl the situation is rather different. According to Freud she already feels castrated as she lacks a penis (Freud sees the female genitals in a negative light, not in terms of what they are, but what they are *not*) and, feeling punished, she rejects her mother and turns to her father. The Electra complex centres around the girl's feeling of penis envy, whereas for boys the Oedipus complex centres around the fear of losing the penis.

In the normal course of events, Freud argued that the phallic stage ends for both sexes in identification with the same-sex parent. This theory is based on the notion that the anatomy of the sexes determines the course of their psychosexual development. However, to psychologists, this theory, despite being highly influential over the last century, is not viewed as a useful explanation. The evidence that exists does not support Freud's views, and many parts of the theory are simply inaccessible to empirical investigation. Other approaches have been viewed as more fruitful.

Cognitive developmental theory

Lawrence Kohlberg put forward a rather different way of looking at gender identity development, centring around Piaget's stages of cognitive development (see Chapter 6). This theory looks at the child's thinking in relation to her or his awareness of gender differences. Kohlberg noted that small children, at around the age of four, identify sex on the basis of superficial characteristics such as hair length and clothes. They are also not aware that sex is an unchanging human quality; a girl may say (like her brother), 'When I'm a big boy . . . ' and be unaware that this cannot be.

Kohlberg argued that once a child 'understands' that he is male, or she is female (that is, achieves gender constancy), the child will want to do things that are consistent with his or her 'category'. Kohlberg thought that it is natural to value things that are consistent with, or like, the self, and thus children will tend to imitate or model their behaviour on those like themselves (for girls, the mother or older sister, and the equivalent individuals for boys). However, Kohlberg additionally argued that children will also want to model their behaviour on persons who are valued because of prestige or power, and, because males rather than females are seen to have these qualities, girls are likely to be influenced by, and want to imitate, both males *and* females. Kohlberg goes on to say that girls, unlike boys, show *complementary modelling*; thus their femininity is defined in terms of males' acceptance and approval.

Kohlberg's view was a reaction against Freud's, and he was also influenced by the work of the Hampsons discussed on p.82. His approach is described as an interactionist approach; he sees biology and the environment as both having a role in shaping the development of gender identity. For Kohlberg, once the child recognizes 'I am a boy', or 'I am a girl', the child will want to do boy or girl things and will find these rewarding. The important aspect of this theory concerns the child's *thinking* about gender, and how he or she comes to make sense of this knowledge.

Social learning theory

A further theory put forward in the 1960s by David Lynn and by Walter Mischel explains gender identity development in terms of social learning. This theory suggests that gender identity occurs through the internalization of characteristics of a person or role through observation, imitation and reinforcement. Initially, children of both sexes are likely to identify with the mother, but through encouragement and reinforcement little boys soon learn to model themselves on males such as the father, since male-appropriate behaviour is reinforced. Little girls are encouraged to be feminine and model themselves on females. Social learning theory predicts, unlike psychoanalytic and cognitive developmental theories, that as children are primarily cared for by females, the process of learning to be feminine is easier for girls than is the process of learning to be masculine for boys.

This theory contrasts with Kolberg's in that the starting point for social learning theory is the role of rewards or reinforcement. Thus, for the boy, 'I want rewards, I am rewarded for doing boy things, therefore I want to be a boy'. On the other hand, cognitive developmental theory holds that general concepts of 'masculinity' and 'femininity' come first; children notice common features in the behaviour of males and females, and identification with our own parents follows on from this.

It may never be possible to test which of these explanations is correct, but there can be no doubt that imitation and identification are powerful forces in forming our own unique personalities.

HOMOSEXUALITY

In our discussions so far there has been an implicit assumption that males and females are heterosexual, but can we take this for granted? Before considering boys and girls growing up, we shall briefly discuss homosexuality.

A homosexual is someone who chooses a sexual partner of the same, rather than the opposite, sex. Their sexual behaviour is like that of a heterosexual individual but the sex of the person with whom they seek to have sexual relations is different. A female homosexual is often termed a *lesbian*, and a male is often termed a *gay*, although the latter term may be used to apply to both sexes.

We know that homosexual behaviour is shown by a significant minority of people. In 1948 Alfred Kinsey reported that over one third of the males whom he studied had displayed some form of homosexual behaviour, although more recent estimates would not necessarily make such a high claim. Cross-cultural studies have found that in over half of the dozens of primitive societies compared, some form of homosexual behaviour is considered normal and acceptable. Homosexual behaviour is also not exclusive to humans; it is displayed by other species. Thus it appears that it is within the range of patterns of behaviour which we might expect in men and women, although it is not present in the majority, just as green eyes or left-handedness are not.

In the past, homosexuality was viewed as a sexual deviation and attempts were made to cure those who showed this form of behaviour. Until the 1960s, homosexuality was illegal in Britain and thus homosexuals could not reveal their sexual orientation without fear of arrest. Fortunately attitudes have changed in recent decades and homosexuality is now accepted by law in Britain. It has also been removed from the *Diagnostic System of the American Psychiatric Association* and is thereby recognized as a 'normal variant' of human sexual behaviour, rather than as a disorder or illness. Homosexual marriage is now on the brink of acceptance in at least one state of America (Hawaii) but this change in attitude is not universal however.

Why are some people homosexual? Several suggestions have been made. Psychoanalysts have suggested that homosexuality may arise if there is incomplete resolution of the Oedipus Complex, Freud's idea which we discussed earlier. Other studies have explored genetic explanations and hormonal imbalances, but attempts to establish a link have so far produced no firm conclusions, although the idea of a 'homosexual gene' has been widely discussed and some authorities believe there may be evidence to support this. Homosexuality may not have one single cause. Studies of the backgrounds of male and female homosexuals, relative to heterosexuals, show that both the homosexual and heterosexual groups of females tend to come from backgrounds which are more similar than are those of the homosexual or heterosexual males; thus the causes of this behaviour both within and between the sexes may be multifaceted. At present we do not understand the cause or causes of this behaviour, just as we do not fully understand what determines heterosexual behaviour.

FROM BIRTH TO MATURITY

The effects of being male or female become apparent as soon as a child is born, and the ways in which boys and girls are brought up to behave differently and to think about each other differently are complex and deep-rooted. In other words, we need to look at the effects sex and gender differences have across the whole life span. It may be possible to trace some of the differences which exist between men and women back to earlier influences in childhood and adolescence, and the life span perspective is a prominent feature of most contemporary research. Soon after birth itself, studies of parents and their young babies have clearly shown that boys and girls are often treated differently. One investigation found that fathers rated their newborn sons as more alert, well co-ordinated and strong, and their newborn daughters as more inattentive, soft and delicate. This was from having only looked at them – they had not yet even picked them up. Since these differences are present so early on, it seems quite likely that some form of *stereotyping* affects parents' attitudes to their baby sons and daughters.

As children grow older and become influenced by the world around them, the influence of these stereotypes becomes increasingly powerful. Gender roles are all-pervasive: children see examples of what is regarded as the appropriate behaviour for boys and girls in newspapers and magazines, on television programmes, in advertisements, in the playground, in shopping centres, in the classroom, and indeed almost everywhere. The enormous power of these influences soon begins to influence children's perceptions of themselves, and this plays a role in the development of gender identity.

It seems likely that there are some early signs of the development of gender identity at around the age of two. Children begin to make verbal distinctions between 'mummy' and 'daddy', and also maybe between 'boy' and 'girl'. Early on these words are likely to be 'labels' that have no consistent reference to sex, but this reference soon becomes established. When this happens, children start to classify themselves as members of one sex or the other, and this can be investigated in different ways. For example, preschoolers have been shown pictures of different toys and games (a football, dolls, and so on), and been asked to say which are for boys and which are for girls. Another technique has been to show pictures of adults engaged in characteristic activities such as washing the car, putting up shelves, cooking dinner, hanging out washing, and to ask similar questions. Research along these lines clearly shows that preschool children have a detailed knowledge of gender roles, and that gender identity is generally thought to be well established by the age of four or so, although, we have noted, not all researchers agree with this (for example, Imperato-McGinley and colleagues.)

The race to grow up

One interesting aspect of sex differences in growing up is the early lead that girls have over boys, and its eventual disappearance. Boys lag behind girls in most areas of early physical development, such as standing, walking, and talking, and this lead carries on into the early school years. Girls are generally ahead of boys in most areas of infant school work, and there are two possible reasons for this. The first is that girls mature physically more quickly than boys, which in turn affects their intellectual development. The second is that in the preschool world, teachers and childminders are nearly all female, and this may have something to do with girls' early developmental lead.

However, girls typically lose their early advantage after the age of six or so. Boys seem to catch up in many areas of school work, and so the 'race' is fairly even in the junior school years. The onset of puberty produces another set of dramatic changes in physical, social and emotional development.

Puberty and adolescence

Puberty typically occurs a year or so earlier in girls than in boys, with the 'growth spurt' being between the ages of 11–13 and 13–15 years respectively. The sudden physical changes which boys and girls experience in adolescence can often give rise to feelings of self-consciousness and awkwardness, and this can have different effects. Research suggests that for boys, early maturation can convey distinct advantages with respect to sporting performance, for example, or indeed in social relationships. In girls, early maturation is more of a mixed blessing: the positive benefits of improved skills and appearing more grown-up can simultaneously be a disadvantage in maintaining friendships within close groups. There is little evidence to link these physical developments with intellectual or scholastic achievements.

Adolescence is a crucial period in the formation of the identity of the emerging adult, and gender is a central part of this. John Archer has suggested that different 'developmental pathways' exist for boys and girls, partly as a result of cultural expectations, and he has made some very interesting observations as a result of his extensive review of the research literature.

First, he suggests that the masculine role is more *inconsistent*: acting in a tough or 'macho' manner for boys may not be typical of the behaviour expected in many adult male roles, for example, whereas 'feminine' behaviour in girls may be more consistent with that in adult female roles. Second, boys seem to be more *rigid* and *inflexible* than girls with respect to opposite sex behaviour: 'tomboys' are much more socially acceptable than 'cissies', for example, and girls can take part in boys' games more readily than vice versa. Third, however, this flexibility differs over the life span for boys and girls. Although girls' interests are more flexible in childhood, they narrow down in the teenage years, centring on physical and sexual attractiveness and personal relationships. Archer refers to this as 'gender intensification', which can seriously limit the horizons, aspirations and capabilities of teenage girls. It does not seem to occur in boys, whose interests typically widen, rather than narrow, in the teenage years.

Of course, developmental pathways in psychological differences between boys and girls are directly linked with social roles and institutions. The pathway that children travel from school, maybe to higher education, and then into the world of work and careers seems to be more clearly defined for boys than for girls. Boys stay on this pathway, and develop a complex of competitive skills and attitudes. Girls are more likely to step on and off at different points in their lives, and can thereby leave their early potential unfulfilled.

THE WEAKER SEX?

We have got used to the idea of female political leaders, doctors, and business executives, though some of us are still unhappy about the idea of female judges, priests, or plumbers. Most people in the West would probably look twice at a female roadmender or

Figure 3.2: The weaker sex?

building site worker although these are reasonably common in Eastern Europe, the USSR, and Japan. Many people would argue that, 'It's not natural' for women to do heavy manual work, saying that this is more naturally suited to the greater height, weight and strength of men. Are they right or wrong? Such questions about what is or is not 'natural', that is, somehow biologically determined, are very important questions. They are also very difficult questions because society's views about the relative roles of men and women are constantly changing.

Are sex differences changing over time?

A great deal of effort has been devoted to identifying exactly what are the main psychological differences between the sexes, and an important landmark was the publication in 1974 of Eleanor Maccoby and Carol Jacklin's book, *The Psychology of Sex Differences*. These two authors carried out a comprehensive review of all the published research literature at the time, and their conclusions received a good deal of attention and discussion. Things have changed in the intervening years, and more recent reviews suggest that some of the originally identified differences seem to be disappearing. However, some new gender differences have been found which were not originally identified by Maccoby and Jacklin, and so the debate continues. Let us look at sex differences in *physical skills, personality, interests,* and *intelligence.*

In the area of physical skills, sex differences were suggested in the sensitivity of some of the sense organs. Women generally have a lower touch and pain threshold than men, so they are more sensitive to pain, but, paradoxically, it is said that they can stand prolonged pain better than men can. They also seem to be more sensitive to sound and smell. For example, they are superior at distinguishing between two very similar sounds, as well as pinpointing exactly where a very quiet sound is coming from. Sex differences are also found in the ways in which males and females carry out everyday tasks. Boys are better at activities involving gross motor skills, such as kicking a ball or pushing a heavy load. Girls may have a corresponding advantage for fine motor skills, such as threading a needle, but the evidence for this is less clear-cut.

Sex, personality and behaviour

Many suggestions have been made about how the personalities of the sexes might differ. Qualities such as *ambition, drive* and *competitiveness* are regarded as typically masculine, whereas *passivity, nurturance* and *emotionality* are seen as typically feminine. It is extremely difficult for researchers to get any clear answers as to whether or not these views have any foundation. Aggression, for example, has frequently been studied in other animals as well as in people. In studies of preschool play, there is no doubt that boys engage in more physical fighting and rough-and-tumble play. When verbal aggression such as taunts and insults are taken into account, however, it is by no means clear that girls are any less aggressive than boys. Other studies in this vein have suggested that boys tend to be more adventurous, independent and competitive, and that girls are correspondingly more affectionate, socially sensitive and emotional.

If we take a life span view of this, the question becomes whether or not the sex differences observed in children carry on into adult life. One common suggestion has been that males may be more interested in objects, or things, whereas females are more interested in people. This is clearly true in children's play. Many studies have shown that boys tend to have mechanical and 'scientific' play interests – in machines, construction games and computers, for example – whereas girls' games tend to revolve around other people, such as playing with dolls, and acting out school, home or hospital scenes.

Can we go on from this to suggest that the interests and behaviour of men and women differ in a similar way? Several new areas of difference are emerging here which were not identified 20 years ago. For example, it appears that women conform more than men in situations involving group pressure; that they are more susceptible to persuasion than men; and that they are more sensitive to non-verbal cues and messages than men. It also seems that men and women have different styles of communication: analyses of conversations show that men are more assertive, and tend to control the interaction to a greater extent than women. We might say that there are important differences in the *power strategies* typically used by men and women.

Sex differences in intelligence

Two prominent ideas about sex differences in intelligence were present in Maccoby and Jacklin's conclusions. The first is that females tend to do relatively better on tests involving words (verbal skills), and that males tend to be correspondingly better on spatial and numerical tasks – at working with shapes and numbers. More recent studies suggest that the second of these differences is disappearing: many studies of mathematical abilities have found no sex differences, and the extent of differences in visual and spatial abilities can often depend on the particular task which is used.

The second, more controversial, idea has provocatively been referred to (by a female psychologist) as the 'mediocrity of women'. If we look at the overall spread of scores of large numbers of males and females on certain intelligence tests, it sometimes turns out that a far greater number of females get scores around the average. More males, correspondingly, get scores that are well below the average as well as scores that are well above it. There may be greater variability, or scatter, in other words, amongst males than females.

Differences such as these may well be reflected in the subjects preferred by boys and girls at school, and here again we see some evidence for a decline in recent years in the gender stereotyping of school subjects. Even so, research carried out in the 1990s still suggests that information technology, physics and CDT (craft, design and technology, which includes traditional male vocational subjects) are perceived as masculine subjects by schoolchildren, and that home economics, personal and social education, and religious education are perceived as feminine. You can find out how much your own school subject preferences correspond with gender stereotypes by completing *Exercise 3.1* at the end of the chapter.

SEX DIFFERENCES OR DISCRIMINATION?

For centuries males have accepted without question the idea that not only are women and men different but also that women are inferior to men. This is captured in Charles Darwin's summary of the differences:

The chief distinction in the intellectual powers of the two sexes is shown by man's attaining to a higher eminence, in whatever he takes up, than can woman – whether requiring deep thought, reason, or imagination, or merely the use of the senses and hands.

As a result of this belief, early researchers in zoology and psychology devoted much time and effort in searching for differences in the brain that favoured males. Their objectivity was highly questionable because on more than one occasion the researchers had to change their views when a site in the brain thought to be larger in males was found to be as large or larger in females. Today this form of work has been abandoned and the debates have become more refined: examining, for example, possible sex differences in the lateralization of function in the cerebral cortex (that is, the extents to which each hemisphere is specialized for particular jobs) or the degree to which each hemisphere is linked by fibres in the corpus callosum.

In the 1990s we have become used to the idea of equal opportunities for both sexes and in some areas, for example, education, there is clear evidence that girls are now out-performing boys. Recent statistics show that girls out-perform boys at age 7 and 14 in all subjects except science, and when GCSE grades in England are studied we find that girls are much more likely to obtain A–C grades in English, foreign languages and history, while boys are more likely to obtain these grades in physics, chemistry and CDT. In both cases, as we have already noted, these are areas traditionally viewed as appropriate for each sex. In considering the core subjects in the National Curriculum (English, Mathematics, a science and a modern language) the proportion of pupils in England with A–C grades is 'much higher for girls than for boys, and the gap has widened over the last five years'. If we examine A-level results, gender differences are less dramatic but over time the trends are of the same general pattern.

Perhaps it could be argued that equality and attempts to ensure that discriminatory practices in education are eradicated, are having an effect. But, some might argue it has gone too far.

In children and young people we find that girls do well or very well but once we look at the destinations of girls in later life there are still very dramatic differences between the sexes (see *Exercise 3.2* which illustrates this point). Males still predominate in jobs thought to be more intellectually demanding, and in positions of greater power. For example, in Britain fewer than one in 12 professors is female, even though women make up one third of university academics. Men earn more on average and the world's wealth is largely in the hands of men. The dilemma for the younger woman is how to combine childbearing and paid work; in the last decade, the percentage of women who are in paid work and have young children has risen rapidly, so that now the majority of mothers with young children earn their living. The traditional notion of a full-time mother at home with her children is outmoded. Nevertheless, combining motherhood and paid work remains a problem area and it is one that is largely viewed as a problem for women themselves, rather than for society in general.

If women tend to be in the lower echelons of many occupations, and have less power, it is hard to see where any motivation for change will come from. Those in power never relinquish it easily, and presumably what is required is a more flexible approach to fitting paid work into the life styles of women who are also mothers. Women will (indeed, must) continue to go on having children, but, as this is not a paid job in itself, they have to rely on their own ability and that of their partners for financial support during this phase of life. Currently, women who achieve high status do this at a price; they are less likely to marry and if they do so, are less likely to have children. Those who do have children generally have them later in life and have fewer of them.

It is hard to see precisely what form equality should take in the workplace when both sexes have paid work, but the major load of childbearing and childrearing falls on the women. Some would suggest that the father's role in caring for children is too limited and that part of equality would be to increase the man's options in the domestic sphere and hence create a more flexible timetable for paid work that is equally available to women and men. But these sort of changes require a major rethink of the traditional ways of working.

There is no doubt that in Britain, compared with the early part of this century when women didn't even have a vote, a considerable measure of equality of opportunity has been achieved. But there are still many areas where women have little opportunity to participate. It is also the case that young women are not exposed to appropriate role models of women in more powerful occupations as young men are. The women who do enter male dominated professions are often perceived as unfeminine and lacking the qualities that many girls aspire to and which are perceived as qualities which make them attractive and desirable.

Greater equality of opportunity for the sexes is evident not only in Britain but also in other parts of the Western world. Nevertheless, there are many areas where sexism is entrenched and shows no sign of disappearing. For instance, the male first rule of succession is still part of the British monarchy and precedence of male heirs over female ones is also the case in many aristocratic families. Whilst sexual discrimination is still part of the fabric of our society it is hard to see how we can truly achieve equality of opportunity. It may be an ideal for some, but of course many people are resistant to the arguments in favour of such equality and in the twenty-first century there will still be much to achieve if equal opportunities is the goal.

References

Archer, J. (1984). Gender roles as developmental pathways. *British Journal of Social Psychology, 23,* 245–256. [Archer's analysis of masculine and feminine 'pathways' in development.]

Bem, S.L. (1975). Sex role adaptability: one consequence of psychological androgyny. *Journal of Personality and Social Psychology, 31,* 634–643. [Sandra Bem's theory of androgyny.]

Bem, S.L. (1981). Gender schema theory: a cognitive account of sex typing. *Psychological Review, 88,* 354–364. [Sandra Bem's gender schema theory.]

Coleman, J.C. and Hendry, L. (1990). *The Nature of Adolescence, 2nd edn.* London: Routledge. [A broad-ranging account of adolescence which highlights the issue of gender differences.]

Colley, A., Comber, C. and Hargreaves, D.J. (1994). Gender differences in school subject preferences: a research note. *Educational Studies, 20,* 13–18. [The study on which *Exercise 3.1* is based.]

Davison, G.C. and Neale, M.N. (1996). *Abnormal Psychology.* New York: John Wiley. [See chapter on sexual disorders.]

Gladue, B.A. (1985). Neuroendocrine response to estrogen and sexual orientation. *Science, 230,* 961. [Homosexuality.]

Hampson, J.L. (1965). Determinants of psychosexual orientation. In F.A. Beach (Ed.), *Sex and Behaviour.* New York: Wiley. [Research on hermaphrodites.]

Imperato-McGinley, J., Peterson, R.E., Gautier, T. and Sturla, E. (1979). Androgens and the evolution of male-gender identity among male pseudohermaphrodites with 5 α-reductase deficiencies. *The New England Journal of Medicine, 300* (*22*), 1233–1237. [Studies of 'girls' who change to boys, quotes on page 1236 and 1234 respectively.]

Jones, S. (1993) *The Language of the Genes.* London: Flamingo. [Discusses the possibility of a homosexual gene.]

Katcher, A. (1955). The discrimination of sex differences by young children. *Journal of Genetic Psychology, 87,* 131–143. [Children's understanding of sex differences.]

Kinsey, A.C., Pomeroy, W.D. and Martin, C.E. (1948). *Sexual Behaviour in the Human Male.* Philadelphia: W.B. Saunders. [Males and homosexuality.]

Kohlberg, L. (1966). A cognitive developmental analysis of children's sex-role concepts and attitudes. In E.E. Maccoby (Ed.), *The Development of Sex Differences.* London: Tavistock. [Cognitive developmental theory.]

Lynn, D.B. (1966). The problem of learning parental and sex-role identification. *The Journal of Marriage and the Family, 28,* 466–470. [Social learning theory.]

Maccoby, E.E. and Jacklin, C.N. (1974). *The Psychology of Sex Differences.* Stanford: Stanford University Press. [The authoritative review of the 1970s.]

Mischel, W. (1966). A social learning view of sex differences in behaviour. In E.E. Maccoby (Ed.), *The Development of Sex Differences.* London: Tavistock. [Social learning theory.]

Morris, J. (1974). *Conundrum.* New York: Harcourt Brace Jovanovich. [A transsexual's story.]

Moss, H.A. (1967). Sex, age and state as determinants of mother–infant interaction. *Merrill–Palmer Quarterly, 13,* 19–36. [Mothers' contact with infant boys and girls.]

Rubin, J., Provenanzo, F.J. and Luria, Z. (1974). The eye of the beholder: parents' views on sex of newborns. *American Journal of Orthopsychiatry, 43,* 720–731. [Fathers' initial reactions to their new-borns.]

Shields, S. (1978). Sex and the biased scientist. *New Scientist, 80* (*11321*), 752–754. [Early research on sex differences and Darwin's quote.]

Smith, P.K. (1986) Explanation, play and social development in boys and girls. In D.J. Hargreaves and A.M. Colley (Eds), *The Psychology of Sex Roles.* Milton Keynes: Open University Press. [Gender constancy and gender stability.]

Social Trends, 26 (1996). London: HMSO [See chapter on education statistics and exam grades referred to here.]

Education Correspondent, (1996). Women kept out of professorships. *The Times*, Friday 26 July, p. 7. [Very few women professors.]

House of Commons (1993–94). *Mothers in Employment*. London: HMSO. [Rapid rise in mothers in employment.]

Recommended Reading

Archer, J. (1995). Sex differences, in A.S.R. Manstead and M. Hewstone (Eds), *The Blackwell Encyclopaedia of Social Psychology*. Oxford:Blackwell.

Archer, J. and Lloyd, B. (1985). *Sex and Gender* (revised edition). Cambridge: Cambridge University Press.

Basow, S.A. (1992). *Gender Stereotypes and Roles, 3rd edn*. Belmont, CA.: Brooks/Cole.

Hargreaves, D.J. and Colley, A.M. (Eds) (1986). *The Psychology of Sex Roles*. Milton Keynes: Open University Press.

Nicholson, J. (1995) *Men and Women: How different are they?* Oxford: Oxford University Press.

PREFERENCES FOR SCHOOL SUBJECTS

INSTRUCTIONS: Please rank order your preferences for the nine school subjects given below. Your most liked subject should get a rank of 1, your second best a rank of 2, and so on.

1. Art and Design
2. CDT (Craft, Design and Technology)
2. English
4. French
5. Humanities
6. Maths
7. Music
8. PE
9. Science

SCORING: You can compare your own preferences with the average rank given to each subject by 52 boys and 41 girls aged between 11 and 13 years in a Leicestershire, UK, middle school in 1993, shown in the table below (do not consult the table until the task has been completed).

Subject	Girls' average	Boys' average
English	2.83	4.61
Maths	4.98	4.76
Science	5.98	4.54
Humanities	3.50	5.24
French	6.50	6.14
Art and Design	4.37	4.80
CDT	5.77	5.08
Music	5.78	6.32
PE	5.35	3.52

THE PORTRAYAL OF WOMEN AND MEN IN THE MEDIA

INSTRUCTIONS: For this exercise select a range of magazines from Sunday newspapers. Taking each magazine, cut out the first ten pictures of males and the first ten pictures of females. Write down for each picture how the male/female is dressed, what s/he is doing (including whether active or passive) and what task s/he appears to be engaged in. Also note any relationship to others in the picture. Record this for all pictures. For example, you might write, 'Female wearing party dress, sitting down drinking wine and looking at a male', or 'Male in smart suit, driving expensive car fast through Manhattan'.

When you have completed the task compare your records for males and for females.

RESULTS: What do your records tell you about the portrayal of males and females? Which sex is portrayed more actively, in positions of greater power or in activities or jobs of higher status?

You may like to repeat this exercise but this time videotape ten TV adverts and then note how the women and men in these are portrayed.

4. *You and Others*

- An eight-year-old schoolboy wears his Chicago Bulls basketball shirt day in, day out and constantly imagines shooting the winning basket for his team.

- A group of teenage schoolgirls follow their favourite Britpop group Oasis to concerts around the country, and model their clothes and hairstyles on their idols.

One theory of personality development – of how we grow up to be the way we are – is that our selves are partly formed by our imitating, or taking on the role of, other people, who are thought of as *models*. The two examples given illustrate two types of model from the worlds of sport and entertainment which commonly influence older children and teenagers.

Younger children are powerfully influenced by more immediate models in the family: boys tend to imitate the behaviour of their fathers, for example, and girls the behaviour of their mothers, as we saw in Chapter 3. These models become more and more varied as children get older, to include perhaps friends, teachers, and neighbours. Adults' role models might include great thinkers, social reformers or politicians. All of these examples show very clearly that people are essentially *social beings*: we constantly act, talk, and think in relation to other people.

SOCIAL ROLES

The process just described is known as *role taking*, and it shows how, to a considerable degree, we think and act so as to fit in with patterns of behaviour laid down by society. Each person is at the centre of a complex web of interrelated roles. You might, at different times of the day, 'act out' the part of parent, motorist, churchgoer, gardener, secretary, and so on: different roles are demanded by different situations. As an interesting exercise, you might like to jot down all the different roles which you fulfil (a) at work and (b) at home, and compare these with similar lists compiled by friends or colleagues.

These roles can be taken on at three different levels. The most superficial is *role enactment*: a person who carries out a disliked job purely for the pay, or a stage actor in an unsympathetic part, is merely 'going through the motions' with no personal commitment to that behaviour. In contrast to this are those people whose commitment to a certain role is so strong that it becomes an essential part of their personality: most doctors would adopt a responsible, caring attitude towards others, for example, whether or not they were on duty. We could say that they have *internalized* the role behaviour, and perform it automatically and unconsciously.

In between these two is the level of *role taking*. At this level, certain parts of the role are identified with and others are not. A schoolteacher, for example, may have completely internalized educational ideals concerning the welfare of her pupils, but, faced with classroom disruption, she may be forced to resort to punishments of which she disapproves. She experiences *role conflict* when this occurs. Some jobs have 'built in' role conflict: prison officers are expected to be both punitive and rehabilitative with respect to their charges, for example, and this can lead to many moral dilemmas. In summary, society prescribes roles for individuals, and they fit into these roles with varying degrees of success. How do we deal with these matches and mismatches at the individual level?

WHAT WE DO AND WHAT WE THINK

- Have you ever gossiped or complained about another person behind their back? Have you ever expressed one view to your boss at work and then expressed a quite different view to your workmates when the boss was not there?

- You are a firm believer in the concept of comprehensive educational provision for all children. The local comprehensive secondary school at which your bright eleven-year-old is due to start in the autumn has a very poor disciplinary and examination record because of its large inner-city catchment area. There is a private school in a nearby town to which your child could travel by train, which has an excellent academic record. What should you do?

Almost all of us must truthfully answer 'Yes' to the first set of questions. We all hold different attitudes in public and in private, and many modern-day politicians seem to have made this into something of an art! It is not quite so obvious how people might respond to the education problem, however. Some would stick to their social principles, electing the comprehensive school: others would put their private interests above their publicly-held beliefs, and send their child to the private school. This very situation interestingly occurred in the UK in the mid-1990s when two prominent Labour politicians (including the party leader) faced a similar moral dilemma. Their decision to take a personal decision which conflicted with official party policy created widespread criticism from their political opponents and from the media.

These dilemmas make it clear that what we say and think are often at variance with what we do: our *attitudes* and our *behaviour* are often inconsistent with each other. The reason for this, once again, is that most of our behaviour is social: it has to take account of decisions that must be taken in relation to other people. The end result is that people sometimes do what seem to be illogical or irrational things, as a result of *social influence*. As social psychologist Elliot Aronson puts it, 'People who do crazy things are not necessarily crazy'.

Social comparison

This idea has been expressed more formally by Aronson's mentor, Leon Festinger, in his theory of social comparison. The basis of this is that people have a constant need to validate their opinions by comparing them with those of others.

Suppose Tina, a successful advertising executive, meets up with her old university friend Hilary, now a primary school deputy head, fifteen years after their graduation. Tina is single, and a frequent international traveller on business expense accounts; Hilary has a husband and a daughter, both of whom (like herself) are committed vegetarians. Tina's invitation to dinner with Hilary's family means that she has to eat food which she finds unpalatable and unsatisfying: Hilary and her family enjoy it immensely. Tina, out of politeness, is quite likely to express the view that, 'I can appreciate that your reasons for eating only vegetarian food are ethically commendable, but I'm afraid it's not for me', or she might even pretend to like it. What she will not do is express the opinion that she would if she were dining with her (non-vegetarian) colleagues. Festinger's theory suggests that our opinions and beliefs are constantly being shaped by this kind of process.

SAVING FACE

In this fictitious story, there is a fundamental inconsistency in Tina's attitudes. She has a negative attitude towards the food, and a positive attitude towards her friend Hilary, but this is incompatible with Hilary's positive attitude towards the food. Tina is most likely to resolve this problem by changing her own attitude, thereby 'saving face', but there are other possibilities. She could, for example, 'agree to disagree' with Hilary, considering that her own carnivorous habits are equally valid. She may even conclude that Hilary's family's eating habits are pretentious, that they only eat in this way in order to appear to be humanitarian and environmentally concerned, and yet simultaneously have no objection to wearing leather shoes.

These different ways of resolving the problem form part of *cognitive consistency theories* in social psychology, and probably the best-known of these is Leon Festinger's *cognitive dissonance theory*, published in 1957. Festinger proposed that a state of dissonance exists when there is inconsistency between the different beliefs and attitudes which people hold, or between those attitudes and their behaviour. The theory suggests that individuals experiencing dissonance are motivated to reduce it, and that there are three main ways of doing this.

The first is to *change attitudes and/or behaviour* so as to make them more consistent: Tina should either convince herself that she does like vegetarian food; become vegetarian herself; or even change her attitude towards Hilary, arguing perhaps that they have 'grown apart' over the years. The second is to *get new information* which supports your attitude or behaviour: Tina might seek information from the food industry which shows that some animals are not always involved in unnecessary suffering, such that it is possible to overcome ethical objections to meat-eating by careful and selective purchasing. The third is to *minimize the importance of the conflict*: Tina could 'agree to disagree' with Hilary and her family and maintain friendly contact. These three strategies are used to change our behaviour and/or attitudes in order to save face.

Lying, boredom, and attitudes

In one study, Leon Festinger and Merrill Carlsmith asked groups of experimental participants to sign up for a study called 'Measures of Performance' which involved carrying out some extremely tedious tasks. One was to fill a tray with 12 spools, then to take them off one at a time, then to refill it, then empty it again, and so on. Another involved a large board with 48 square pegs – participants were asked to turn each peg one quarter-turn clockwise, then do them all one more quarter turn, and so on for half an hour. In an elaborate experimental design, the participants were divided into three groups. The *control group* was simply told that they were to rate the dull, boring tasks for 'interest' and 'scientific value' as a check on other experiments being conducted in the psychology department. The *one dollar group* was paid one dollar for telling new participants, just about to start on the tasks, that the tasks were 'intriguing', 'enjoyable', and 'a lot of fun'. The *20 dollar group* was paid 20 dollars for misinforming the new participants in the same way.

Participants in both of the groups who were paid also rated the tasks for 'interest' and 'scientific value' after finishing them, and there were some clear and surprising differences between the average ratings of the three groups. The control group, predictably, gave low ratings on the two scales (an average of –0.45 on a scale from –5 to +5). The 20 dollar group gave slightly higher ratings than this (–0.05), but the one-dollar group's ratings were considerably higher (1.33). The dissonance theory explanation for this result is based on the fact that participants in the two paid groups had to deceive the new participants, that is, to make attitude statements which were inconsistent with their own knowledge of the tasks. The 20 dollar participants were well paid, they had a good justification for lying, and so they experienced relatively little cognitive dissonance. The one-dollar participants, on the other hand, got a trifling reward for lying, and so experienced considerably more dissonance. The latter group apparently reduced this dissonance by upgrading their ratings of the task itself: they 'saved face' by convincing themselves that it was indeed 'interesting' and of 'some scientific value'.

This is a powerful result because it is counter-intuitive. The most obvious common sense prediction would be that people who receive a large reward for saying that the tasks were enjoyable would themselves rate them as such, in comparison with those who only receive a small reward. Exactly the opposite seems to be the case. In this case at least, psychology seems to involve more than just common sense.

STEREOTYPES

Are the Japanese industrious, ambitious and intelligent?
Are Americans materialistic, pleasure-loving and conventional?
Are Jewish people ambitious, industrious and shrewd?
Are women more nurturing, caring and submissive than men?
Are bespectacled people intelligent?
Are professors eccentric and absent-minded?

Some people would answer 'Yes' to many of these questions, and would therefore have certain expectations about the behaviour of any new Japanese, American, Jewish, female, bespectacled or professorial person they might encounter. There can be no doubt that these expectations are faulty. Some Japanese are sloppy and imprecise. Some Americans are quiet and reserved. British people can be extrovert and sociable, and so on.

Such *stereotypes* about distinguishable groups of people persist nevertheless. They involve overgeneralization: people erroneously attribute all the characteristics of the stereotype to individual members of the group, even though only some (if any) of those characteristics are truly applicable. Stereotypes can be based on a number of different group characteristics: in the example at the beginning of this section, we have chosen nationality, race, gender, physical characteristics and occupation as the basis for them, but they might also be based on other sources of difference such as age, social class or even attitudes and preferences.

Exercise 4.1 shows how *musical preference* can be used as a basis for stereotyping: the knowledge that someone is a fan of pop music or a classical music listener can influence many other aspects of people's views about their attitudes and personality. The exercise is based on a study of university students by one of the authors and his colleague, Adrian North, at Leicester University, UK. We asked these students to complete questionnaires dealing with three musical styles (classical music, chart pop, and indie pop), and found that very strong stereotypes existed about the perceived characteristics of enthusiasts of these three styles.

These stereotypes can be a defining feature of lifestyle in teenagers. Knowledge of someone's preferred musical styles can be the key to explaining clothing preferences, hairstyles, preferred clubs and leisure haunts, and various other attitudes, likes and dislikes. The same author asked his two teenage sons to list 'the main styles of pop music', and they produced the following list: grunge/ indie, rock/heavy metal, rap, house/dance, jungle, soul/swing, acid jazz, chart pop. The boys also explained that each of these styles is linked with characteristic styles of dress and attitude. This list is of course specific to a certain time (1995) and place (the UK), but it shows how detailed the distinctions can be.

Are stereotypes always wrong?

The eminent social psychologist Roger Brown has suggested that views about ethnic and racial stereotypes have changed over time. He points out that the term 'stereotype' was first introduced by the political commentator Walter Lippman in his book *Public Opinion*, which was published in 1922. Lippman's clear view was that national and racial stereotypes were erroneous – that it was not only irrational but also potentially dangerous to propagate oversimplified stereotypes about why Jews, Negroes or Hispanics had such and such a personality.

This liberal view about the irrationality of stereotypes was (and probably still is) commonplace, and many sociologists and social psychologists spent a good deal of time propagating it to their students and others around them. Some well-known empirical evidence about ethnic stereotypes was provided in a classic study carried out by David Katz and Kenneth Braly in 1933, who asked 100 Princeton University students to assign 'typical' personality traits (for example, industrious, intelligent, materialistic, sly, progressive, treacherous) to each of ten ethnic groups (such as Germans, Italians, Jews, Negroes). The researchers found clear evidence of stereotyping, but argued that because there were such wide variations in what was considered to be 'typical' of each group, the stereotyping displayed by their subjects was indeed irrational and divisive.

This progressive point of view was given some support by a follow-up study of a further group of Princeton students in 1951 in which it was found that the level of stereotyping had declined in the intervening years. However, a further study in 1967 by Marvin Karlins, Thomas Coffman and Gary Walters showed that the stereotyping had increased ('rebounded') once again to 1933 levels, which suggests that the beliefs expressed may not have been so irrational after all. The problem here, as in many areas of social science, lies in the relationship between scientific evidence and the political context in which it occurs. In the 'politically correct' 1990s it is more dangerous than ever to express what might be seen to be any kind of prejudiced opinion about members of ethnic or other minority groups.

However, Roger Brown's perhaps wiser and more mature view is that it is naïve to suggest that there is no basis whatsoever for ethnic or other group stereotypes. Although it may still usually be wrong to try to describe what is *typical* of a given group, it may nevertheless be possible to define what is 'somewhat' or 'slightly' characteristic of them: the tendency to categorize is a basic aspect of human cognition, and it seems odd that stereotypes persist so strongly if they have no basis in reality whatever. The problem is that the answers to scientific questions such as these are inseparable from the political, social and cultural context in which they take place, and there is no doubt that stereotyped thinking can lead to terrible consequences for members of minority groups, as was clearly seen in the Second World War.

STEREOTYPING AND PREJUDICE

Even if stereotypes do have some basis in reality, they can be very damaging when they are used to convey generalized negative or

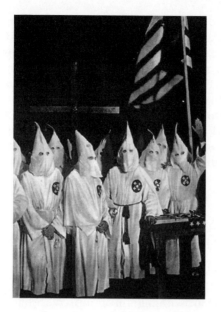

Figure 4.1: The use of stereotyped thinking against minority groups is termed 'prejudice'.

hostile attitudes towards groups of people. The use of stereotyped thinking against minority groups is what we might call *prejudice*. A very visible, offensive example of this is of course racial prejudice: some people really believe that blacks are stupid, lazy and oversexed, or that Jews are selfish, grasping and dishonest. Prejudice can be defined as 'an attitude (usually negative) toward the members of some group based solely on their membership of that group'. Impressions that are formed of particular individuals have nothing to do with the actual behaviour of those individuals, but are based instead on their membership of particular groups.

It's only a joke

Prejudice is at the heart of a good deal of racist humour: the basis of 'Irish jokes' in Britain is that the Irish are stupid, and there are similar Polish equivalents in the USA, for example. Do these jokes simply serve to 'let off steam'? Do we express prejudiced attitudes to other members of the group in a harmless, joking context (such as the revue in the social club) because we do not really hold them? Or is it that the humour itself creates prejudice: that sharing jokes about Irish or Polish stupidity, Scottish meanness or about mothers-in-law actually reinforces our stereotypes of these groups?

This latter idea is the first of four possible explanations of prejudice: that once we have acquired a stereotype about a particular group, we tend to take much more notice of information that fits in with it than of that which does not. This explanation is that we form *negative schemata*, systematically biased ways of thinking about that group, and that these stereotypes become self-confirming. In fact, if we receive new information which doesn't fit the stereotype, we go out of our way to find further information to rationalize this!

Competition

The second explanation is that prejudice arises from competition between different social groups: that when desirable economic resources such as jobs, good schooling or housing are in short supply, prejudiced attitudes can be fuelled. In Great Britain, for example, there is ill-feeling amongst some unemployed indigenous whites towards immigrant groups who have jobs, such as the Asian communities in cities like Leicester and Birmingham. One might reasonably expect this to reinforce stereotyped and prejudiced attitudes against individual Asians.

Social categorization

The third explanation is based on people's natural tendency to divide those around them into two basic groups, 'us' and 'them'. We identify ourselves with certain *in-groups*, whom we value highly, and correspondingly undervalue members of *out-groups*. A good example of this is in present-day Northern Ireland: the divisions between Catholic and Protestant members of the population are powerful and long-standing, and strangers are quickly categorized as members of one group or the other. When this happens, the processes of stereotyping and overgeneralization come into play so that certain attitudes and behaviour are attributed to the newcomer. These are automatically also seen in a negative light, and lead to dislike or hatred.

Social learning

The fourth and final explanation is that prejudiced attitudes are learnt from early childhood onwards – that they are shaped by parents, peers and other powerful social influences. This is easy to see in the example of Northern Ireland just mentioned: generation after generation of children are taught within the family to despise the members of the opposing group. When such attitudes are implanted at an early age, it is easy to see that they are likely to be particularly strong and resistant to change. *Social learning* also takes place as a result of the models and roles that children see in the world around them: in magazines, newspapers, and on TV, for example.

Gender stereotyping is strongly prevalent on television, for example. Women are typically seen in subservient roles in many advertisements and programmes, and men are much more likely to be seen in powerful or dominant parts. You may have already noticed this if you tried *Exercise 3.2* in Chapter 3. The broadcasting authorities are aware of this problem of course, and are doing their best to break down stereotypes. For example, there are now many more female TV and radio presenters than there were a decade or two ago. There is also a noticeably higher proportion of presenters who are members of ethnic minority groups, and who have regional accents rather than the received pronunciation (RP) for which the world-famous BBC used to be renowned.

HOW DO OTHERS INFLUENCE US?

Consider the following questions:

- When you are carrying out an everyday task, do you think that you would behave in exactly the same way when on your own as you would in the company of others?

- If you were to collapse in the street would you assume that you would get more help if you were amongst many others, than if there were very few or just one person nearby?

- If you found yourself in a group in which others were saying something that was contrary to the evidence of your own eyes, would you speak out and tell them so?

The answers to these questions may seem obvious. If you are 'your own person' and confident of yourself then you probably do not see yourself as swayed or influenced by others. Obviously you would speak the truth as you see it, or assume that if more people were around then more help would be available should you need it. In fact, research by social psychologists has shown that in each of these situations the answer is quite likely to be 'No'. People's behaviour and decision making is influenced by the presence of others and this may apply even if there is no direct interaction between them.

Being true to oneself would therefore seem to be a contradiction, because you could almost say it depends on the situation that you find yourself in. Of course, it's not quite so simple as this, but, as we shall see, social influences on our behaviour and cognition are varied and complex.

Social loafing

Probably the first social psychological experiment was by a Professor Ringelmann. He was actually an engineering professor, but was able to show that in a tug-of-war team, the more members of the team there were, the less hard each member pulled on the rope. In this case the effect of the others seemed to inhibit the performance of each team in trying to out-tug the other. Later, this finding was labelled *social loafing* by Bibb Latané and others because they found similar results, particularly in situations where someone was in distress or requiring help. These studies have shown that a person may get less help from members of a crowd or group than if there is just one bystander. The murder of Kitty Genovese in 1964 is a real example of this; despite many people (there were 38 witnesses) hearing her cries for help, not one person came to her aid or even called the police. This research led psychologists to conclude that, 'The larger the number of onlookers, the smaller the individual probability of helping, and the longer the delay'. Other studies do not find this inhibitory effect of the presence of others – indeed, quite the reverse.

Social facilitation

Robert Zajonc and many others have reported that individuals perform better when others are around than when they are alone. In a number of tasks it was found that people working together, or in the presence of others, perform at a faster rate. These effects have been termed *coaction* and *audience effects*. However, the presence of others works best on simple or well-learned tasks; if the task is new or difficult then the presence of others impairs performance. (Have you ever tried to find something in the presence of someone who is eager for you to find it? Why is it you can never find it while they are there, but find it as soon as they've left the room?)

Social facilitation is not just a feature of human behaviour – we can see similar effects in a variety of non-human animals including some intriguing studies on cockroaches. In humans it applies particularly in the context of sports and familiar everyday tasks. But why does it appear that the presence of others can have both inhibitory and enhancing effects on us?

Mary Brickner and co-workers have suggested that the importance of the task and the cultural context are factors that may explain the two apparently opposing findings. They argued that loafing was more likely to occur in relation to unimportant tasks. Studies of different cultures indicate that a situation producing social loafing in the West may actually produce an enhancing effect in China and Japan. Perhaps it depends on whether a culture stresses the importance of the individual or the group in its ideology.

Social influences on decision making

A number of researchers have shown that it's not just what you do but what you *think* that can be influenced by others.

Psychologists have found, as we saw in the Introductory chapter, that group decisions can often be more extreme than an individual's decision made alone. This is known as the *group polarization phenomenon* and the example we cited in the Introduction was the *risky shift*, a particular form of the phenomenon discovered by James Stoner. Stoner was surprised to find this because we generally think that decisions made by boards and committees are likely to be safer decisions where an extreme view will be stifled. As we outlined, there are two main hypotheses which explain why this might arise and it has been suggested that in groups where there is an exchange of information, the group may wish to define its identity more clearly, hence producing a pressure to move to the extreme.

Other research indicates that the presence of others may result in pressure to conform and this is exemplified in a classic study by Solomon Asch.

CONFORMITY

In 1951 Solomon Asch published an experiment on visual perception in which participants were asked to match a standard line
with one of three alternatives, is a task which all people with normal vision can do quite accurately. Tests were run using groups
of seven to nine people who were asked to answer aloud.
However, the experiment was rigged. Asch used only one true
participant – and the others were confederates whose answers
had been pre-determined. Each naïve participant was placed
towards the end of the row so that the majority of the confederates' responses were given first.

Asch determined in advance that on two-thirds of the tests confederates would unanimously respond with one of the wrong alternatives. How would the naïve participant react when confronted
by this? On testing over 100 naïve participants, he found that only
25 per cent of them remained independent. Across the whole
sample the error rate was 36.8 per cent of judgements, whereas in
normal circumstances it would have been less than 1 per cent.
Why did the participants 'give in' or conform to the majority judgement, despite the indisputable evidence before their eyes?

Why does conformity occur?

The high level of conformity found in the Asch study prompted a
number of further experiments. Asch found that the size of the
group, providing that it was of at least three confederates, did not
affect the degree to which a single naive participant conformed.
(Later research indicated that conformity increases up to a group
size of seven confederates and thereafter does not rise. A larger
crowd does not appear to enhance the effect.) The attractiveness
of the group, and the confidence of the naïve subject in his or her
ability, also influence conforming behaviour. Participants who
perceive the group as desirable, and who feel that they are less
competent than average will, experiments show, be more likely to
follow the lead of the group rather than stick to their own view.

In addition to this, other research suggests that there is also a
physiological pressure to conform. Measures of the fatty acid levels in the blood of participants in an experiment of this type
show an increased level of blood fatty acids when they held out
against the confederates' wrong responses, but this was lower for

participants who conformed and also gave wrong responses. Evidently not conforming is an uncomfortable experience.

How did participants explain their conformity? Asch found that many participants complied whilst privately rejecting the majority view which was voiced. But they still underestimated the extent to which they conformed and voiced wrong answers. This suggests that their judgement was partly distorted by group pressure.

More recent reviews have argued that Asch's findings have been misinterpreted and it has been pointed out that participants managed to resist conformity pressures on about two-thirds of the judgements and that thus conformity was the exception, rather than the rule.

Resisting the pressure to conform

Having an ally is one important way that can enable a participant to resist group pressure. If two naïve participants were present in an Asch-type experiment, conformity dropped to 5.5 per cent of the judgements given. The support of someone else agreeing with the participant's view clearly enabled her or him to resist strong group pressures.

Other research indicates that conformity varies depending on the consistency of the confederate's judgements – the greater the consistency shown, the greater the conformity from the naïve participant and vice versa. Cultural factors also play a part and research on conformity in different countries has found some variations but in general there are still quite high levels of conformity wherever research is carried out. Only one study, reported in the 1980s, found that a group of engineering students showed minimal conformity in an Asch-type experiment: the researchers argued that this was because the students' training encouraged precision and accuracy.

The research on conformity is shocking in some respects. Most of us would hope that we could resist pressure of this kind, but even though some resistance was occurring, it is still a matter of concern that group pressure can be so potent.

COMPLIANCE AND OBEDIENCE

Having considered a fairly subtle form of pressure, let us now explore how people react to being given quite specific instructions on what to do. Would you obey instructions when you felt what you were being asked to do was harmful?

Some controversial experiments on obedience were carried out by Stanley Milgram. His 'teacher' participants, who thought that they were taking part in an experiment on the effects of punishment on memory, were told to deliver electric shocks of increasing intensity when a 'learner' subject, out of sight in an adjacent room, made an error in a task. Shocks ranged from 15–450 volts, and shock buttons were labelled from 'Slight shock' to 'Danger: severe shock' at the top of the scale. The learner, who was actually an actor confederate of the experimenter, behaved as if he actually received the shocks (in fact, he did not) and could be heard crying out as they were apparently given. The true aim of the study was to explore the extent of the 'teacher' participants' obedience to the instructions.

All the participants in Milgram's experiment were men of above average intelligence and yet two-thirds of them obeyed the instructions, delivering shocks up to the danger zone, whilst showing great distress in doing so and even pleading with the experimenter to stop the study. The power of the experimenter was extraordinary. Psychiatrists asked to estimate the level of obedience had predicted that no more than one per cent would obey instructions to this degree. Obedience to authority appeared to override humane considerations.

Milgram's experiment and the subsequent variations which have been carried out have been severely criticized. Many believe that trust in psychologists, and the health and dignity of the participants, were greatly at risk. The fact that the participants were debriefed only goes part of the way towards allaying these ethical objections. Nevertheless, the results clearly show that authority is very powerful. It is hard for a single person to resist, though obedience was found to be greatly reduced if two naïve 'teacher' participants were allowed to work together.

THE POWER OF AUTHORITY

Stanley Milgram's experiment reveals to us the power of an authority figure, in this case the experimenter. This person is seen as a professional, carrying out important research. After all, understanding more about learning is something that most of us would believe to be of value in psychological research. The catch is that if the 'professional' is unethical in what she or he requires of us we may fall into the same trap as the participants in Milgram's experiment.

An authority figure, someone we see as having legitimate power, can make us feel unable to question what is required of us. In the last few decades there has been a considerable amount of research on management and the ways in which leaders or bosses can be trained to manage others effectively. Styles of leadership or management have been identified and large organizations have spent time and money on training of this type for supervisors, managers or anyone who has subordinates or teams to work with.

Leaders do not always gain power through their official position in an organization; leaders can emerge in groups where all the members start out on an equal footing. In recent years, the concept of *charisma* has re-emerged as a possible explanation for the power of some leaders. What distinguishes the charismatic leader from others is that such a person is able to establish an *intense emotional bond* with their followers and he or she has a shared vision with those who follow of what the future might be. Studies of charismatic business leaders have been carried out by Alan Bryman. We do not have space to explore leadership, of whatever type, in detail here, but its relevance to our discussion is that those who gain power by whatever means may be those whom it is hard for us to disobey.

One of the authors well remembers, while carrying out research on mothers and babies, observing an angry nurse 'ticking off' a new mother on the maternity ward as she placed her newborn baby on its back in the cot (a tradition of the Asian community from which she came). Obediently the mother placed her baby on its tummy. Several years later, after more authorities had researched cot deaths, one could well imagine the reverse scenario with babies being turned from tummy to back. Such a situation reveals that the views of authorities are subject to change and there are times when the ability to resist or rebel is important.

It is of some comfort to report that studies of the Milgram type carried out in Australia, Germany and the Netherlands have shown that obedience, in certain conditions, can be minimal. The main factor that enabled the individual to resist was having an experimental accomplice who refused to obey instructions. Just as we saw in the Asch study, so too in the Milgram situation support from one other individual makes a crucial difference. Perhaps what we can learn from this is that standing alone in our views is a very difficult thing for most people; if we have no support we need to look for it, and this seems to provide the strength to resist those in authority.

Being independent is not easy, as we have seen, and the increasing number of books and courses on 'assertiveness training' (mentioned in Chapter 1) are an aid to those who feel they are 'Yes-people' – people who cannot, or dare not, speak out against individual or group pressure.

Being assertive does not mean always getting what you want when you want it; it means negotiating with others to reach a fair or equitable solution when a conflict of interest arises. When conflicts arise, emotions are involved, and many people are unable to cope when confronted by an angry person, especially when the person is felt to have some power over us, for example, boss, parent, and even spouse or child. One technique for dealing with conflicts when one feels the need to resist pressure and refuse a request is the *broken record technique*. *Exercise 4.2* illustrates this technique.

THE INFLUENCE OF THE MASS MEDIA

The growth of the mass media in the last four decades has led to a great increase in the size of the group which can influence us. Today there are films, radio, television (numerous channels), newspapers, magazines, and, most recently, computer-generated images in computer games, as well as the myriad of information available world-wide on the Internet. Whilst this makes available to people an almost infinite amount of information, such immediate access to the world can also have a down side and there is now concern about the possible adverse influence of some of this material, in particular violent or pornographic information. We shall consider the impact of violent images in this section.

Since the arrival of television there has been a burgeoning of research investigating the effects of observing violence on people's behaviour and attitudes. Indeed, in North America it has been estimated that children have probably seen 18,000 TV murders by the time they have graduated from high school. This has contributed to the very strong gut feeling expressed by the public that a heavy diet of violent programs (be they cartoons, videos or films, or news coverage) can do nothing positive for children.

Aggression and violent images

The definition of what constitutes aggression is the first problem encountered in carrying out the research (see Chapter 5 for a fuller discussion). Researchers must look not only at the incidence of aggression but also at the way in which it is portrayed. A violent event in a 'Tom and Jerry' cartoon is unlikely to be comparable to one reported in a news programme, but even cartoon images may not be innocuous in their effects. Several hypotheses have been put forward about the effects of observing violence. Seymour Feshbach, amongst others, has suggested that it is 'cathartic'; that watching screen violence may reduce viewers' likelihood of subsequently displaying violence. Others believe the opposite – that it may increase the chances of violence and aggression in the observers, and current thinking tends to support this view.

In 1994, Elizabeth Newson, of Nottingham University, UK, circulated a paper on video violence and the protection of children. In this paper she voiced her very deep concern about these issues, and her views were endorsed by 25 professionals working with children. These issues have also been tackled in a report, *Children and Violence*, published in 1995, and in this it was claimed that:

There is an authoritative body of psychological opinion internationally which believes that higher levels of viewing violent images are correlated with increased acceptance of aggressive attitudes and aggressive behaviour.

These publications indicate a higher level of concern than has been expressed in earlier research studies where a rather more cautious line had been taken. However, the belief that such images can cause increased levels of aggression is not unanimous among the professionals. Guy Cumberbach, an eminent researcher in this field, takes the view that much of the research which is used as evidence for these claims is flawed and he feels that in normal circumstances the majority of mass communication has a very limited effect on its audience. He also challenges the view that children are particularly vulnerable.

Research of this type is not easy to conduct; much of it is in a contrived setting, or involves acts of aggression that may be perceived as relatively minor ones because of the ethical difficulties of using very violent images in such research studies. In an attempt to investigate these issues on a large scale, Stanley Milgram carried out research in America on this topic. He contrived that a TV show shown in some areas would contain two anti-social acts: breaking a charity box, and making an abusive phone call. A 'control' programme, which did not contain these acts, was shown in parallel broadcasts in other viewing areas. Many people watched the shows in viewing studios containing charity boxes and telephones, but no significant differences in subsequent anti-social acts were found between the two viewing areas. This result provides no immediate evidence for the large-scale imitation of TV violence, and of course it tells us nothing about the long-term effects of such viewing. Other studies do find positive correlation between observing violence and its imitation, but of course this does not indicate a causal link.

A number of researchers who have compared children who have observed TV violence with those who have not indicate that there is some evidence for increased aggression in children in the former group and this research implicates even the cartoon as a possible means of promoting aggressive acts.

It would seem that in spite of the conflicting evidence, the current mood amongst psychologists is to be inclined to the view that if there is any positive evidence linking the viewing of violence with adverse changes in behaviour and attitudes then steps should be taken to protect people, especially children, from exposure to such material. Indeed an American Psychological Association (APA) Commission on Youth and Violence recommends that teaching children critical viewing skills at home and at school could be one way of mitigating the effects of television violence, and they add that 'television can be an effective and persuasive teacher of pro-social attitudes and has the potential to make a major contribution towards reducing violence'. This statement recognizes the capacity of television as having potential as a force for good, but if so then it must also be recognised as having equal potential in the opposite direction.

THE POWER OF SOCIAL INFLUENCE

This chapter has spelled out the immense power of other people upon our behaviour as individuals. Social influence shapes what we do, what we think, and indeed, most aspects of our personalities. It determines our impressions of other people, and our attitudes and behaviour towards them. The mere presence of others can alter and distort our judgements, even when we disagree violently with those others.

Under certain circumstances, social pressures may force us to do things which we would not otherwise have contemplated. Recent stories of atrocities in Bosnia, for example, make it clear that those who committed them did so as a result of intolerable social pressure. The study of football hooliganism, in Great Britain at least, seems to suggest that some of the worst offenders are law-abiding, unexceptional citizens who hold down respectable jobs in everyday life. It is only when they are in certain social situations, notably crowds, that they become anti-social and potentially harmful to others.

Social influence can be used for the good of humankind as well as for its ill, however, as the recent and regular charity relief appeals such as 'Comic Relief' clearly show. The power of the mass media is skilfully used to bring the plight of famine-stricken inhabitants of the Third World to the notice of the affluent West. Many Westerners who would otherwise have ignored charity appeals have in this case made generous donations to the cause, partly because they are responding to the actions of their friends, neighbours and colleagues.

The power of social influence in the 20th century is becoming ever greater as electronic communication and information storage becomes increasingly efficient: the potential effects and increasing access to the Internet, for example, are only just beginning to be realized. As we approach the millenium, the insights of social psychological knowledge will become increasingly important in analysing the implications of the tremendous changes in human communication which are taking place.

References

Argyle, M. and Colman, A. (Eds.) (1994). *Social Psychology*. Harlow: Longman. [Cross-cultural studies of the Milgram type experiment.]

Aronson, E. (1995). *The Social Animal*. San Francisco: W.H. Freeman. [Includes quote on craziness.]

Asch, S.E. (1955). Opinions and Social Pressure. *Scientific American, 193*, 31–35. [Studies of conformity.]

Brickner, M.A., Ostrom, T.M. and Harkins, S.G. (1986). Effects of personal involvement: Thought-provoking implications for social loafing. *Journal of Personality and Social Psychology, 51*, 763–769. [Social loafing and social facilitation.]

Brown, R. (1986). *Social Psychology, 2nd edition*. New York: The Free Press. [Many aspects of the topic of social loafing.]

Bryman, A. (1992). *Charisma and Leadership in Organisations*. London: Sage. [Research on charisma.]

Feshbach, S. (1961). The stimulating versus cathartic effects of a vicarious aggressive activity. *Journal of Abnormal and Social Psychology, 63(2)*, 381–385. [The effects of viewing violence.]

Festinger, L. (1957). *A Theory of Cognitive Dissonance*. Stanford: Stanford University Press. [Festinger's original statement of his theory.]

Festinger, L. and Carlsmith, J.M. (1959). Cognitive consequences of forced compliance. *Journal of Abnormal and Social Psychology, 63(2)*, 381–385. [Compliance and why it occurs: strategies of 'face-saving'.]

Gilbert, G.M. (1951). Stereotype persistence and changes among college students. *Journal of Abnormal and Social Psychology, 46*, 245–254. [A follow-up to the Katz and Braly study.]

Gulbenkian Foundation Commission. (1995). *Children and Violence*. London: Calouste Gulbenkian Foundation. [Includes references on Newson on pages 69–70 and Cumberbatch.]

Karlins, M., Coffman, T.L. and Walters, G. (1969). On the fading of social stereotypes: studies in three generations of college students. *Journal of Personality and Social Psychology, 13*, 1–16. [The latest of three studies of stereotyping.]

Katz, D. and Braly, K.W. (1933). Racial stereotypes of one hundred college students. *Journal of Abnormal and Social Psychology, 13*, 1–16. [The first attempt to identify ethnic stereotypes.]

Kravitz, D.A. and Martin, B. (1986). Ringelmann rediscovered: The original article. *Journal of Personality and Social Psychology, 50*, 936–941. [The tug-of-war study.]

Latane, B., Williams, K. and Harkins, S.G. (1979). Many hands make light work: The causes and consequences of social loafing. *Journal of Social Psychology, 27*, 822, 832. [Social loafing.]

Lippman, W. (1922). *Public Opinion*. New York: Harcourt, Brace. [Original discussion of the term *stereotype*.]

Milgram, S. (1974). Conversation. *Psychology Today, June*, 71–80. [TV and its influence on violence.]

Milgram, S. (1963). Behavioural study of obedience. *Journal of Abnormal and Social Psychology, 67(4)*, 371–378. [Experiment on obedience to authority.]

Moscovici, S. (1980). Cited in Argyle, M. and Colman, A.M. (Eds), *Social Psychology*. Harlow: Longman. [Conformity and consistency in the confederates.]

North, A.C. and Hargreaves, D.J. (1997). Musical preference and social cognition in adolescence: music as a 'badge'. *Manuscript submitted for publication*. [An attempt to identify attitudes associated with three musical styles.]

Perrin, S. and Spencer, C.P. (1981). Independence of conformity in the Asch experiment as a reflection of cultural and situational factors. *British Journal of Social Psychology, 20(3)*, 205–309. [Conformity and engineering students.]

Sanson, A. and Di Muccio, C. (1993). The influence of aggressive and neutral cartoons and toys on the behaviour of pre-school children. Special Issue: The Psychology of Peace and Conflict. *Australian Psychologist, 28(2)*, 93–99. [Cartoons and violence.]

Stoner, J.A.F. (1961). Cited in Argyle, M. and Colman, A.M. (Eds), *Social Psychology*. Harlow, Essex: Longman. [The risky shift.]

Zajonc, R.B. (1965). Social facilitation. *Science, 142*, 269–274. [Social facilitation.]

Recommended Reading

Aronson, E. (1995). *The Social Animal*. San Francisco: W.H. Freeman.

Baron, R.A. and Byrne, D. (1987). *Social Psychology: Understanding Human Interaction, 5th edn*. Boston: Allyn and Bacon.

Brown, R. (1986). *Social Psychology: The Second Edition*. New York: The Free Press.

Eiser, J.R. (1986). *Social Psychology*. Cambridge: Cambridge University Press

MUSICAL STEREOTYPES

INSTRUCTIONS: *Karen Green* and *Karen Brown* are described below. Read the description of Karen Green to one group of people and ask them to assess her character by selecting one member of each pair of statements in the 'Questionnaire' below. Carry out the same procedure for Karen Brown with a separate, equivalent group of people.

Karen Green is 15 years old, goes to a local secondary school, and has two younger brothers. She is quite interested in tennis and reading, but her main leisure interest is music. She listens to a lot of classical music and has over 50 CDs, including recordings of the music of Mozart and Beethoven.

Karen Brown is 15 years old, goes to a local secondary school, and has two younger brothers. She is quite interested in tennis and reading, but her main leisure interest is music. She listens to a lot of pop music and has over 50 CDs, including some by Blur and Oasis.

Questionnaire

1. Concerned about her appearance — Unconcerned about appearance
2. Pro-establishment — Anti-establishment
3. Fun-loving — Serious
4. Sees technology as a good thing — Uninterested in technology
5. Keen on women's rights — Uninterested in women's rights
6. Enjoys thinking about things — Not very reflective
7. Likes to be popular — Not concerned about others
8. Unconventional — Conventional
9. Fond of tradition — Not keen on tradition
10. Religious — Not religious
11. Sophisticated — Unsophisticated
12. Has intellectual interests — Anti-intellectual

RESULTS: How did your two groups of people differ in their descriptions? Is this result surprising?

THE BROKEN RECORD TECHNIQUE

This is a technique which enables you to be persistent in asserting your needs or wishes. Like the broken record, all that you do is repeat over and over again in an assertive manner, what you want or need. Broken record is useful in a variety of situations:

● when faced with someone who won't take 'No' for an answer and persists in asking for reasons for your refusal;

● when in a situation where you are continually being diverted from your own goals by clever, but irrelevant points;

● when you wish to save time and curtail unproductive discussions.

In the following example of a refusal, this technique can be used from the outset or after you have given the explanation which you feel is a fair and adequate one in the situation. If you feel that the person making the request disregards your rights, then no explanation is required.

EXAMPLE: Refusing another drink. 'A' asks the questions, 'B' makes the responses.

A response lacking in assertiveness	*An assertive response*
A. 'Would you like another drink?'	A. 'Would you like another drink?'
B. 'No thanks – I've had plenty and I don't want another one.'	B. 'No thanks – I've had plenty and I don't want another one.'
A. 'But we're all having one, you must join us.'	A. 'But we're all having one, you must join us.'
B. 'No, I'm driving and must watch my drinking.'	B. 'I don't want another one.'
A. 'Oh come on, the police never breathalize round here.'	A. 'Oh come on, just one more.'
B. 'No, I don't want to risk it, I need my car for my job.'	B. 'I don't want another one.'
A. 'Oh don't be such a wimp, can't you hold your drink then?'	A. 'Oh don't be such a wimp, can't you hold your drink then?'

continued

continued --

THE BROKEN RECORD TECHNIQUE

B. 'Well I'm not used to beer and I feel a bit . . . '

Etc. etc., numerous complicated and fruitless explanations which make you feel weak and foolish, probably leading you to accept a further drink.

B. 'I don't want another one.'

Etc. etc., this dialogue can go on and on, but you retain your dignity and you stick to your original decision of refusing a drink.

COMMENT

Note, in the example given, that the assertive person achieved his/her goal, whilst the person lacking assertion probably ended up by having, 'Well, just one more then', as well as going into enormous detail about him or herself and effectively agreeing that s/he was a wimp. The outcome of the latter is that the person offering the drink learns that the other is weak and will give in, if persuaded, whereas the assertive response shows clearly what the assertive person's limits are. The technique helps you set and keep your own limits and it also enables you to teach others your particular limits.

ROLE PLAY

If the dialogue on the left in this example sounds familiar and you recognize yourself in it, then role play this with a friend. Get your friend to take on A's role and try to persuade you to do something that you want to refuse (but often find it hard to). First, role play your usual type of response, then try the broken record technique in role play. Ask your friend to comment on your performance and repeat the dialogue again until you can refuse assertively.

5. *Your Emotions*

Humans can experience a wide range of emotions, and at times, emotions can be switched on or off with amazing rapidity. We only have to watch a baby laugh, cry and go red in the face with anger all in the space of a few moments to know that one emotion can overtake another in rapid succession. We are less likely to witness such dramatic changes in adults, whose emotional expressions are kept under greater conscious control. Nevertheless, each of us is aware, in our day-to-day lives, of feeling happy, annoyed, sad, bored, irritated, depressed or any of a multitude of feelings without any conscious effort. We may not express these feelings as a baby or toddler might, and there are marked cultural differences in the extent to which emotional expression is permitted, as we saw in Chapter 1, but we experience these feelings nonetheless.

What are emotions? We often talk of emotions or feelings as being one and the same. It is true that a key element in emotion is a bodily change – a physiological response such as a beating heart, sweating, flushed or pale face, weakness at the knees, or butterflies in the stomach – accompanied by a particular strong feeling, such as love, terror, anger or fear. Emotions seem to be separate from the thinking part of our mind; we may say 'I just can't help loving him/her' despite what appear to be numerous reasons that may make us not even *like* the person. But emotions are not separate from the rational, thinking part of our minds, as we shall see.

In general, emotion and cognition are bound up together, and although we can identify an emotion as 'a state of agitation' which has measurable physiological changes, emotional experience is linked with an attribution process. (For a fuller explanation of 'attribution process' see Chapter 2.) We actively seek an explanation for our feelings; the physiological changes are not a sufficient condition for the occurrence of an emotional experience. A rapidly beating heart may be due to love, anger or even vigorous exercise; the emotional experience depends on various cognitions that enable us to determine which. However, the interpretation of our feelings or bodily changes is not always as simple as we might believe.

This is illustrated in an intriguing study by Donald Dutton and Arthur Aron. In their experiment, one group of men was required to cross a very high, swaying bridge above rocks and rapids. The bridge had a low guard rail and was predicted to produce a feeling of anxiety (or high arousal) in the men crossing it. Another group of men crossed a low and sturdy bridge (the control group). On the opposite side of the bridge, men in both groups met a woman confederate of the experimenters, who administered a personality test to them all. Men in the experimental (swaying bridge) group showed more sexual imagery on the test and were judged to be more attracted to the woman confederate than those in the control group. More men from the experimental group telephoned her afterwards to find out further details about the experiment – she had offered her phone number for this reason to all participants. The men in the experimental group, it was argued, attributed their feelings of high arousal, at least in part, to the attractions of the woman, rather than solely to the anxiety caused by their nerve-wracking bridge crossing. This study has been criticized, but subsequent work has confirmed that it is possible for us to attribute bodily sensations to the incorrect source, as was suggested here. In reviewing this research, Bernard Murstein points out that this misattribution is most likely to occur in situations where the true cause of the feelings is minimized.

In the past, psychologists believed that some emotions were instinctive, a term used to describe both the inbuilt drive (or motivation) underlying behaviour, and/or the unlearned behaviour patterns themselves. It was thought that instincts were inbuilt into the individual, and there was much speculation concerning which emotions were fundamental. Drives, for the satisfaction of physiological needs such as hunger and thirst, were felt to be fundamental motives, but an emotion such as love, for instance, was often described as a secondary drive. Such a drive, it was said, arose through association with a primary drive. A baby's love for its mother was considered by some to fit this category, because the mother, by feeding her baby, satisfied the primary drive of hunger, and thus a need or love for mother was derived by association. As we shall see, research on love and attachment in infants throws some light on the truth of this.

Humans are capable of experiencing very many different emotions and in this book we cannot hope to do justice to all of these. We have therefore decided to concentrate on just two areas of emotional experience: 'attachment and love' and 'anger and aggression'.

LOVE AND ATTACHMENT

We use the word love in many different ways to describe our feelings for people, for non-humans, for food and drink, inanimate objects (home, work) and much more. We shall confine ourselves in this chapter to animate objects.

Psychologists have suggested that love or attachment is 'an affectional tie that binds one individual to another', and that such an emotion is likely to be manifest in certain types of behaviour, such as that designed to promote proximity and physical contact with the object of the attachment. This definition makes it possible to identify patterns of behaviour which are signs of an attachment and thus to measure the emotion.

First Love

When does a baby first feel love? Does love develop rapidly after birth or is it a gradual process? Studies of non-human animals, such as those by Konrad Lorenz, have been influential in shaping our ideas. Lorenz was an ethologist who observed that goslings form a strong attachment to their mother, or, if they were separated from her at hatching, would follow, and become attached to,

Figure 5.1: Imprinting.

almost any reasonably large animal, or object, to which they were exposed. Their attachment was so strong that Lorenz likened it to a pathological fixation and termed it 'imprinting'. Imprinting was found to have long-term effects on behaviour, in particular social and sexual behaviour, and Lorenz showed that if he hand-reared goslings, later on they chose him as their mate, rather than a member of their own species. Lorenz went on to demonstrate that the young of a variety of bird species, in particular the precocial ones (those that are mobile and well developed at hatching) such as ducklings, chicks of domestic fowl and turkey poults, also show imprinting. Other researchers began to investigate this topic in mammals and it led to speculation about 'human imprinting'.

Researchers became interested in the relationship between the human baby and its mother after birth and the notion that perhaps both baby and mother bond quickly after birth. Some researchers, such as Lee Salk for example, even discussed the idea of the baby becoming imprinted on features of the mother, such as her heartbeat, *before* birth. Later studies have discounted the idea of imprinting as it is observed in precocial birds but studies have shown clear evidence of preferential responding to a variety of maternal cues. Babies show preferential responses to the smell of the mother's milk and to her voice very soon after birth but a true attachment to the mother seems to take some months to develop.

Rudolph Schaffer demonstrated that love for the mother (or carer) does not develop rapidly. It takes months for a specific attachment to be formed. Signs of attachment between babies and specific individuals include smiling, following with the eyes, crying in the absence of the mother, and greeting responses such as lifting the arms. Although these may occur in the first months of life in response to a range of individuals, such patterns are typically shown only in relation to particular individuals after six months of age. Schaffer found that by studying babies in the home and during short and longer separations from the mother, specific attachments are formed between six to nine months of age, and this has been described as the *sensitive period* for attachment in human babies.

Many parents will be aware that these stages occur in their own children because a small baby of just two or three months will smile at a stranger, or can be comforted by an unfamiliar adult when distressed. By seven months the same baby has become more choosy. Typically, he or she will only smile at specific individuals, and will only be comforted by those same individuals. If a stranger smiles at them, or tries to comfort them when they are upset, they will become even more upset. At seven or eight months a baby is likely to be described as 'clingy' by the parents, and at this time the baby finds both short and long-term separations from those to whom they are attached very distressing.

THE NATURE OF INFANT LOVE

Mary Ainsworth has studied in depth the nature of the relationships between a baby and his or her carers and she has shown that there are qualitative differences in the types of attachment shown by babies for their carers. Their love is expressed in different ways, and she described this in terms of the *level of security* shown in the infant's attachment. Ainsworth devised an intriguing way of measuring attachment in human babies. As we have already noted, babies become discriminating in their behaviour towards particular individuals, smiling selectively or only permitting certain individuals to comfort them. Mary Ainsworth used this to develop her standardized method of assessing infant attachment.

She developed the *Strange Situation*, a procedure in which the infant and caregiver undergo a short series of seven episodes, each lasting about three minutes. The infant, the caregiver (such as mother or father) and a stranger take part in these. The idea is that the baby experiences a series of situations in which it is with the caregiver and/or stranger, or alone. Each stage of the procedure is slightly more stressful for the infant (although a given episode is always shortened if the baby becomes more than mildly distressed), and by videotaping the whole session, attachment in the infant is assessed. Signs of attachment measured include proximity and contact seeking, contact maintaining, resistance, avoidance, search, interaction at a distance, and the infant's response when reunited with its caregiver.

The attachment or love shown by the infant leads to classification in one of three categories following assessment in the 'strange situation'. These are *securely attached* infants (Type B), and two categories of *anxiously attached* infants: those showing avoidance (Type A) and those showing *resistance* or *ambivalence* in their relationship to the caregiver (Type C). The category given applies to the *one* relationship measured and not to all the baby's relationships; thus, a baby could be securely attached to the mother but anxiously attached to the father, or vice versa – it is not possible to generalize.

A number of researchers have warned against assuming that this classification is appropriate universally because in different cultures the styles of interaction between caregiver and baby can be so different. In some cultures less than half of babies assessed in the *Strange Situation* were classified as securely attached and to assume that this indicates a problem with the parent–baby relationship may be unwise. For example, in cultures where babies are never away from their mothers, but carried with them constantly, any form of separation may be extremely distressing, leading to a distorted assessment of the relationship.

The *Strange Situation* has been widely used and is generally thought to be a reliable indicator of the nature of a particular relationship, not merely a measure of the infant's temperament. Initially, it was used for infants aged between 12 and 24 months but a similar form of assessment has been used with children up to the age of six, and with older children and adolescents questionnaire forms of separation anxiety have been devised to measure attachment between children and parents.

Love unlimited?

John Bowlby has been highly influential, over the past four decades, in shaping our views on how infants love and to whom their love is directed. Bowlby believed that a warm, intimate and continuous relationship with a mother (or mother substitute) was essential for mental health. He put forward the notion of 'monotropism', the idea that the baby is unable to form attachments to more than one person. Later Bowlby recognized that babies do indeed become attached to others, but he still believed that the mother was generally the primary figure to whom babies become attached. Other research, such as that by Rudolf Schaffer and Peggy Emerson showed that babies might have several attachment figures and the mother was not necessarily the person to whom the baby was most attached. In some families, fathers or other caregivers may be the primary figure. A number of studies show that infants do not suffer if they have several regular caregivers (for example, mother, childminder and grandmother), and this applies so long as there are not more than four or five such carers and they are all a regular part of the baby's life.

The importance of the first love or loves of the infant has been stressed by Bowlby, and before him Freud emphasized the damaging long-term effects on the individual of not having a satisfactory early loving relationship. Similarly, in non-human animals Lorenz has reported the later severe social and sexual problems that can arise in the absence of an early attachment.

Fortunately there are few people who have been without *any* opportunity to become attached to someone in infancy or childhood, but the evidence available suggests that, for those who have not loved or been loved, the effects are marked. Such a person develops into the so-called 'affectionless character', unable to feel any attachment for others in later life and unable to form loving relationships with other people. For those who have been orphaned in childhood, or have been separated from those they love, the long-term effects are much less serious. Loving in adult life appears to be built on early experiences of loving in childhood, and it is undoubtedly better for babies and children to have loved and lost than never to have loved, in terms of the long-term effects on adult relationships.

ADULT LOVE

First love, that between a baby and, typically, its mother, has been the focus of much research by psychologists, perhaps because the

Figure 5.2: For most people, being loved and loving someone is central to their lives as an adult.

mother–infant relationship is seen as the prototype of all love relationships that follow it. Love between adults has been much less studied, but, for most people, being loved and loving someone is central to their lives as an adult and so this relative lack of interest by psychologists is hard to explain.

Why do adults love each other? We can see an argument for infant love and mother love because the infant is so dependent on the mother for care, but is this the basis of adult love? Lawrence Casler sees love as a sign of inadequacy, a sign that the individual does not have the inner resources to stand alone. Others (for example, Erik Erikson) take just the opposite view and see the ability to love and form an intimate close relationship as an adult as a sign of adequacy and normality in an individual. Some believe that the role of love is to motivate people to be parents and take on the tasks of parenthood. Finally, Elaine Walster sees love as a label we give to a certain state of intense physiological arousal felt in a particular context. There is some evidence in support of this idea, as we saw earlier in the experiment by Donald Dutton and Arthur Aron.

Love between adults can take several forms: we may love those of the same sex as us, or of the opposite sex, and sexual attraction may or may not be included in our feelings. The definition of attachment given earlier makes no distinction between sexual love or love without this component, nor does it reveal whether liking is merely love of lesser intensity, or an entirely different emotion. Zick Rubin examined the relationship between love and liking, asking a large sample of students to answer various questions about their relationships with a lover and with a platonic friend. Careful statistical analysis of the answers revealed that love is made up of at least four components: *needing, caring, trust* and *tolerance*. Later research showed that for any individual the amount of each of the components in their own conception of love may vary.

Liking, in Rubin's terms, emerged as an emotion that is quite different from love; it is characterized by a person recognizing someone as mature and competent. Respect for a person seems to be central to the concept of liking. However, liking and love can go hand in hand, and a relationship described as one of liking or friendship may contain love elements.

THE NATURE OF ADULT LOVE

Signs of love

Bernard Murstein suggests that signs of love come in three forms or characteristics, as we see in *Table 5.1(i)*. We feel it, but this is not a reliable index of love because a man may love his partner, but, at a given moment, feel angry with her. Yet most of us would not say this temporary state overrides his love for her. A similar problem can occur when we consider an individual's behaviour, as loving behaviour is not always exhibited in those who claim to love. So finally we are left with love as a judgement, a '*cognitive decision by the individuals that they love one another*'. This decision may of course be reversed, but it seems that this is the key to adult love, be it based on feelings or behaviour, that it is a conscious decision.

The development of love

Three stages of love have been identified (see *Table 5.1(ii)*): *passionate, romantic* and *conjugal*, but the sequence of these stages

Table 5.1: Love in adults

(i) The characteristics of love: within the individual

Behaviour	–	responding to the other's needs
Feelings	–	physiological correlates, such as palpitations
Judgement	–	a cognitive decision

(ii) The development of love

Passionate	–	the initial stages, intense arousal
Romantic	–	the idealization of the loved one
Conjugal/companionate	–	occurs later in the relationship, involves liking and trust, knowledge replaces fantasy

(iii) Sternberg's triangular theory of love: three components within a relationship

Intimacy	–	feelings of closeness and being bonded
Passion	–	the drive to satisfy the love physically
Decision/commitment	–	the decision to love and then maintain that love

(iv) Lee's colours of love: love styles

Primary Colours
Eros	–	powerful physical love
Ludus	–	playful love
Storge	–	companionate love

Secondary Colours
Mania	–	desperate and mad love
Pragma	–	pragmatic love
Agape	–	selfless, altruistic love

has not been studied. Passionate love involves intense arousal, and romantic love involves idealization of the loved person. If you would like to find out the strength of your passionate love for your loved one, then fill in the *Passionate Love Scale* in *Exercise 5.1*. The least intense form of love is conjugal because it occurs after marriage (or a full partnership) is established and the couple habituate to each other and live their day-to-day existence together; passion may well be there, but liking and trust are the key elements in the relationship.

Types and styles of love

Is there just one type of love, or is love made up of a number of dimensions as are personality (see Chapter 2) or intelligence (Chapter 10)? We shall consider two theories – those of Robert Sternberg and John Alan Lee.

Robert Sternberg identifies three components of love in his Triangular Theory (see *Table 5.1(iii)*). These are intimacy, passion and commitment. Each of these is said to vary in different love relationships; thus, love at first sight will be higher on passion and lower on the other two components. This approach is a good beginning but needs further refinement to deal with all the complexities and subtleties of love.

Another approach to love has been John Alan Lee's analysis of the styles of love. Lee is less concerned with the definition of love, but more in enabling those who love to define the 'different colours' of love, as represented in *Table 5.1(iv)*. Lee investigated Canadian and British people's loving relationships by asking them to complete lengthy questionnaires on their relationship. Lee sees love as arising from blends of three 'primary' colours; these are *Eros, Ludus* and *Storge*.

Primary and secondary colours of love

The first colour of love is *Eros*. This is a love based on physical attraction and a quest for the lover's ideal beauty. *Ludus*, the second colour, is a playful love, unconcerned with commitment and skilled at the tactics of the game. The final primary colour is *Storge*, a love that is compassionate rather than passionate. Lee found that few love affairs are pure examples of one type, and the 'primary colours' of love blend to give a new type with its own unique properties. Three main blends of love were identified: *Mania, Pragma* and *Agape*. These are the secondary colours of love. A blend of Eros and Ludus produces Mania. The manic lover swings from ecstasy to despair, unlike erotic lovers who do not suffer pains with their pleasure. Some people describe this as a neurotic type of love. Pragma is a blend of Ludus and Storge, or, as Lee describes it, 'love with a shopping list; a love that seeks compatibility on practical criteria'. The last blend, Agape, is less common than the others. This is the classical Christian view of love; an altruistic love lacking in jealousy or impatience. This love is a mix of Storge and Eros. Lee goes on to say that there are many more mixtures or combinations in the 'colours of love', just as there are with true colours. He also discusses ludic eros and storgic ludus, for example, (see Further Reading for more information).

Lee studied people of all ages, classes and educational background and found that his classification of loving styles fitted all his groups. He also studied homosexual males and again the typology fitted their styles of loving. It should be emphasized, however, that this analysis has not been applied to other cultures, so we do not know whether it accurately reflects women's and men's love universally.

Just as it is possible to identify signs of attachment in a baby, so can this be identified in adults who love one another. Research has confirmed what we might have expected, in that typical signs include: displaying love verbally, displaying love physically in hugging and kissing, in being more relaxed in the presence of a loved one, in giving material evidence of love in gifts and helping behaviour, in showing emotions and moral support, and quite simply by increased mutual gaze. These different measures of the behaviour of love reflect what we might expect from the components in Rubin's study (p.135). Finally, is it possible to make predictions about how long love lasts, and whether a relationship can survive a long-term commitment such as marriage? John Lee believes that a lasting relationship is more likely if a couple share the same style of loving, but of the various types, the storgic lovers are most likely to survive together longest. Liking for the lover also seems to predict a longer-lasting relationship.

The conception of love in Western culture is that it *precedes* a long-term commitment and is something that is not under full rational control; thus it is common to hear people worrying over whether they love enough to make such a commitment as marriage. In other cultures, love is expected to *follow*, rather than precede, marriage; this shows us how entirely different are these two views of love, for clearly here it is what is *thought* which influences and shapes the loving which follows.

Let us now turn to entirely different emotional experiences: anger and aggression.

ANGER AND AGGRESSION

Psychologists have often been accused of having little to say about what the man or woman in the street regards as the 'real' issues and concerns of everyday life. This certainly applies to our topic of adult love, but, happily, there are many areas of psychological research which do not support this generalization, and few more so than human aggression.

Aggression, anger and hostility feature prominently on many people's lists of important concerns and have been widely researched. Most of the major schools of thought in psychology have had something to say about this form of behaviour, and some of these ideas have sprung directly from personal concern about the extent of human suffering caused by aggressive behaviour and from fears for the future of the species.

Once again, the first major difficulty lies in defining the term 'aggression'. A useful starting point is to distinguish aggression from the related concepts of anger and hostility. 'Anger' refers to a state of emotional arousal typically accompanied by activation of the autonomic nervous system and by characteristic patterns of facial expression (described in Chapter 1). It is clear that a person may be angry without being physically destructive. Equally, aggressive behaviour might occur without the aggressor feeling angry prior to the action. 'Hostility' refers to negative appraisals or evaluations of people or events. Psychologists frequently use the term 'cognitive' to describe this aspect of aggression. It would, of course, be possible to appraise a particular group in society (capitalists or communists, for instance) in very negative terms without feeling angry or behaving aggressively, though, as we noted earlier, as a rule cognitive and emotional processes are intricately linked.

Aggression, then, refers to overt or observable behaviour, though precisely what sort of behaviour may be deemed to be aggressive is controversial. Many contemporary psychologists suggest that the term 'aggression' is restricted to acts resulting in personal injury or destruction of property, while accepting that injury may be psychological as well as physical. Even this apparently simple definition has some difficulties. Are we to class as aggressive an injurious act that was 'accidental' (for example, shooting a person unintentionally) or an act that was intended to injure but 'failed' (attempting to shoot another, but missing)? In general, the definition of an act as aggressive involves a value judgement on the part of the observer. Injurious acts may not be labelled as aggressive when they are socially prescribed or approved; thus capital punishment or smacking a child are often not construed as acts of aggression. In this sense, labelling a behaviour as aggressive *always* has a social and political dimension to it.

HOT AND COLD AGGRESSION

It is useful to make a distinction between two kinds of aggression. These are *angry* and *instrumental*, or what some have called *annoyance-motivated* and *incentive-motivated* aggression. The former is proceeded by strong feelings. The person is in an aroused, psychologically-activated state, often induced by environmental frustration of some sort. This is *hot* aggression. In instrumental aggression, on the other hand, the aggressive act is used as a way of obtaining some environmental reward and heightened emotion may not be present, as in the case of someone using violence to rob a bank. There is a clear difference between a *cold* act of this sort and someone assaulting a neighbour following an angry argument. The two classes are, of course, not entirely independent, in that aggression is also intended to some extent to secure a 'reward' from the environment, though in this case the reward obtained is likely to be that of inflicting pain or injury itself.

Rewards for aggression

The many sources of instrumental aggression have been well-documented in psychological research. That some aggressive behaviour is indeed learned socially because it is effective in securing environmental rewards or because aggressive models for imitation exist is now widely accepted. The rewards for aggression are many and powerful. Young children may learn to become physically aggressive because initial attempts at fighting off a bully by 'hitting back' proved to be effective; the reward in this case is the alleviation of pain. Similarly, the marked differences between societies in the levels of violent crime are probably attributable in part to the differing extent to which violent behaviour is rewarded and punished. There exist cultures, and also sub-cultures within societies, in which violence is so strongly reinforced that it is pervasive. In such circumstances, aggression may be necessary for success and even essential for survival.

Anger in society

In recent years there has been increased interest in the study of angry forms of aggression and it is on this emotion that we shall focus for the rest of this chapter. It is striking that anger is an important feature of much of the violence which causes social concern. Studies of homicide, for example, suggest that this violent act is often a response to intense anger. The violent person is often described as in a 'fury' or in a 'rage', directed in many cases at a person with whom he or she has an intimate relationship (such as a wife or husband). Anger may also be involved in less obvious ways. There is evidence, for example, that many rapes show features of aggression. Nicholas Groth interviewed a large number of rapists and found that a substantial number of them were in an angry/frustrated state prior to the assault, and appeared to be motivated to hurt and degrade the victim rather than to obtain sexual relief. Thus the popular notion that the rapist has been overtaken by strong sexual feelings is a misleading one.

THE NATURE OF ANGER

Most people have experienced intense anger at some time, yet it is an emotion that we rarely analyse in any rational and objective way. One of the authors of this book carried out some research on anger by asking a group of students to recall, and write in detail, about a recent experience of anger in their everyday lives. Here are two representative incidents which were recalled.

The house we had just moved into was promised to be ready for the start of term by the landlady. But the downstairs was still undecorated and this was causing us a lot of inconvenience. What made me angry was the fact that the things we had been promised had not occurred. The landlady always had some poor excuse as to why things were going wrong. I got fed up with her excuses. I felt my blood boiling. It didn't last long because I started to laugh and then calm down. I thought to myself, 'It's no use getting annoyed over the situation because it wouldn't help matters', and I cooled down.

I was sitting on a bus, while the bus-driver was collecting the tickets. When he came to the back seat there were three black guys and one white sitting there. They couldn't find their tickets straight away, and fooled around a bit while looking for them. Suddenly the bus-driver stated that he had had enough of their fooling around and ordered them off the coach, threatening them with the police if they refused. I couldn't believe my ears at first. Then, I started getting really upset – I was almost on the point of physically showing my anger.

What does psychology have to say about experiences of this sort? It is possible to identify four components in the experience of anger: the *environment, cognition, emotional/psychological arousal* and the *aggressive behaviour* itself. That these components have very complex inter-relationships is now clear (see the account by Raymond Novaco). All four are likely to be involved in the incidents just described and the first two of these elements, in particular, have been the focus for recent experimental investigation.

PROVOCATION?

Anger and angry aggression are generally preceded by a triggering environmental event. In the incidents detailed, for example, the triggers are the landlady's failure to carry out her promises and the unjust treatment of the passengers. There are a number of theories concerning the nature of the events that are likely to be important. The *frustration-aggression* theory, for example, suggests that the blocking of activities directed towards an important goal for the person is likely to be crucial. This is more obvious in the first incident than in the second. Leonard Berkowitz has argued persuasively that environmental events elicit aggression to the extent that they are 'aversive' for the person or animal. Thus the absence of an expected reward (as in the first incident), or the blocking of goal-directed activity, produce aggression because they are unpleasant. Experiencing failure, being insulted, unjustly treated, or attacked, share the property of aversiveness and are capable, therefore, of producing anger and aggression. Leonard Berkowitz suggests that humans and other animals are born with a readiness to flee or to fight when confronted by an aversive stimulus. Which reaction will occur depends on previous learning experiences (flight, for example, may have been found to be more effective in the past) and on the nature of the particular situation (a situation where the person has a sense of being 'in control' may make a fight more likely). A number of laboratory and naturalistic studies give support to this theory, showing, for example, that pain is a powerful elicitor of angry aggression. Unpleasant smells, 'disgusting' visual stimuli (for example, pictures of diseased and suffering animals), and high temperatures have also been found to lower the threshold for aggression, though in the latter case the effect is curvilinear: that is, fairly high temperatures make us more irritable, but very high temperatures may actually reduce aggression, perhaps because their tendency is to make us sleepy and lethargic.

It is important to recognize that when we become angry we are not reacting just to an immediate trigger. That trigger is 'embedded' (as Raymond Novaco describes it) in a broader social context which often involves stress for the individual. For example, a father may lose his temper one afternoon while trying to control his 'naughty' three-year-old, but his reaction is likely to be affected by prior exposure to frustration and stress earlier in the day. Somehow, he transfers his anger and frustration from the earlier situation to the later one. It has been suggested that 'residual excitation' (at a physiological level) may account for this transfer. This raises the question of whether an individual's exposure to unpleasant and aversive social conditions, such as unemployment, poor housing conditions, or financial problems, may contribute directly to anger, and even violence, in response to the familiar frustrations of everyday life.

FEATURES OF ANGER

Psychologists such as James Averill have conducted diary studies of anger and aggression with a view to finding out what we report as making us angry in everyday life, rather than relying on rather unnatural laboratory studies. If you would like to keep an 'Anger Diary', see *Exercise 5.2.*

Diaries tend to confirm the importance of aversive/frustrating events for anger but also suggest a feature of anger not always apparent in the laboratory – that it is predominately elicited by *interpersonal events.* Other *people*, rather than things or impersonal occurrences, make us angry. James Averill reported that people become mildly to moderately angry in the range of several times a day to several times a week, and that only six per cent of incidents are elicited by a non-animate object. The frustrating person in over half the episodes was someone known and liked – friends and loved ones are common sources of aversive experiences.

The second component of anger, the cognitive aspect, is concerned with the way in which we appraise, interpret and construct the social environment. Attribution theory has been a major force in cognitive theorizing and attributions are now widely believed by psychologists to be relevant to anger and aggression. Attributions are best explained as the person's attempt to explain *why* an aversive or frustrating event has happened. The nature of the explanation a person arrives at determines in part how they feel and what they will do. An everyday example may make this clearer. Suppose that you are knocked off your bicycle by a car while travelling home from work. This painful and aversive event may be attributed by you to your own inadequacies ('I failed to look where I was going',) or to chance ('Given the number of cars and bicycles on the road, it is inevitable that accidents occur'). Neither of these attributions is likely to produce anger or aggression. If you made the attribution, however, that the car driver deliberately intended to knock you off your bicycle, or was driving carelessly, your threshold for anger and aggression is likely to be considerably lowered. Attributions of 'malevolent intent' of this sort have been shown to be important in understanding human aggression.

Psychologists have tried to tease out the factors which determine whether hostile attributions are made. Social judgements of this sort prove to have complex origins. Studies suggest that to assess a person's responsibility for the harmful event, the perceiver attempts first to establish whether the act carried out by the person was intended or unintended. If intended, the action may be construed as malevolently or non-malevolently motivated. It may be the case, of course, that particular individuals are biased in their appraisals. The person who is generally more angry and aggressive than others may habitually see the worst in other people's intentions and motivations and fail to undertake a rational evaluation of what caused a particular event to occur.

Psychological studies strongly suggest that cognitive processes of appraisal and attribution are crucial determinants of anger and of our emotions in general. One of the exciting developments of the late 1980s and 1990s has been the increasing interest shown in the emotions by cognitive scientists. Gerald Clore and his colleagues have tried to specify the cognitive conditions giving rise to anger and a range of related emotions. It appears that the appraisals underlying anger are complex, with subtle differences being found between anger and emotions such as resentment, reproach and frustration. You might find it useful to try to specify the conditions and appraisals giving rise to the emotions of anger and, say, sadness, based on your own experiences of these emotions. You might compare your account with the theories put forward by cognitive scientists such as Gerald Clore and Andrew Ortony.

But is appraisal necessary?

Some find contemporary theories of anger and other emotions to be excessively cognitive. Is anger necessarily preceded by appraisal and attribution of the person causing offence? Might anger sometimes be an automatic and immediate reaction, with little extended thought occurring between stimulus and response? It is likely that distinctive cognitive appraisals are not *necessary conditions* for the experience of anger, at least in its less intense forms.

The third and fourth components of anger are physiological arousal and the aggressive act itself, which may or may not follow anger arousal. 'I felt my blood boiling', in the first anger incident recalled on p.142, probably refers to the effects of the autonomic activation (increase in blood pressure, heart rate, respiration, muscle tension and so on) which we know accompanies the angry state. The precise role of physiological changes in the genesis of emotion is still controversial, as is the question of whether the pattern of physiological arousal that accompanies anger can be discriminated from that occurring with other strong emotions such as fear or anxiety. In particular individuals, the physiological component of anger can be strong and even overwhelming. One of the authors of this book had in therapy a client whose main problem was his inability to control his temper in a range of situations. He reported intense physical symptoms (sweating, muscle tension) for up to two days following an angry upsetting incident. A reaction of this intensity is probably rare but it does highlight the importance of physiological events.

Most experiences of anger in everyday life are not followed by physical aggression, as we saw in the two incidents described. James Averill found that less than ten per cent of angry episodes induced physical aggression. What he called 'contrary reactions', that is, activities opposite to the instigation of anger, such as being friendly to the instigator, were twice as frequent as physical aggression. Anger may produce a range of other reactions, and the previous learning experiences of the individual are clearly important in determining whether frustration and anger are responded to with withdrawal, help-seeking, constructive problem-solving, or what Albert Bandura has called 'self-anaesthetisation through drugs and alcohol'.

As suggested, there are likely to be complex and bi-directional relationships between the environmental, cognitive, physiological and behavioural components of anger. Ways of thinking and appraising may induce anger, but equally the emotional state of anger may make it more likely that we will think angry thoughts. Environmental frustration may cause aggression, but behaving aggressively may also expose the person to even more frustration (being disliked by others or even becoming subject to a retaliatory attack from them). Untangling these complex inter-relationships will be a major task for psychologists in years to come.

It is likely that our future understanding of anger will be increasingly influenced by psychologists working therapeutically with individuals who have problems of anger control. Anger management has become an important treatment within clinical and forensic psychology, particularly for individuals whose anger gives rise to violence. Treatments of this sort have a clear basis in psychological theory. It is to be hoped that therapeutic practice will, in turn, lead to advances in our understanding of this important emotion.

References

Ainsworth, M.D.S. (1982). Attachment: Retrospective and prospect. In C.M. Parkes and J. Stevenson-Hinde (Eds), *The Place of Attachment in Human Behaviour*. New York. Basic Books. [The Strange Situation.]

Averill, J.R. (1982). *Anger and Aggression: An essay on emotion*. New York: Springer-Verlag. [A stimulating book, covering many social, psychological and cultural aspects of anger.]

Berkowitz, L. (1982). Aversive conditions as stimuli to aggression. In L. Berkowitz (Ed.), *Advances in Experimental Social Psychology, Vol.15*. New York Press. [Argued that environmental events elicit aggression.]

Bowlby, J. (1971). *Attachment and Loss. Volume 1: Attachment*. Harmondsworth: Penguin. [Attachment in infants and monotropism.]

Dutton, D.G. and Aron, A.P. (1974). Some evidence for heightened sexual attraction under conditions of high anxiety. *Journal of Personality and Social Psychology, 30*, 510–517. [Men on swaying bridge experiment.]

Groth, A.N. (1979). *Men Who Rape*. New York: Plenum. [A clinical account of sexual aggression.]

Hatfield, E., and Sprecher, S. (1986). Measuring passionate love in intimate relations. *Journal of Adolescence, 9*, 383–410. [Passionate love scale.]

Lee, J.A. (1988). Love styles. In R.J. Sternberg and M.L. Barnes (Eds), *The Psychology of Love*. New Haven: Yale University Press. [Style/colours of love.]

Main, M. and Cassidy, J. (1988). Categories of response to reunion with the parent at age 6: Predictable from infant attachment classifications and stable over a 1-month period. *Journal of Youth and Adolescence, 14*, 267–283. [Attachment in older children.]

Murstein, B.I. (1988). A taxonomy of love. In R.J. Sternberg and M.L. Barnes. (Eds), *The Psychology of Love*. New Haven: Yale University Press. [Love classified: includes comment on Casler, Erikson and Walter.]

Novaco, R.W. (1994). Clinicians ought to view anger contextually. *Behaviour Change, 10*, 208–218. [Demonstrates the social embeddedness of triggers for anger.]

Ortony, A., Clore, G.l. and Collins, A. (1988). *The Cognitive Structure of Emotions*. Cambridge: Cambridge University Press. [An influential example of the cognitive approach to understanding emotions.]

Rubin, Z. (1970). Measurement of romantic love. *Journal of Personality and Social Psychology, 16(2)*, 265–273 [Love and liking.]

Salk, Lee (1962). Mothers' heartbeat as an imprinting stimulus. *Transactions of the New York Academy of Science, 24*, 753–763. [Imprinting in humans.]

Schaffer, R. (1977). *Mothering*. London: Fontana. [Mother–infant attachment: includes comment on Freud and Emerson.]

Sluckin, W. (1972). *Imprinting and Early Learning*. London: Methuen [Imprinting: includes comment on Lorenz.]

Smith, P.K. and Cowie, H. (1991). *Understanding Children's Development*. Oxford: Blackwell. [Measurements of attachment.]

Sternberg, R.J. and Barnes, M.L. (1988). *The Psychology of Love*. New Haven: Yale University Press. [Discusses adult love; includes comment on Casler, Erikson and Walster].

Wyer, R.S. and Srull, T.K. (Eds) (1993). *Perspectives on Anger and Emotion: Advances in social cognition, Volume VI.* Hillsdale NJ: Lawrence Erlbaum Associates. [A series of papers focusing on the work of Leonard Berkowitz, but also illustrating contemporary theories. See also the chapter on 'Where does anger dwell?' by Clore and others.]

Recommended Reading

Archer, J. (1994) (Ed.). *Male Violence.* London: Routledge.
Archer, J. and Browne, K. (1989) (Eds). *Human Aggression: Naturalistic approaches.* London: Routledge.
Berryman, J.C., Hargreaves, D.J., Herbert, M. and Taylor, A. (1991). *Developmental Psychology and You.* Leicester: BPS Books (The British Psychological Society).
Sternberg, R.J. and Barnes, M.L. (1988). *The Psychology of Love.* New Haven: Yale University Press.

MEASURING PASSIONATE LOVE

If you would like to find out how you feel about someone you love, then Elaine Hatfield and Susan Sprecher's *Passionate Love Scale* will interest you. In this scale you are asked to describe how you feel when you are passionately in love. Some common terms for this feeling are *passionate love, infatuation, love sickness,* or *obsessive love.*

Think of the person whom you love most passionately *right now.* If you are not in love at the moment, think of the last person you loved passionately. If you have never been in love, think of the person you came closest to caring for in that way. Keep this person in mind as you complete this section of the questionnaire. Try to describe how you felt at the time when your feelings were the most intense.

SCORING: For each item, give your answers as a score from 1–9 as shown. Then total your score for all questions.

Possible response to each item:

1	2	3	4	5	6	7	8	9
Not at all true				Moderately true			Definitely true	

PASSIONATE LOVE SCALE

1. Since I've been involved with _____ , my emotions have been on a rollercoaster.
2. I would feel deep despair if _____ left me.
3. Sometimes my body trembles with excitement at the sight of _____ .
4. I take delight in studying the movements and angles of _____'s body.
5. Sometimes I feel I can't control my thoughts: they are obsessively on _____.
6. I feel happy when I am doing something to make _____ happy.
7. I would rather be with _____ than anyone else.

continued

MEASURING PASSIONATE LOVE

8. I'd get jealous if I thought _____ were falling in love with someone else.
9. No one else could love _____ like I do.
10. I yearn to know all about _____.
11. I want _____ physically, emotionally, mentally.
12. I will love _____ forever.
13. I melt when looking deeply into _____'s eyes.
14. I have an endless appetite for affection from _____.
15. For me, _____ is the perfect romantic partner.
16. _____ is the person who can make me feel the happiest.
17. I sense my body responding when _____ touches me.
18. I feel tender toward _____.
19. _____ always seems to be on my mind.
20. If I were separated from _____ for a long time, I would feel intensely lonely.
21. I sometimes find it difficult to concentrate on work because thoughts of _____ occupy my mind.
22. I want _____ to know me – my thoughts, my fears, and my hopes.
23. Knowing that _____ cares about me makes me feel complete.
24. I eagerly look for signs indicating _____'s desire for me.
25. If _____ were going through a difficult time, I would put away my own concerns to help him/her out.
26. _____ can make me feel effervescent and bubbly.
27. In the presence of _____, I yearn to touch and be touched.
28. An existence without _____ would be dark and dismal.
29. I possess a powerful attraction for _____.
30. I get extremely depressed when things don't go right in my relationship with _____.

COMMENT: The authors of this scale have used it to assess passionate love in a variety of relationships and in both sexes. In general, they have found that women and men do not differ in how much love is experienced and research on

--- *continued*

continued --

MEASURING PASSIONATE LOVE

a number of different ethnic groups found that women and men love with equal passion.

Researchers have found that passionate love scores vary with the stage of the relationship. If you would like to see how your scores compare with Hatfield and Strecher's, see their findings below.

MEASURING PASSIONATE LOVE

Passionate Love Scale
Following are shown the mean or average scores of passionate love as a function of gender and dating stage in the women and men assessed by the authors of the scale.

	Mean of Passionate Love	
	Men	Women
Occasional dating/regular dating	177.50	164.83
Exclusive dating	215.45	220.89
Living together and/or engaged	216.67	218.31

How does your total score compare with the average?

ANALYSING YOUR OWN ANGER

Your own experience may be a rich source of ideas about the nature of anger and aggression. An 'Anger Diary' is simple to keep and often revealing. Keep a diary over a period of two weeks and fill it in at the same time every evening. Write an account of your experiences of anger that have arisen in the course of the day. For each experience, try to answer the following questions:

1. What was the precise event that elicited my anger? What irritated me most?
2. Was the source of my anger another person? Myself? An object or thing?
3. What interpretations did I put on the frustrating event? Are there other interpretations I did not consider? What sorts of things did I say to myself following the frustration that made me more angry?
4. What physical sensations accompanied the anger experience?
5. What behavioural reaction did I show? Was my response verbal aggression?

COMMENT: A series of incidents analysed in this way will reveal the patterns of your own experience of anger and may encourage you to formulate your own ideas and to compare them with those discussed in this chapter and in the Recommended Reading on p.148.

6. *Growing Up*

'Spare the rod and spoil the child.'
'Children should be encouraged to express themselves.'
'Children have lost their innocence in the video age.'
'The moral decline of modern youth stems from unemployment.'

It goes almost without saying that the future of any society is determined by the way it brings up its young, and so the truth or falsehood of statements like those above are of immense importance to all of us. The first two come from the wealth of folk wisdom that exists about how children should be brought up, and ideas about this have changed dramatically over the last century. The first statement would have been commonplace in Victorian society, but such harsh ideas were replaced in the 1960s and 1970s by sentiments along the lines of the second.

As we approach the millennium, however, the pendulum has swung back in the opposite direction. In the UK at least, the liberal, 'permissive' ideals of self-expression and creativity are out of fashion once again. The economic realities of the 1990s have produced a massive growth in private education, and the resurgence of ideas like 'back to basics', in which the development of the 'three Rs' and of vocational, functional skills are seen as much more important than fostering intellectual curiosity or independent thinking.

The pace of change

This shows us that 'expert' recommendations about parenting and education are moulded to a considerable degree by social and cultural change, and the pace of social change is probably as rapid as it ever has been. The traditional nuclear family, with its mother, father and 2.4 children is now the exception rather than the rule. Children are these days much more likely to be brought up by caregivers outside the family, or in one-parent families. The incredible pace of technological change, and the ubiquity and increasing networking of personal computers in particular, is already leading to changing patterns of working. Working from home and part-time working are now much more viable proposi-tions than hitherto, and this in turn is likely to affect many aspects of people's lives.

Changes such as these are affecting many aspects of our lifestyle, and so it is difficult to pin down the causes of particular problems. Official statistics show that young people are involved in crime (with new developments such as the inaptly-named 'joyriding'), with drugs, and with sexual health problems at much earlier ages than hitherto. So how should we react to statements like the third and fourth ones listed at the beginning of this chap-ter? The putative 'moral decline' of youth (and maybe of modern society as a whole) is variously blamed on parents, on politicians, on economic conditions, on schools and teachers, on the decline of the authority of the church, and even on the individuals them-selves. The concepts of 'evil' or 'wickedness' were recently used to explain the particularly horrific murder of one child by two oth-ers, and the murder of a headmaster at the school gate by a teenager. What contribution might psychologists make to the explanation of these problems, and can they recommend how child-rearing *should* be carried out?

STUDYING DEVELOPMENT

The field of *developmental psychology* deals with these issues, and has important contributions to make to child-rearing and educa-tional policy-making. It has undergone some important changes in recent years, and we will pick out three features in particular.

Do children train their parents?

One significant new feature is the understanding that children train their parents just as much as the reverse. Early ideas about child development saw it as a one-way process in which the child was something like a shapeless blob of clay which was gradually moulded and shaped by parents, teachers and others. Research on babies' smiling, crying, babbling and gazing makes it quite clear that the relationship between parent and child is *reciprocal*: the infant takes the lead in the first interactions and non-verbal 'conversations', and this gradually develops into a relationship in which each partner takes into account the behaviour and perceived intentions of the other. Far from being passive blobs of clay, babies exert a considerable influence over their own upbringing.

The life-span approach

The second feature is what has become known as the *life-span* approach. Quite simply, this is that human development should be studied across the full age span, from conception right through to old age and death. Until the last decade or so, developmental psychologists devoted most of their attention to pre-schoolers and school-aged children. Early infancy was neglected, although this is a very active area of current study, and adolescence has always been a difficult period to research, perhaps because it is the period of transition between childhood and adulthood. The worst neglect, however, was that of adult life. With the exception of some studies of ageing, very little attention was paid to the changes that take place in people's lives between the ages of about 18 and 60. This may be partly because the study of marriage, careers, family patterns and so on has taken place in related disciplines such as sociology and anthropology, but the life-span developmental approach is now, at last, beginning to fill some of these gaps.

The ecology of development

We have noted that the pace of social change has led to some important changes in patterns of child care. There is now a much greater demand for nursery provision, childminders, and other forms of day care than existed in the past. Present-day fathers are also more likely to take an active part in childcare than were their predecessors. These changes are reflected in the *ecological approach* to the study of development, which proposes, in short, that all of the different influences upon the child should be taken into account. Psychologists have tended to concentrate almost exclusively on the mother–child relationship; indeed the well-known early work of John Bowlby stressed the overwhelming importance of this bond (see Chapter 5).

Now that mothers are no longer automatically their children's primary daytime caregivers, ecological research has begun to look more closely at the influence of fathers, siblings, other relatives, baby-sitters, childminders, and so on. An important aspect of this research is the recognition that all the relationships within the family system are interdependent. For example, when the first baby arrives, the parent–child bonds that are formed inevitably affect the existing relationship between mother and father. The arrival of the second-born, similarly, has effects upon the existing relationships between father, mother and first-born, in addition to all the new bonds that are formed.

THE WORLD OF THE INFANT

It used to be thought that newborns came into the world with very few skills other than some basic physical reflexes, and the infant's *learning experiences* were seen as crucial for development. In recent years, psychologists have moved away from this view, and current research is uncovering more and more abilities that seem somehow to be 'built into' babies, or 'pre-wired', at birth. The study of infancy is now one of the most active areas of developmental psychology.

Perceptual development

One of the first people to try and map out the changes that take place in infancy was the famous Swiss psychologist Jean Piaget (1896–1980). Piaget proposed that, from birth until the age of about two years, all children pass through six substages, moving from the use of simple physical reflexes through to the beginnings of *symbolism*. Piaget proposed that in the first three of these sub-stages (up to the age of eight months or so), 'thought is action'.

Figure 6.1: Jean Piaget (1896–1980).

What babies do to toys and other objects *is* what they think about them. The objects could thus be said to possess what might be called 'motor meaning', and one consequence of this is that they have no 'permanence'. A baby's taps on a rattle, for example, represent his or her 'thinking' about the rattle at this early stage. If the rattle goes out of sight, it effectively ceases to exist.

This idea was captured by the well-known expression 'out of sight is out of mind'. Piaget proposed that *object permanence* – the recognition that objects do not cease to exist when they are out of sight – only gradually develops over the fourth, fifth and sixth substages of infancy. Acquiring object permanence is an extremely significant 'liberation' from the physical world. No longer is the infant's thinking tied to the 'here and now', that is, to given situations at given points in time, because he or she can now form *symbols*, or *internal representations*, of objects. Objects are thus not now always 'out of mind' when they disappear from sight.

As with many parts of Piaget's theory, the idea that 'out of sight is out of mind' has subsequently been challenged by experimental researchers. Studies have been carried out in which infants' head movements and heart rate have been monitored as they track different objects moving in front of and behind screens, and the emerging map of perceptual development in infancy turns out to be more complicated than Piaget first proposed. Under certain circumstances babies *do* seem be able to demonstrate object permanence at earlier ages than Piaget suggested. But the explanations which have been suggested for these results vary, since factors such as motor skills and memory also need to be taken into account. The realization that infants' perceptual development takes place in a *social world* is an increasingly important feature of contemporary research: babies draw on the people around them in constructing meaning from the wealth of sensory input they receive.

Social development

The most significant early social relationships for most infants are those formed with their parents. Research clearly shows that these relationships are *reciprocal* ones in which the parent responds to the child just as much as vice versa. In one study by Glyn Collis and Rudolph Schaffer, mother–infant pairs were videotaped whilst playing together with several toys in a novel situation. Analysis of the tapes showed a typical pattern of *turn-taking* in the timing of the actions of mother and child. For example, a sequence of actions might be started by the child looking at one particular toy. The mother might then look at the same toy and 'elaborate' upon the child's attention towards it by talking, pointing, or maybe touching. This response by the mother might in turn stimulate the child to explore the toy further, and so a kind of 'chain' of actions is built up by means of turn-taking. Social development can thus be seen as a whole series of interrelated and increasingly complex 'chains' such as these.

A key feature of each 'chain' is that mother and infant work together, as a team, with their actions very precisely phased in time with one another. This *synchronization* has been demonstrated in vocalizations, as well as in gestures (such as pointing), and in visual gaze. Daniel Stern's research, for example, clearly shows that when mothers respond verbally to (non-verbal) babbling noises by their babies, they tend to time their 'conversational' responses just as they would in a normal verbal conversation with an adult. They 'converse' with their infants by creating imaginary replies, and these interactions have the important function of laying the foundations of later social interaction.

Born social

The precision with which this phasing takes place in parents' interactions with even very young babies has led psychologists to conclude that infants are born with a tendency to respond to other human beings; that they are 'born social'. There is a good deal of evidence that babies can distinguish between people and things very early on. They are much more likely to attend to faces than to scrambled pictures of facial features, for example, and to the sounds of human speech rather than to the many other sounds they might hear.

It has also been suggested that parents and infants 'interpret' each others' actions, and mutually 'construct the meanings' of the chains of action that they build up. The baby's smile, for example, might be interpreted by the mother as meaning that he or she likes a certain toy which happens to be present, and so starts off a 'chain' such as that described. The sequence of actions is built up and kept going by the baby's interpretation of the mother's behaviour, as well as vice versa. This takes us a long way from the view of the baby as a helpless 'blob of clay'!

'THEORY OF MIND': PERCEIVING EMOTIONS IN OTHERS

Infants' understanding of the social world – how they perceive themselves in relation to other people, and how they develop awareness of the mental states of others – has been the subject of a substantial body of research over the last two decades. The first stage in this is the development of self-recognition. One well-known study by Michael Lewis and Jeanne Brooks-Gunn used the 'mirror test'. In their study, infants in six age groups between nine and 24 months were placed in front of a mirror, and observed for about 90 seconds. Their noses were then daubed with rouge, and they were observed again for the same period of time. In the first period, most of the 96 babies in the sample smiled at their reflection in the mirror, and many reached out to touch it, although very few touched their own nose. In the second period, however, whether or not they touched their nose was closely related to age. The younger infants tended not to do so, even though they could see their own red nose, but the majority of the older ones (over 18 months) did. This suggests that the understanding of self, in terms of a reflection in the mirror, develops at about this age.

By the age of about two years, children have not only developed self-awareness, but are also able to express their own emotional states to others. This leads on to the recognition and prediction of beliefs, desires and emotions in other people. When they do so, they are in effect forming hypotheses about what is going on in the minds of others, and this has become known as the development of a 'theory of mind'. Paul Harris has developed a theory of how this might develop, based on the idea that children use an 'as if' or pretence mechanism to imagine themselves in the other person's position. Apart from self-awareness, the ability to do this requires the capacity for pretence, or make-believe, as well as the ability to distinguish between reality and pretence.

Predicting false beliefs

There is currently a good deal of debate about the basis of 'theory of mind', and Harris' view is not the only one. Others, such as Alan Leslie and Josef Perner, have argued that pretence is only one factor in predicting the mental states of others, and place more emphasis on the child's developing 'knowledge base' about the world than on emotional states. One way of testing some of these different interpretations has been to use what have become known as 'false belief' tasks. The first of these was devised by Hans Wimmer and Josef Perner, and involved a story about a boy called Maxi who had been out shopping with his mother. Mother helped Maxi to put away some chocolate they had bought in a blue cupboard, and Maxi went out to play. Whilst he was playing, his mother moved the chocolate into a green cupboard, and Maxi came back in. The children doing this task are then asked, 'Where will Maxi look for the chocolate?'

Wimmer and Perner found that three-year-olds typically failed on this task, predicting that Maxi would look in the green cupboard. This incorrect answer is based on the actual location of the chocolate rather than on an accurate prediction of Maxi's point of view. A higher proportion of four- and five-year-olds gave the correct answer, and almost all the six-year-olds did so. Many other variants of the false belief task have been devised, one of which appears as *Exercise 6.1*. Different testing conditions and formats have given rise to differing success rates at different ages, but there seems to be little doubt that most children have the ability to form theories of other people's minds by the age of five.

LANGUAGE DEVELOPMENT

The acquisition of language is a remarkable human achievement. Early in their lives, children are able to communicate subtle meanings to each other and to adults, and have internalized some complex grammatical rules. Psychologists have tried to explain the ways in which the speech-like sounds produced in babies' babbling gradually turn into recognizable syllables and words, and how these are put together to form meaningful sentences. The child who says, 'I rided my bike' or 'I eated my biscuit', presents a fascinating problem. It is only because of the irregular (and ever-changing) nature of the English language that these utterances are considered to be 'wrong'. In adding the past tense ending '-ed' to the verbs, the child is applying a standard grammatical rule in a perfectly logical and consistent manner. The identification of these rules, and of the part they play in thought as a whole, is one of the central tasks of research in this field.

Children seem to acquire language in a similar series of phases, regardless of the actual language learnt in particular cultures. In the early months, parents are able to identify cries of hunger, anger and pain, and 'oo' sounds are frequently made in pre-verbal 'conversations' with parents. Babies vary the pitch and stress in these vocalizations, and repeat sounds in 'vocal play'. By the age of 12 months, the first 'words' start to appear. These are often inventions which refer to whole classes of objects. One of the authors' sons, for example, used the word 'gam' to refer to all the foods which interested him at the time. This included porridge, ketchup and other baby foods as well as 'jam'. He also used the word 'jus' to refer to all of his drinks. These 'words' are typically delivered with speech-like intonation and stress.

By the age of 18 months children have typically acquired about 20 words, and this rapidly grows to about 200 by the age of 21 months. Towards the end of the second year babies produce what has been termed 'telegraphic speech', a highly condensed form which contains the first two-word sentences – 'allgone jus' or 'allgone gam' were frequently heard at mealtimes! Sentences then get longer, and three to four word sentences, which may appear ungrammatical, but which nevertheless involve the application of grammatical rules (for example, 'I no want gam'), are produced by two- to three-year-olds. Between three and four years vocabulary increases to about 1000 words, and the length and complexity of children's sentences are such that they can easily be understood by adults who have not met them before. By the age of five, children's speech is very similar to that of adults, and they are able to modify features like the length of sentences and grammatical complexity according to the characteristics of the listener.

Speaking and learning at home

Judy Dunn and her colleagues carried out detailed observations of pre-school children in their homes with their families. They observed the conversations of children aged three and four with their mothers, siblings and friends, and then analysed episodes which were especially likely to reveal children's social understanding, such as arguments, jokes and pretend play. The analyses showed that children with advanced levels of understanding of others were more likely to have engaged in extended pretend play when they were two years old; to have more 'connected' interactions with friends at age three; to have taken part in conversations about why people behave as they do; and to have witnessed an intense relationship between two other family members.

These findings contradict the well-known Piagetian idea that young children tend to be 'egocentric': that they can only see things from their own point of view. Far from being 'egocentric', the children in Dunn's study seemed not only to be able to respond to, but also to anticipate or even pre-empt, what the other person might say or do. Dunn and her colleagues have also shown that children's emotional understanding shown in social relationships at age three is related consistently to their understanding as measured by tests at seven, and this once again confirms the importance of the social context of learning.

FROM HOME TO SCHOOL

The social context of learning changes dramatically for most children when they make the transition from home to school, pre-school playgroup, nursery school or kindergarten. There is usually a substantial increase in the number of children and adults present and most children form new friends who are unknown to their own parents. There is also a clear increase in the amount of time spent

Figure 6.2: Varieties of play in children.

away from the home. They are expected to enter into *formal* learning relationships with adults, and sometimes also with other children. They learn that they have to compete for the teacher's attention, and to start distinguishing between informal and formal learning relationships with peers, teachers, and other adults.

We have suggested that pre-schoolers have developed a clear understanding of the roles and mental states of others, and that they are skilful and active learners. However, Martin Hughes reported that the reception teachers he interviewed consistently described new children coming to school as 'egocentric, immature, lacking in confidence, over-dependent, and lacking in basic skills and knowledge . . . unable to socialise . . . with little evidence of any social training in the home, . . . and frequently bad-mannered, disruptive and disobedient . . . there was a reluctance to ask questions, discuss stories or relate experiences'. These do not on the face of it sound like descriptions of the same people which suggests that children's learning relationships in school may be very different from those at home or out of school.

Conversations at home and at school

Barbara Tizard and Martin Hughes recorded 30 four-year-old girls' conversations with their mothers at home and with their nursery teachers at school, and contrasted the language and learning in these two settings. They found that the girls asked significantly more questions at home, and that the adults' answers at home were much more detailed than at school. The girls asked three main types of question, namely *business questions* (for example, 'Where are the scissors?'); *curiosity questions* (such as, 'What's that?' 'How do you do that?); and *challenge questions* (for example, 'Why should I?'). Challenge questions only formed about one tenth of the children's questions, but seemed to be particularly effective in gaining new information in the mothers' answers. Tizard and Hughes also identified conversations in which the child asks a sequence of questions which take account of the adults' answers, often finding them unsatisfactory and thus actively pursuing understanding.

Formal school or nursery settings, on the other hand, seemed specifically to discourage children from asking challenging questions and from persisting in their questioning. It seems from this research that children's intellectual and language needs are much more likely to be met at home than at school, as there is a great deal more scope for active learning by dialogue and interaction. This completely turns on its head the common idea that what teachers do in classrooms is essentially 'educational' and that what goes on in domestic conversation is more humdrum and routine.

LOGICAL THINKING IN SCHOOLCHILDREN

We referred earlier in this chapter to Jean Piaget's well-known *stage* theory of child development, and in particular to his important concepts of *object permanence* and *egocentrism*, which Piaget proposed were central features of the *sensori-motor* (0–2 years) and *pre-operational* (2–7 years) stages respectively. Perhaps the single most influential and controversial part of the theory deals with the changes which take place in children's thinking at around the age of seven. Piaget believed that this age marks the transition into the third *concrete operational* stage. He gave an extremely detailed account of the sudden advances in logical thinking ability that children make around this age, and his theory has formed the basis of various curriculum schemes for mathematics and science in the first school.

Conservation

One of the central concepts in Piaget's account of this transition is that of *conservation*. In the well-known *conservation of volume* task, for example (see Question 2 in the Introduction), children are shown two identical containers of liquid and asked to compare them. Most will agree that there is the same amount in each. The liquid from one of the two is then poured into a third differently-shaped container so that the two levels of liquid are now different. According to Piaget, the pre-operational child will typically now say that there are different amounts of liquid in the first and third container on the basis either of height or width. When the liquid is poured back into the two original containers, the child typically reverts to the original answer that there is the same amount in each. Piaget's explanation is that these answers reveal a lack of understanding of conservation: that the volume is conserved despite its physical appearance in different-shaped vessels. Only with the acquisition of concrete operations will children realize that the volume does not change throughout the experiment.

Piaget devised similar tasks in many areas of school mathematics, including number, distance, time, and classification, and the same basic principles underlie his explanation of the acquisition of concrete operational thinking in each case. In essence, this is the ability to *decentre*: to be able to recognize that two dimensions of a display can interact to determine a higher-order property like volume, rather than just focusing on one of these dimensions. In *Exercise 6.2*, you can try out another of Piaget's well-known conservation tasks if you can find some playdoh and some willing children.

Making 'human sense'

Piaget's theory of transition into the concrete operational stage has been subjected to a great deal of critical scrutiny from within as well as from outside psychology, perhaps because it has had such a profound influence upon adults' views of children's capabilities, and upon the practice of teaching. Many experiments have been able to show that young children are capable of displaying conservation abilities at a much earlier age than the theory would predict, and this has been done by varying the task in a number of ways. One of the most interesting of these is based on the idea that the social understandings inherent in test settings exert a strong influence upon the judgements that children make. Margaret Donaldson has suggested that children try to make 'human sense' of the test situation rather than simply responding literally to the questions.

This was demonstrated in a pioneering study by James McGarrigle and Margaret Donaldson at Edinburgh University, who used the standard Piagetian number conservation tasks such as those illustrated in *Exercise 6.1*. Most of the four- to six-year-olds in their study failed in these tasks when the experimental transformation was intentionally carried out by the experimenter. When they ingeniously made the transformation appear to be accidental, however, by means of a 'naughty teddy bear' who 'spoilt the game', the number of children who succeeded on the task more than doubled.

This is a convincing demonstration that pre-operational children can display conservation abilities when the conditions are appropriate. It also illustrates once again the importance of the social context of learning. Piaget himself realized this – whatever the ultimate implications of 'situational' research for his theory, he was well aware that relationships between peers can be particularly powerful. In school, children are often expected to work with other children on common tasks, such as making a model or making up a story. Peer learning takes place in informal relationships, such as children's friendships, and also in formal learning relationships, such as co-operative groups.

CO-OPERATIVE LEARNING IN SCHOOL

In co-operative learning, children work together on some common task. Group work has been seen by educationalists as a cost-effective use of teacher time as compared with the use of individualized programmes of learning. Teachers who use it argue that it raises children's levels of achievement levels, promotes social development, and also increases children's levels of self-esteem. How might developmental theorists like Piaget account for these kinds of benefit?

Conflict or co-operation?

Piaget believed that cognitive development is more likely to occur when children work with peers than when they work by themselves, or interact with older children or adults. This is because his theory suggests that development is brought about by the resolution of *conflict* between what the child already knows and any contrasting views that might be put forward by others. Whereas children are quite likely to give way if adults' or older children's interpretation of an event differs from their own, they are more likely to argue with friends or peers. This challenge or disagreement will force children to attend to aspects of the event which they might have missed if working alone. Conflict therefore creates *disequilibrium* in children's minds, which motivates them to reconstruct their understanding of the event, and in turn to moving them towards a higher level of understanding.

Other prominent theorists, notably the Russian developmentalist Lev Vygotsky, stress on the other hand that development occurs through social *co-operation* rather than through conflict. The essence of Vygotsky's theory is that children draw on the more experienced members of the social groups of which they are

Figure 6.3: Co-operative learning. (*From Dave Roberts.*)

part, absorbing cultural expectations, approaches, and methods as a natural part of the learning process. Development will take place when a more experienced child, parent or teacher guides the child's participation in particular tasks; and this process of guidance has been described as 'scaffolding'. By recruiting and maintaining the child's attention, setting appropriate task limits, and drawing attention to its critical features, the instructor provides a kind of framework or 'scaffold' which makes it much easier for learning to take place.

Co-operative group work and peer tutoring

'Co-operative group work' has many meanings and purposes in schools, including working together in small groups, as well as the technique of 'peer tutoring' in which a more able or experienced child works with a less able or experienced child. There are also distinct national variations in the forms that these approaches take. Keith Topping contrasted the 'extremely rigid, rule-bound and prescriptive' North American versions of co-operative group-work with their 'warm, fuzzy and comfortable' British equivalents, for example. There is growing evidence that structured group work is effective in promoting cognitive gains, that it can lead to social and affective developments, and that it can specifically be used to promote team work and co-operative attitudes.

Peer tutoring, particularly when used in the teaching of reading, has been shown to produce improvements in children's attitudes and achievements regardless of gender, race and social class divisions, especially for the children who act as tutors. The evidence for similar gains in self-concept, self-esteem and self-image is less strong, in spite of teachers' claims for this kind of benefit. Perhaps most encouraging of all is the consistent finding that co-operative grouping can be particularly beneficial in multi-ethnic classes. Improvements have been demonstrated in social relationships, liking for others, and in reduced negative stereotyping of other racial groups.

ADOLESCENCE AND BEYOND

The abrupt and profound physical changes which mark the onset of puberty have far-reaching consequences. From the base of the brain, the pituitary gland secretes hormones into the bloodstream which give rise to dramatic changes in primary sexual characteristics (the development of the genitals; the onset of ovulation in girls, and of ejaculation in boys) as well as in secondary ones (sudden increases in height and weight and the growth of pubic hair in both sexes; breast development in girls; growth of body hair and a deepening of the voice in boys). Both sexes experience a sudden *growth spurt*, and all of these developments start and finish a year or two earlier in girls than in boys.

These physical changes naturally affect the whole of psychological development, and one of the most obvious outcomes is the awakening of sexuality itself. Adolescence is a time of major readjustment: the teenager must suddenly come to terms with new-found sexual feelings, and powerful emotional attachments towards others. The whole pattern of social relationships is changed, with parents and family, with peers, and with those in the world of school or work such as teachers, supervisors and other authority figures. The adolescent is neither a child nor yet an adult, but is in a confusing, embarrassing, and often bewildering, period of transition.

Is there an identity crisis?

One prominent psychological idea which derives from psychoanalysis is that wrestling with this 'identity crisis' creates a great deal of 'storm and stress', and that protest, rebellion and *regression* to earlier forms of behaviour are fairly common and natural reactions to this. Sociological theories, on the other hand, emphasize the changes in social roles that teenagers suddenly experience, and there are three main types of these.

Role conflicts are common: to be a 'son' and a 'boyfriend' at the same time might well lead to problem situations when parents and girlfriend are both present. Role *discontinuities* are experienced, for example, when the 'schoolchild' is suddenly thrust into work experience, and has to relate to adults in a quite different way than hitherto. Role *incongruence* also occurs because the adolescent is torn between two conflicting sets of values: with the conventional social attitudes represented by parents and school on the one hand, and with those of peer cultures, which quite often oppose authority, on the other. The mass media play a large part in defining peer cultures, which are often linked to current style in pop music. The clothes, hairstyles, and leisure interests of grunge, indie, or rap fans in the late 1990s have all in part been created or developed through the media, since the teenage market represents considerable spending power.

Modern-day psychologists draw on both of these types of explanation, and tend to play down the idea of an 'identity crisis' in which the problem issues just described surface all together. The basis of John Coleman's 'focal theory', for example, is that different issues 'come into focus' at different parts of adolescence. Anxiety over heterosexual relationships is a common worry early on, for example. Fears of rejection from, and problems with, different peer groups typically surface somewhat later: and conflict with parents may come to the fore later still. This theory sees the adaptation to adult life as gradually unfolding over time with respect to these different issues of concern, so that the idea of a period of intense 'storm and stress' is not now widely accepted.

The modern world is a rapidly-changing place, and today's teenagers are sophisticated and well-informed to an unprecedented degree. This is indeed an essential part of survival in the sense that youngsters face the problems of crime, drugs, and sexual health at earlier ages than ever before. Other social changes such as increases in youth unemployment, changes in patterns of working and changes in family structure mean that the world is an increasingly uncertain place both outside the home and inside it. Feelings of immobilization, depression, and uncertainty are perhaps not so surprising, and these feelings are quite likely to be taken out on parents since they are usually on the spot, or 'in the firing line'. This is the origin of the so-called 'generation gap' which can clearly be seen in Western society, but which is not necessarily present in all cultural groups.

Adult careers and family life

Somehow, most of us manage to survive the trials of adolescence, and to adapt to the typical adult roles of our society. The course of development in adulthood is probably best explained in terms of the ways, as individuals, in which we fit into patterns of work and career, of parenthood and family life. These developments seem to be quite different for men and for women. In Western society at least, most men have a clearly defined career pattern, followed by retirement, with parenting largely as a background or support role. The typical female life span is much more inconsistent: the relative importance and priority of the roles of worker, caregiver and homemaker vary considerably over adult life.

One effect of this is that women tend to report lower levels of life satisfaction than men, and to suffer more from depressive illnesses and problems, according to the findings of many research studies. It has also reliably been found that single and divorced women seem to suffer less in this respect than those who are married. The moral seems to be that it is better for men to be married, and for women to stay single, though this presents some obvious practical problems!

Traditional gender role behaviour seems to be at its strongest in the years of active parenting, in the 20s and 30s. In later life, at least in married couples, 'role blurring' occurs and the interests, attitudes, and behaviour of both sexes become less stereotyped. In men, it seems very likely that this is a direct result of retirement. The man gives up his active 'breadwinner' role. He is based at home, where the jobs to be done are domestic, and so it seems fairly natural that he should take on some of the characteristics of the 'homemaker'. In women, the picture is much less clear. One suggestion invokes the so-called 'empty nest syndrome' – that having devoted a considerable amount of time and effort to parenting and homemaking, women one day find that their 'birds have flown', and this can present another disruptive role change.

This picture of later adult life is of course based on conventional two-parent married families in Western society, and therefore leaves a great deal unexplained. Today's women are much more likely to have full-time or part-time jobs than in the past, and many other changes are taking place in family structure and patterns of working. The growth of part-time work and the possibilities of working from home which are afforded by computer networking seem to be increasing female employment in particular, and it remains to be seen how further technological advances will shape the lifestyles of the future.

References

Bowlby, J. (1971). *Attachment*. Harmondsworth: Penguin. [Bowlby's theory of parent–child bonding.]

Bremner, G. (1993). *Infancy, 2nd edn*. Oxford: Blackwell. [A comprehensive guide.]

Coleman, J.C. and Hendry, L (1990). *The Nature of Adolescence, 2nd edn*. London: Routledge. [Includes the 'focal theory'.]

Collis, G.M. and Schaffer, H.R (1975). Synchronisation of visual attention in mother–infant pairs. *Journal of Child Psychology and Psychiatry, 16*, 315–320. [Research on mothers and babies looking at things together.]

Dunn, J. (1995). Studying relationships and social understanding. In Barnes, P. (Ed.), *Personal, Social and Emotional Development of Children*. Milton Keynes: Open University Press. [Dunn's research on conversations at home].

Frith, U. (1989). *Autism: Explaining the Enigma*. Oxford: Blackwell. [Includes the false belief task used in *Exercise 6.2*.]

Harris, P.L. (1989). *Children and Emotion*. Oxford: Blackwell. [Includes Harris' account of 'theory of mind'.]

Hughes, M. (1991). The child as a learner: the contrasting views of developmental psychology and early education. In Desforges, C. (Ed.), *Early Childhood*

Education. British Journal of Educational Psychology, Monograph Series No. 4. Edinburgh: Scottish Academic Press. [Now out of print.]

Leslie, A.M. (1990). Pretence, autism, and bases of 'theory of mind'. *The Psychologist, 3,* 120–123. [Work on pretence.]

Lewis, M. and Brooks-Gunn, J. (1979). *Social Cognition and the Acquisition of Self.* New York: Plenum Press. [Includes research on the infant's acquisition of self.]

McGarrigle, J. and Donaldson, M. (1974). Conservation accidents. *Cognition, 3,* 341–350. [The social setting affects children's conservation abilities.]

Stern, D. (1977). *The First Relationship: Infant and mother.* London: Fontana. [Studies of synchronization between infants and mothers.]

Tizard, B. and Hughes, M. (1984). *Young Children Learning: Talking and thinking at home and school.* London: Fontana. [Different characteristics of talk at home and at school.]

Topping, K. (1992). Co-operative learning and peer tutoring: an overview. *The Psychologist, 5,* 151–162. [Broad-ranging review.]

Vygotsky, L. (1961). *Thought and Language.* Boston, MA: MIT Press. [Vygotsky's increasingly influential theory of teaching and learning.]

Wimmer, H. and Perner, J. (1983). Beliefs about beliefs: representations and constraining function of wrong beliefs in young children's understanding of deception. *Cognition, 13,* 103–128. [False belief task about a boy called Maxi.]

Recommended Reading

Berryman, J., Hargreaves, D.J., Herbert, M. and Taylor, A. (1991). *Developmental Psychology and You.* Leicester: BPS Books.

Donaldson, M. (1978). *Children's Minds.* London: Fontana.

Durkin, K. (1995). *Developmental Social Psychology.* Oxford: Blackwell.

Smith, P.K. and Cowie, H. (1991). *Understanding Children's Development, 2nd edn.* Oxford: Blackwell.

Wood, D. (1988). *How Children Think and Learn.* Oxford: Blackwell.

FALSE BELIEFS: THE SALLY-ANNE TASK

Figure 6.4: The Sally-Anne task.

INSTRUCTIONS: Tell the story of Sally and Anne by talking children through the five cartoon pictures shown above. Try this with children aged between three and six years old. The correct answer is that Sally should look in the basket, since she (unlike the children answering the question) does not know that the marble has been moved. Was there any increase with age in the number of correct answers?
(This task is adapted from Frith, 1989)

CONSERVATION OF MASS

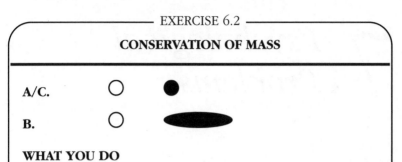

A/C.

B.

WHAT YOU DO

A. Take 2 pieces of different-coloured playdoh (say red and green, or whatever else is available) and roll them into balls of identical shape and size. Ask the child, 'Do the red and green balls have the same amount of playdoh, or are they different?' If the child says they are different, change one of the two until the child agrees they are the same.

B. Roll out the green ball into a sausage shape, and repeat the question.

C. Roll the green 'sausage' back into the shape of a ball, and ask the question once more.

Try A–C with a five-year-old, a seven-year-old and a nine-year-old.

YOUR FINDINGS

Piaget's theory predicts that younger children (under the age of seven) are likely to say *either* that there is more playdoh in the green sausage than the red ball in B because 'it's longer', *or* that there is more in the red ball than the green sausage in B because 'it's fatter'. They focus on just one dimension of the display, and only realize that the length and width jointly determine mass as they get older. Do your results support this theory?

7. *Psychological Problems*

Throughout this book we have been trying to show ways in which psychologists have attempted to understand and explain particular aspects of human experience and behaviour. Some areas of psychology are explicitly concerned with applying psychological theories to the problems and distress that arise in everyday life. Clinical psychology, for example, is about the application of psychological theories and methods in psychiatric, medical and related settings. The range of clinical psychology is now great, encompassing the fields of behaviour problems in childhood, the difficulties of the elderly, the effects of brain damage, delinquency and antisocial behaviour, as well as mental disorders such as depression and schizophrenia. In recent years other branches of professional psychology have developed and advanced very rapidly. Health psychologists focus on the interface between medical illness/health and psychological processes. Counselling psychologists use psychological principles to help individuals cope with the wide range of problems that occur in everyday life. Forensic psychologists, on the other hand, work with the social problem of crime and its management by the justice system.

Whilst there are many types of applied psychologists, in general these various professionals have much in common. They share basic training in psychology as an applied science and endeavour to increase human well-being and reduce distress through the application of psychological theory and research.

It is not possible in a short chapter to give an overview of this work. What we shall try to do is to give a flavour of the psychological approach by picking out three areas. The problem areas we have chosen are those of anxiety, childhood sexual abuse and psychological aspects of schizophrenia. Clinical psychologists were not the first to tackle these problems but they have brought new perspectives to bear on them.

ANXIETY AND RELATED PROBLEMS

Let us start by considering one particular case in detail.

Ms J is a 23-year-old nurse. She was referred for help with a problem which had developed over the preceding year. Prior to this she had few serious psychological difficulties. She had been brought up in a conventional middle-class home along with a brother and sister. She had always viewed herself as the 'nervous' and 'emotional' member of the family but never considered herself as having any major problems. A year prior to her referral she had been working a series of night shifts at a general hospital. When alone on the ward during the night a patient to whom she was very attached died. She was upset at the time but not unduly so. Two weeks later, while working on the ward at night, she was telephoned from home and told that her father was seriously ill. He died a few days later. Over the ensuing weeks bouts of anxiety would arise if she was working alone on a night shift. She would feel dizzy, her legs would shake and she had a feeling of desperately wanting to leave the ward. On occasions she actually left the ward at night when these 'panics' came on. She eventually gave up night shifts but her fear generalized to some degree to working during the day. She was then unable to go to work. Even the thought of work upset her. She was concerned to re-establish her normal work pattern as she was planning to marry and needed the income.

Phobias

Problems of fear and anxiety, of the kind just described, formed the bread-and-butter work of many clinical psychologists in the

1960s and early 1970s, particularly for psychologists of the behavioural school. Today, even though the range of problems tackled is much wider, fear and anxiety are still a common reason for consulting a clinical psychologist. The problem just described is an example of a *phobic disorder*: the degree of fear experienced is out of all proportion to the objective threat the feared situation poses and is of such an intensity as to restrict and impair the individual's daily life. Phobias are fairly common. One American survey found that more than seven per cent of the population reported a mildly disabling phobia but that severe, crippling phobias were found in only two people in every thousand. A range of phobias can be found in the community, including fears of illness, injury, storms, animals (such as rats, mice, spiders, cats, dogs), heights and crowds. The most commonly treated one is agoraphobia.

Agoraphobia

Agoraphobia begins most commonly between the ages of 18 and 35 and is found predominantly in women. Fear-arousing situations include being away from home, being in crowds, being confined, travelling on trains or buses, and even going shopping. As with other phobias, the feared situation is often avoided and the person's life becomes very restricted as a result. Agoraphobics often experience a state best described as 'panic' in the feared situation. Their heart may thump; they may feel dizzy, sweat or experience a range of other unpleasant sensations. Panic symptoms like these can seem like a real physical disorder such as heart disease and sufferers may even believe they will pass out or die.

Panic disorders of this sort are usually distinguished from *generalized anxiety* disorders in terms of the duration of the anxiety experience. For panic disorder the anxiety is sudden and limited in duration. For generalized anxiety disorder, the feeling of apprehension is present over a long period of time and is unrelated to the perception of any specific danger.

THE COMPLEX NATURE OF FEAR AND ANXIETY

Psychologists and doctors have made a number of contributions to our understanding of conditions of this sort. An important beginning has been to reveal the complexity of fear and anxiety.

Anxiety seems to involve four systems which interrelate in a complex and, as yet, poorly understood way: a cognitive/verbal system, a physiological system, a subjective/emotional system, and a behavioural system. In some instances of anxiety all four systems are activated. The person perceives and expects danger (cognitive), he or she sweats, trembles and feels dizzy (physiological), feels anxious and frightened (subjective), and avoids the threatening situation (behavioural). But it is possible that these systems can become desynchronized. The person may show all features, except the cognitive perception of a particular threat (for example, in generalized anxiety, where the person does not perceive any particular danger). It is also possible to be fearful without marked physical changes, and vice versa. Equally the person may experience the cognitive, physiological and subjective aspects of anxiety in a particular situation and yet not avoid it. The clear implication of all this is that treatments may need to tackle these many different aspects of the problem if they are to be effective.

SOURCES OF PHOBIAS AND ANXIETY

There have been many attempts in psychology to explain how phobias are acquired. Indeed, two of the most famous case histories in the history of psychology were presented as attempts to study and explain phobias in a young child.

Little Hans

In 1909, Sigmund Freud published a case history entitled 'The analysis of a phobia in a five-year-old boy'. This became known as the 'Little Hans' case after the name of the boy concerned. Little Hans had developed a fear of horses and of going out. The phobia was explained by Freud in terms of the Oedipus complex. This refers to a conflict which psychoanalysts believe arises during the 'phallic' stage of development. The conflict is one between the male child's sexual impulses towards his mother and his fear of castration by the father. The Little Hans case demonstrates that complex (some would argue, fanciful) interpretations can be made of fear reactions in children and adults, but such hypotheses prove difficult to test scientifically.

Little Albert

In 1920, John Watson, the American behaviourist, reported on an equally famous boy, 'Little Albert' (see also Chapter 9). Watson detailed an attempt to establish a phobia in an 11-month-old boy by classical conditioning; that is, learning through the temporal association of two events (discussed in detail in Chapter 9). Briefly, Watson tried to condition fear to a white rat. Whenever a white rat was placed in front of Albert a loud noise was made by hitting a hammer on a metal bar close by – it was known that Albert was frightened of loud noises. After a number of pairings of rat and noise Albert became frightened of the rat and subsequently generalized his fear to rabbits, cotton wool and other similar things.

It is almost certainly true that phobias *can* be acquired through classical conditioning of this sort and the phobias produced can appear irrational to someone not familiar with the conditioning history.

Learning and unlearning

One of the authors of this book has a young daughter who, for some time as a baby, became upset and cried if the word 'hot' was said in the course of conversation. This puzzled many visitors to the house, though it had a simple conditioning explanation – in the preceding months she was at the stage where she spent much time exploring the house and its corners. She would often be spotted about to put a hand on something that might burn, such as a radiator and would be warned: 'Don't touch that, it's *hot*', typically just at the moment when she did in fact touch it. 'Hot', then, became a conditioned stimulus signalling pain.

Some clinical cases of phobia can be shown to be based on conditioning experiences of this sort. The case of Ms J mentioned earlier seems to be explainable in this way. Ms J's avoidance of the feared situation (the ward at night) prevents her 'unlearning' her fear reaction. She gives herself no opportunity to learn that she can be on the ward at night without anything tragic happening. In many, perhaps most, clinical cases, however, conditioning experiences of this sort cannot be found in the person's history. What the other routes to a phobia might be are not yet clear.

Passing on fear

Social modelling may be an important factor. It can be demonstrated in laboratory studies that young monkeys with no experience of snakes can develop a strong fear by observing their parents react with fear to a snake. It is not difficult to see how agoraphobic reactions, phobic fear of illness, or a range of other fears could be acquired by humans in this way. Parents may teach fears by direct modelling and such learning may be accentuated by the parents' and child's capacity to encode such experiences in a verbal way. A fear of mice or spiders can run in the family.

Phobias can make good sense

Recently, it has been argued that the assertion that phobias can be acquired by conditioning needs considerable qualification. The conditioning of phobias is highly selective. Only *some* objects and *some* situations are easily linked with fear while others are not. Martin Seligman and others have pointed out that the objects or situations most feared by phobic people are the ones that *were* dangerous in the early stages of human history. The argument goes that evolution will have selected for those individuals who would readily associate particular dangerous situations with fear. People and other animals who quickly learned to be afraid of heights, or strangers, or separation would have reproductive advantages over those without this capacity. Learning of this sort is referred to as *biologically prepared*. People do not readily acquire phobic reactions to electrical plugs or guns because such objects have appeared too recently in human culture for them to have featured in natural selection. Clearly, we are primed to develop only particular kinds of fears or phobias. What other factors, apart from biological preparedness, promote the acquisition of particular fears, is, as yet, largely unknown.

Who is vulnerable?

Conditioning theories have been relatively unsuccessful in accounting for more complex phobias such as agoraphobia or for generalized, non-specific, anxiety states. For agoraphobia, there is rarely an obvious traumatic conditioning event that can be pointed to. A theory of the origin of agoraphobia, therefore, will need to look at a broader range of influences, such as the ones proposed by a team of British researchers, Andrew Mathews, Michael Gelder and Derek Johnston. They suggest that there are three *vulnerability factors* which predispose the person to develop agoraphobic symptoms:

1. The early family environment. Families in which there is instability, over-protectiveness or lack of parental care may increase the tendency to be dependent on others and to avoid difficult situations.
2. A general 'anxious' temperament (possibly influenced by genetics).
3. Exposure to general stress in the environment.

The likely sequence for the development of the disorder is as follows. The anxiety-prone person with a 'bad' family background is exposed to stress (conflicts, domestic crises, and so on) which induces a high level of anxiety and physical arousal. When the person then finds him or herself in an overstimulating environment (for instance, a crowded shopping centre or store in the case of agoraphobia), the physical arousal is increased and, eventually, the person experiences a full-blown panic in that situation. An additional factor then determines whether the person becomes agoraphobic or develops a generalized anxiety state. The person will become agoraphobic if he or she attributes the panic experienced to the external situation (the crowded place) rather than internally. The person now sees the panic as being caused by the setting and learns to avoid it in future. Once the agoraphobic habit has been produced it will be maintained and confirmed if staying at home is rewarded by family and friends and if the person now avoids going out from fear of having another panic attack. It may be that the panic attack itself is now feared as much as the crowded street or shop.

Looking for danger

This account, of course, does not fully explain why some people are anxiety-prone in the first place nor why only some individuals are made anxious by life stresses. One promising line of recent research suggests that anxious people 'selectively process' information relating to personal danger. It is as if the anxious person is attuned to threats in the environment in a way that the non-anxious person is not. The 'dangers' in this case may be social (for example, rejection) as well as physical (for example, illness).

Andrew Mathews has suggested that the anxious person may be locked in a 'cognitive-anxiety loop'. Cognitions or thoughts about danger cause a state of anxiety. The state of anxiety, in turn, activates 'danger schemata'. In everyday terms, perceived danger produces anxiety, which makes the person even more aware of thoughts and memories relating to danger. Such a loop produces an escalation of distress until a state of panic is reached.

THE TREATMENT OF FEAR AND ANXIETY

The treatment of phobias has been one of the success stories of modern clinical psychology. A very large number of studies have been conducted in the last 30 years evaluating the effectiveness of various therapeutic approaches. With considerable consistency, the research points to the effectiveness of *exposure to the feared situation* in reducing phobic reactions. There have been several variants of exposure treatment which have been popular for a time.

Systematic desensitization

In the 1950s Joseph Wolpe developed *systematic desensitization* as a treatment for phobias. The technique has three components. First, the client is trained in *deep muscle relaxation*, to produce a physical state that is incompatible with the experience of anxiety. Second, the client is helped to devise a *hierarchy* of fear-inducing situations. At the top of the hierarchy are situations of maximum fear; at the bottom situations of low fear. An actual hierarchy for Ms J, the nurse, is shown in *Table 7.1.*

Finally the client is asked to imagine each scene, starting at the bottom of the hierarchy, while deeply relaxed. When the fear diminishes the client moves up the hierarchy until the most frightening scene can be imagined without fear. This simple method proved to be effective with a number of simple phobias. Subsequent experiments showed that the relaxation was not essential for this method to be effective.

Implosion

A variation on this particular technique is to use *implosion*. Here the client is immediately induced to imagine the worst possible

Table 7.1: Hierarchy of fear-inducing situations for Ms J

☐ Maximum fear:	(1)	Working on the ward alone at night when a patient is dying.
	(2)	Working on the ward alone at night when no one is seriously ill.
	(3)	Working with another nurse on a night shift.
	(4)	Working alone on a day shift.
	(5)	Working with another nurse on a day shift.
	(6)	Visiting the hospital at night but not on duty.
	(7)	Visiting the hospital in the day but not on duty.
☐ Minimum fear:	(8)	Walking past the hospital.

situation and to experience it fully, without graduated exposure. It is now widely accepted that for systematic desensitization and implosion to work, they need to be accompanied by real life exposure to the feared situation. Graduated exposure is the approach most likely to be effective with Ms J. as it is with most agoraphobics. In most cases, the method produces significant changes which are maintained over time, although clients are often left with residual difficulties even at the end of treatment. Why exposure works and how the effect is to be explained remain matters of debate within clinical psychology. It is unlikely that it can be explained in mechanical conditioning terms. It is more likely to be the client's thoughts, expectations and general appraisal of him or herself and the situation that are changed in the course of 'facing up' to feared situations.

The interest of clinical researchers has moved away from investigating whether exposure treatments work (they do) to asking how exposure can be made even more effective. How long should exposure sessions be? How many times per week? How effective are 'homework' sessions for the client? Are follow-up 'booster' exposure sessions useful? It is likely that research into these questions will lead to further advances in treatment methods in the future.

Psychological treatments for generalized anxiety, where there is no identifiable trigger, are rather less advanced. Effective therapies await a greater understanding of the psychological processes involved. As with many other problems, the attention of contemporary clinicians and researchers is increasingly focused on the role of higher-level 'cognitive' activities in the causation and cure of these anxieties.

Treating panic

One of the most rapidly developing areas in the last decade has been the psychological treatment of one type of anxiety – *panic disorder*. Panic refers to recurrent attacks of intense fear and anxiety. During an attack, the sufferer may experience a range of disturbing symptoms, including a racing heart, sweating, shaking, nausea, numbness and choking. Sometimes panics of this sort are associated with agoraphobia. It is the intensity of the physical symptoms, and their short duration, which distinguish panic disorders from generalized anxiety disorder. While pharmacological interventions play a part in the contemporary treatment of panic, psychological intervention is also essential. Generally speaking, effective treatment programs for panic include a broad range of procedures and methods. These include training the person to modify their overbreathing (a likely contributor to feeling panicky) and teaching the person to consciously produce the physical symptoms of panic. There is also an important emphasis on helping the person to identify automatic catastrophic thoughts ('I'm going to die') which accompany physical sensations of panic, and to substitute more realistic thoughts ('My heart is racing because I have been overbreathing'). Using such methods, many clients are able to control and reduce the terrors of a panic attack.

CHILDHOOD SEXUAL ABUSE

Occasionally in the development of clinical psychology and psychiatry new 'discoveries' or new theories arrive which have a dramatic impact on the thinking and clinical work of practitioners. Some would argue that the past 20 years have witnessed such a phenomenon – the 'discovery' (or re-discovery) of the importance of childhood sexual abuse as a social and psychological problem. One of the authors of this book trained as a clinical psychologist in the 1970s. At that time childhood sexual abuse was rarely raised as an important issue in either the academic or clinical aspects of training. In the clinical setting it was rare to ask questions of patients or clients about their experience of abuse as a factor contributing to psychological or psychiatric disorder.

In the 1990s the clinical world has changed. Childhood sexual abuse is covered as an important topic in clinical education and practitioners are trained to routinely identify whether sexual abuse has occurred and what the implications for the client's distress and disorder might be. This is a topic which elicits strong emotions and the challenge for psychologists and other professionals is to achieve a balance between scientific detachment and the feelings of indignation and anger which are naturally elicited by the abuse of children. These latter emotions should not be overlooked in that they have been an energizing and activating force in encouraging research and the development of therapeutic interventions for child victims and for perpetrators.

Why does abuse occur?

It is difficult, if not impossible, to devise successful preventative programs to eliminate child sexual abuse without having a model of why abuse occurs. One of the most influential attempts to provide an explanatory framework has been by David Finkelhor in America. In 1984, Finkelhor put forward what he called the *Precondition Model.* He states four necessary conditions for the occurrence of abuse; that is, abuse will not occur, according to the theory, when these four conditions are not present. The theory tries to specify both *intra-perpetrator* factors and factors in the *situation* that might be important.

The first precondition is that the potential perpetrator is *motivated* to sexually abuse a child. Three factors are seen as contributing to motivation –'emotional congruence', 'sexual arousal' and 'blockage'. By 'emotional congruence' Finkelhor means the emotional liking for the company of children that some perpetrators report. It is not unusual for a perpetrator of abuse to say he has always found children easier to relate to than adults. 'Sexual arousal' refers to physiological sexual arousal. 'Blockage' refers to major difficulties in relating to adults. It is now clear from research studies that perpetrators (sexual offenders against children) frequently have serious problems in establishing intimate, longer-term relationships with adults.

For Finkelhor, motivation is only the first step. For abuse to occur, the potential offender must move to Step 2, *overcoming the internal inhibitors* that the vast majority of people would have about abusing a child. Alcohol, mental disorders, brain damage and anger are all factors which can sometimes produce disinhibition.

Situational factors

Even the motivated, disinhibited person may not progress to offending unless two further steps occur. Firstly, potential *external inhibitors* must be overcome. In general, society successfully inhibits abuse by providing good supervision, by families and others, of children at risk. The breakdown of supervision, therefore, is a significant risk factor. Finally, abuse still will not occur unless the potential victim's (the child's) *resistance is overcome* in some way. Research suggests that sex offenders often target children who will find resistance difficult or who have emotional difficulties which make them vulnerable.

A theory in practice

Finkelhor's theory is a good illustration of how powerful a theory can be in suggesting intervention and prevention methods. Psychologists' efforts are increasingly directed at prevention, as theories such as Finkelhor's suggest many avenues for producing change, including changing the characteristics of perpetrators in rehabilitation programs and changing the social environment itself. The psychological treatment of sex offenders causes heated debate in the press and amongst some groups in the community. Nevertheless, it is the case that substantial treatment programs for sex offenders exist in many countries of the world, including the United States, Canada, Britain, Australia and New Zealand. At a recent international conference reviewing such treatment programs there was much optimism about the effectiveness of these programs in reducing recidivism (relapses). The psychological treatment of sex offenders provides a vivid and controversial example of applied psychology at the coal face.

Psychologists have devised intervention programs based on theory and research findings and also produced some evidence that such programs work, at least for some offenders. Whether governments and communities will invest resources in such programs, and view rehabilitation as being as important as punishment in dealing with sex offenders, is far from clear.

Prevention

Prevention is a much broader task than the treatment of perpetrators, as Finkelhor's theory would suggest. Prevention programs devised by psychologists such as Deborah Daro emphasize education for children and adolescents, better training of professionals working with children, education for parents, changes within child and welfare agencies and the raising of public awareness about sexual abuse as all being vital.

Finally, part of the preventative effort has been focused on preventing and offsetting the negative consequences of childhood abuse for children and for adults. As psychological studies progressively identify the effects of childhood sexual abuse as leading to later psychological and psychiatric disorders, it will become increasingly important to devise and evaluate therapeutic interventions for those who have been the victims of abuse.

PSYCHOLOGY AND SCHIZOPHRENIA

Clinical psychology has a relatively short history, many of the important developments in the discipline having occurred over the past 30 years. Behavioural and cognitive clinical psychologists quickly made important contributions to the understanding and treatment of some of the 'neurotic' disorders (see the section on anxiety problems, for example). Contributions to the more severe 'psychotic' disorders, such as schizophrenia, have been less obvious. There are a number of reasons for the past neglect of such conditions by psychologists. Schizophrenia is often viewed as strongly biologically determined, and as needing an exclusively medical approach to management. Additionally, some psychologists, and even some psychiatrists, have questioned the validity of the disorder as a discrete disease of the nervous system, suggesting that it represents a *group* of problems rather than a single one.

What is schizophrenia?

Schizophrenia is a severe psychiatric disorder affecting approximately one per cent of the population. Its presentation varies in different individuals, but amongst the most common symptoms are *delusions, hallucinations* and *thought disorder.* Delusions are false and abnormal beliefs (for example, that the government has implanted a radio transmitter in your brain to control your actions). Hallucinations are sensory experiences in the absence of an external stimulus; the most common form of hallucination is hearing a voice which often gives instructions, or comments in a negative way on the person's behaviour. Hallucinations commonly cause much distress to the person, though not necessarily so. Thought disorder refers to a disorganization of speech, sometimes in the form of a loosening of associations, so that speech becomes confusing and disjointed for the listener.

The psychological perspective

Psychologists are increasingly making a contribution to the understanding and treatment of schizophrenia, often in innovative ways. The general view of psychologists tends to be that the likelihood of a schizophrenic episode occurring depends on the person's vulnerability (which has a likely biological/genetic basis) in combination with the level of stress they experience. It is generally believed that the psychosocial stressors may be more relevant to the *maintenance* of schizophrenia (why it continues or recurs) than to its initial onset.

In addition to the psychosocial contribution to the maintenance of schizophrenia, it is also clear that schizophrenia causes major impairments for the affected individual. Apart from the symptoms of the condition itself (delusions, hallucinations, thought disorder), the person suffers subsequent disabilities (poor social and community survival skills, poor self-image) and social problems (unemployment, family discord, diminished social networks).

How to intervene

Psychologists such as Max Birchwood and Nicholas Tarrier in the United Kingdom have described and evaluated a range of interventions for schizophrenia. These are normally complementary to medical interventions, rather than alternatives to them. One approach has been to directly tackle the symptom itself and to assist the person to cope more effectively with it. For hallucinations, for example, the first step would be to conduct an analysis of the factors controlling and influencing the hallucinatory experience, of the emotional consequences, of how the person copes, and of how they might cope more effectively. Treatment would involve devising and enhancing coping techniques through practice and rehearsal. Paul Chadwick and Max Birchwood have shown that the person's appraisals and interpretations of the hallucinatory agent (the voice) are important determinants of adverse emotional and behavioural reactions to the hallucinations. It follows that in therapy we may need to help individuals change their interpretations and beliefs concerning the voice. Cognitive therapy for schizophrenia is a new but rapidly developing area of psychological practice.

Change through the family

There is evidence that family stresses contribute to the likelihood of a person with schizophrenia relapsing after discharge from hospital. For this reason, interventions need to focus on the family as well as on the individual sufferer. Nicholas Tarrier suggests that family interventions need to include educating the family about schizophrenia, stress management, goal setting for the patient and improving communication. It appears that a consensus is emerging that the problem of schizophrenia requires a multidisciplinary response in which the biological, psychological and social aspects are all addressed in an integrated and co-ordinated way.

In conclusion, in this chapter we have only been able to sketch some examples of how psychology can contribute to solving, or at least helping individuals cope better with, human problems. Anxiety, childhood sexual abuse and schizophrenia are very diverse phenomena, but all three contribute to human distress. There are grounds for a cautious optimism that we will see psychology make an increasing contribution to solving such problems in the future.

References

Andrews, G., Crino, R., Hunt, C., Lampe, L. and Page, A. (1995). *The Treatment of Anxiety Disorders: Clinician's guide and treatment manuals*. Cambridge: Cambridge University Press. [An advanced book, but covers most of the work on anxiety mentioned in this chapter].

Birchwood, M. and Preston, M. (1991). Schizophrenia. In W. Dryden and R. Rentoul (Eds.), *Adult Clinical Problems: A cognitive-behavioural approach*. London: Routledge. [A good, brief overview of work on schizophrenia.]

Birchwood, M. and Tarrier, N. (Eds) (1992). *Innovations in the Psychological Management of Schizophrenia*. Chichester: Wiley. [An example of current innovations, with contributions from many workers in the field.]

Chadwick, P. and Birchwood, M. (1994). The omnipotence of voices: a cognitive approach to auditory hallucinations. *British Journal of Psychiatry, 164*, 190–201. [The person's appraisals of the hallucinatory agent.]

Daro, D. (1991). Prevention programs. In C.R. Hollin and K. Howells (Eds), *Clinical Approaches to Sex Offenders and Their Victims*. Chichester: Wiley. [Discusses principles of prevention of child sexual abuse].

Finkelhor, D. (1984). *Child Sexual Abuse: New theory and research*. New York: Free Press. [An influential book by an internationally recognized authority.]

Mathews, A.M., Gelder, M.G. and Johnston, D.W. (1981). *Agoraphobia: Nature and treatment*. London: Tavistock. [A comprehensive account of the treatment of agoraphobia.]

Seligman, M.E.P. (1970). On the generality of the laws of learning. *Psychological Review, 77*, 406–418. [Discusses prepared learning.]

Wolpe, J. (1958). *Psychotherapy by Reciprocal Inhibition*. Stanford, CA: Stanford University Press. [Systematic desensitization.]

Recommended Reading

Dryden, W. and Rentoul, R. (Eds) (1991). *Adult Clinical Problems: A cognitive-behavioural approach*. London: Routledge.

Peterson, C. (1996). *The Psychology of Abnormality*. Fort Worth, TX: Harcourt Brace.

WHAT IS 'NORMALITY?'

An enduring problem in clinical psychology and psychiatry is the definition of normality and abnormality. When, and by what criteria, can a person's behaviour be considered 'abnormal' and thereby in need of 'treatment'? In this chapter we have considered phenomena such as delusions and hallucinations. You might think that these would be considered abnormal by both professionals and the general public. But what about other behaviours and experiences? If possible, try the following task in a group, but start out by thinking about it on your own.

Consider the following three behaviours and write down whether you would consider them as abnormal and requiring treatment.

- *A person repeatedly trying to commit suicide*   YES/NO

- *A person repeatedly committing serious crimes*   YES/NO

- *A person who feels deeply depressed most*   YES/NO
  days over a period of several months

Now list *why* you have this view; that is, by what *criteria* is this behaviour abnormal?

Compare your judgements and your criteria with other people in your group. Do you agree with each other? Turn to p.193 to see criteria often suggested as important to our judgement of abnormality.

continued

continued ---

WHAT IS 'NORMALITY?'

Criteria often suggested as important to our judgement of abnormality

(a) Deviation from statistical norm (most people do not act this way).
(b) Norm violation (breaks formal or informal rules about how we should act).
(c) Causes distress to the person.
(d) Causes distress to others.
(e) Impairs the person's functioning.
(f) Has a biological cause.
(g) The person seeks treatment for the problem.

(For a discussion of whether crime meets these criteria, see: Raine, A. (1993). *The Psychopathology of Crime: Criminal behaviour as a clinical disorder.* San Diego: Academic Press.)

8. Your View of the World: Perception and Memory

How does a profoundly deaf child whose hearing is restored by the insertion of a cochlear implant, know what he or she is hearing? Does the meaning of every sound have to be learned and remembered? Does the relative importance of different kinds of sound also have to be learned so that the appropriate sounds are paid attention to?

In this chapter we will look at the processes involved in perceiving things, in paying attention and remembering. These three aspects of human functioning are all related, as without memory we would not be able to recognize objects in our environment, nor be able to allocate our attention appropriately. We will look at each in turn, although we will see some overlap in the explanations of the processes involved.

PERCEPTION

Making sense of the world

How do you know that the thing you are looking at is a book? This knowledge is more than the sum total of the visual image you are receiving from your eyes and the feel of the book from your hands – it depends also on your prior knowledge of what a book is.

The sensory receptors in our eyes, ears, noses, tongues and skin receive information from our environments and transform this into electrical impulses which are transmitted to our brains. This is the subject of sensory physiology. As psychologists, we do need to have some understanding of the processes involved in detecting environmental events or stimuli. However, perception involves more than just taking in information from our senses; perception is concerned with our *interpretation* of the sensory information we receive. We only perceive something when we become aware of it and this occurs in the higher centres of the central nervous system where the sensory information is not just received, but is processed. Perception involving the sense of vision is the area that has been most studied as for the majority of us this is the *modality* (type of information) on which we are most dependent, although other species rely on scent, hearing, or even perception of electrical impulses to a greater extent than vision. We will use sight to illustrate perceptual processes.

THE VISUAL SYSTEM

The eyes and vision

The retina at the back of the eye contains two types of cell which are sensitive to light energy. These light sensitive cells, which are called *rods* and *cones* because of their shape, form one of five layers of cells in the retina and can be thought of as rather like the film in a camera. There are approximately 3,000,000 cones and 100,000,000 rods in the retina of each eye. Rods are highly sensitive to light but give us no information about colour, which is why in poor light in the evenings we may be able to see, but not to distinguish colour. When the light is brighter, we use our cones and can see in colour. After passing through the retina, where light energy is converted into electrical impulses which can travel along nerves, signals proceed along the optic nerves to the optic chiasma. Here, some of the signals from the right eye swop over to be transmitted to the left side of the brain and vice versa, as shown in *Figure 8.1*.

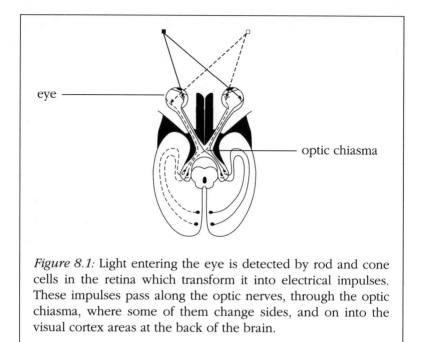

Figure 8.1: Light entering the eye is detected by rod and cone cells in the retina which transform it into electrical impulses. These impulses pass along the optic nerves, through the optic chiasma, where some of them change sides, and on into the visual cortex areas at the back of the brain.

When the signals reach the primary visual cortex area at the back of the brain, recordings of electrical activity in single cells have shown that they are received by cells which are only sensitive to specific shapes, directions of movement, sizes and so on. This was first found by David Hubel and Torsten Weisel in 1959. But the important physiological discovery of these *feature detection cells* still leaves us a long way from understanding how we interpret the light patterns falling on our eyes as corresponding to particular objects in the environment.

Seeing objects

When we look at an object, we see it in relation to a background. Indeed, it has to be sufficiently distinct from the background in order for us to be able to see it at all (this is also true of hearing sounds, touching, smelling and tasting). It was pointed out by a group of German psychologists that the distinction between figure and background cannot be measured simply in terms of physical

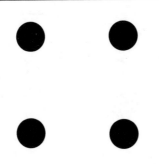

Figure 8.2: What do you see here? Chances are that you 'saw' the four corners of a square. In fact, there are just four black dots in the figure. The tendency to see a square is termed 'closure' by Gestalt psychologists and is one aspect of our perception of 'good' figures even when they are not actually present.

boundaries. The demonstrations by these 'Gestalt psychologists' of what they called *laws of perceptual organization,* show that in perception, the whole is greater than the sum of its parts. For example, the four isolated dots shown in *Figure 8.2* are 'seen' by most people as the corners of a square, not as four isolated dots.

Another example of this principle of grouping is in our interpretation of ambiguous figures such as that shown in *Figure 8.3.* You may see one face, or you may see two faces in profile kissing, but almost certainly you will not see both figures at the same time or any sort of compromise between the two.

Size constancy, distance cues and visual illusions

When this book is held close to you, the light reflected from it stimulates large areas of your retinae. When the book is on the table at the far end of the room, it stimulates a much smaller area of your retinae. So does the book look smaller the further away it is? A silly question perhaps, but why? Almost certainly the book looks to be about 20cmx15cmx2cm however near or far away it is. This is because of a phenomenon known as *size constancy.* One way in which we can explain size constancy is to suppose that the brain is receiving information not only about the size of the retinal image, but also about how distant the object is from us.

Figure 8.3: What do you see here? Is it one face or two people in profile, kissing? Our perception of ambiguous figures such as this one tends to alternate between the possibilities.

We can fool the brain by giving conflicting clues, as in visual illusions. *Perspective* is one clue as to the distance away an object is. Parallel lines, such as railway lines or the edges of a straight road, will appear to converge in the distance. *Figure 8.4* shows a variation on the Ponzo illusion, which uses this perspective phenomenon to demonstrate size constancy.

The converging lines are interpreted as parallel lines receding into the distance and most of us perceive the two ladders as being of different lengths, when in fact they are the same (measure them if you aren't convinced).

This, and other evidence that we seem to make assumptions about the nature of the objects in our environment, led Richard Gregory in 1966 to propose the theory of *perceptual hypotheses*. The idea is that we use what we already know to make the best guess we can about the sometimes sketchy and ambiguous material our senses present to us. One difficulty with this is that it cannot explain how we come to learn what things are in the first place.

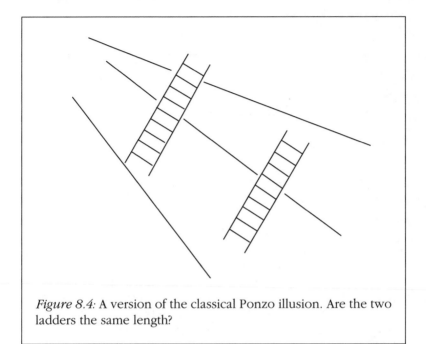

Figure 8.4: A version of the classical Ponzo illusion. Are the two ladders the same length?

Gregory's theory can be classed as a 'top down' theory, as it is based on the idea of information stored in the higher centres of the brain being used to interpret incoming information from the senses. A completely different approach to perception was hinted at earlier when I mentioned feature detection cells. This is the idea that information is processed from the 'bottom', where it enters at the retinae, and 'up' as it progresses through the various levels of analysis in the central nervous system. One problem here is that there would have to be so many feature detectors in order to discriminate not only between all the shapes, directions of movement, colours and so on, but also between the same information in different contexts. The ambiguous shape in *Figure 8.5*, although identical, is interpreted as an H in the first word, but as an A in the second by a fluent reader of the English language.

This is difficult to explain by a purely *bottom up*, or *data-driven*, theory of perception. Perhaps a theory incorporating both extreme approaches may come nearer to explaining how perception operates. Ulrich Neisser's cyclic model is such a theory. He suggested that we have an idea, or an *anticipatory scheme*, of

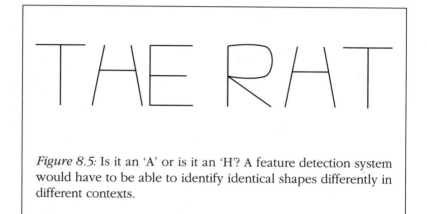

Figure 8.5: Is it an 'A' or is it an 'H'? A feature detection system would have to be able to identify identical shapes differently in different contexts.

what we are likely to be seeing (top down), and we test this continuously against features coming in from our eyes (bottom up).

One other rather different explanation of perception should be mentioned before we leave this topic. This is the theory of *direct perception*, developed by James Jerome Gibson. This explanation doesn't consider stages of processing or the features of isolated objects, but instead explains perception as occurring as a result of the information gleaned from the whole environment as we move in it and it moves around us.

ATTENTION

Focusing attention on one thing at a time

A lot of the time we select what we will pay attention to. For example, while reading this book you cannot also read the newspaper or watch the television. When listening to music you may focus on the brass section of the orchestra and be unaware of the violins. The *single channel* theory of attention, proposed by Donald Broadbent (1926–1993), was based on the common experience of being able to attend to only one thing at a time. This theory views the brain as an information processing system where information enters the senses, is temporarily stored in a sensory buffer store and is then passed through a selective filter which allows only one channel from all the incoming information to pass. Experiments using headphones to relay different signals to the two ears offer evidence for the single channel theory.

A typical experiment would involve playing three different pairs of numbers to each ear, with the first pair of numbers going to left and right simultaneously, followed by the second and third. When asked to recall the numbers, it is much easier to recall all numbers presented to one ear together, than it is to recall the two presented at the same time, one to each ear. This seems to show that input to one channel (one ear) is selected. More recent elaborations using Broadbent's basic method have shown that the information from the selected-out channel is not completely lost. Indeed this split span procedure can give different results if, for example, the information given to the two ears consists of words which can be combined to make a meaningful message. In the type of experiment illustrated in *Figure 8.6*, participants are able to report hearing 'Have a drink', or '294' as easily as they can report '2 a 4' or 'Have 9 drink'.

This involves switching between channels (ears) and suggests that we are able to select on the basis of meaning.

Figure 8.6: An illustration of the split span procedure used to illustrate the finding that sounds are selected for attention on the basis of meaning. The character in the illustration is able to switch between channels (ears) and report hearing 'HAVE A DRINK'.

The cocktail party phenomenon

Anne Treisman modified the theory to allow for the unattended information being reduced in strength rather than lost. When in deep conversation with one person at a noisy party, you can be completely unaware of what anyone else is saying until someone on the other side of the room mentions your name. This shows that the unattended conversations apparently are not completely blocked, and if their content becomes sufficiently pertinent, they can catch your attention. Treisman's modification of the single channel theory of attention incorporates this *cocktail party phenomenon*. She suggested that the unattended information is attenuated, not lost, and that our attention has different thresholds depending on the possible interest to us of the information.

Dividing attention between different things

Anyone who has tried to listen to a small child while helping an older one with homework, planning what to have for tea and wondering what the puppy is up to in the next room, will be all too well aware that there is a limit to our capacity to process information. Perhaps, though, you can knit and watch television or read a book at the same time? Or perhaps you can drive a car and hold a conversation? If you are an accomplished keyboard operator, perhaps you can copy-type one passage at the same time as repeating another passage spoken to you over headphones? Under certain circumstances we can pay attention to more than one thing at a time. We can usually only do this if the two tasks require the use of different input and different output modalities (*channels*). Another important point is that with practice we are able to carry out some tasks without having to pay attention. That is to say, some processes are carried out automatically. If one task is being done automatically, for example driving a car, another act such as holding a conversation can easily be performed. If, as the driver of the car, you suddenly find yourself having to carry out evasive action because the lorry in front has jackknifed, the chances are that your conversation will come to an abrupt end. Your driving skills have become attentional processes again and you are no longer able to attend to your conversation. There is a limit to our capacity to divide our attention, but automatic processes take up very little of this capacity, which is why they can usually be performed at the same time as other tasks. In general though, our resources seem to be allocated by a central processor and may be spread over several tasks which require little mental capacity, or may be concentrated on one, more demanding, task.

MEMORY

Much of what we have said so far in this chapter has depended on the existence of memory. Indeed, without memory of how written English works, we would have been unable to write any of it and you would have been unable to read it. So, how does memory work?

One way to look at memory is to consider it in three stages. The first, *encoding*, involves transformation of input from our senses to a code suitable for the memory to store; the second is *retention*, or holding the information in a store or stores; and the third, *retrieval*, the processes involved in getting information out of the store(s). At any one of these stages something may go wrong and we will have forgotten the information we had hoped to remember. The types of errors we commonly make can tell us quite a lot about the codes used and the organization of information in our memories, as we shall see later.

THE INFORMATION PROCESSING MODEL OF MEMORY

The storage system just described is often thought of as being divided into short- and long-term memory stores. According to this way of looking at things, all the information which passes the encoding process is passed on to the short-term memory. This is as far as something like a telephone number which we look up, use immediately, and then forget, ever gets. This type of memory has a capacity of about seven items (when telephone numbers are longer than this we have to group the digits together in order to remember them), and lasts for a few minutes at the most. We can only keep material in the short-term memory for longer than this if we keep repeating it, or *rehearse* it. Experiments have shown that information in the short-term memory is often stored in an *acoustic* code; that is, according to the way it sounds. This is shown by looking at the mistakes we make – these are to 'recall' wrong, but similar sounding, words to those we were actually trying to remember. This applies even to material presented visually, so if you were shown a list of letters and asked to recall them, you would be more likely to substitute F for M (which begins with the same sound) than for E (which is physically more similar). A visual code is used in short-term memory, for information such as the positions of shapes in a grid, which cannot easily be expressed in an acoustic form.

Material to be stored for longer than the few minutes possible in short-term memory must be held in another store. The traditional view is that it is passed from the short-term to a long-term memory store. This store is thought to have almost unlimited capacity and storage duration. All kinds of information stored for the long-term, is classified into *episodic* memory for personal experiences and particular events in our lives, and *semantic* memory for general knowledge and meanings of things. Furthermore, there is evidence that information stored in long-term memory is organized in a complex network of connected, related concepts. One version of this model is known as the *spreading activation model* and it assumes links which may be more or less long and strong between words. *Figure 8.7* illustrates this, showing 'car', 'truck' and 'bus' connected by strong short links to 'vehicle'. Thinking of one concept, for example, 'vehicle', would make it easy to recall 'car', 'bus' or 'truck'. 'Wheels', 'carburettors' and 'exhaust pipes' would also be more accessible once you were thinking of the concept 'vehicles', than they would if you were thinking along different lines, for example 'houses'.

Try to recall the names of teachers you had at your very first school. The chances are that you will recall the names of other teachers you have known (category: teachers), or of other people you knew when you were at that school (category: people I knew when I was aged 4–11), perhaps before you are able to come up with the appropriate names. This theoretical model of categorical organization in memory has recently received some support from PET scanning, which shows the location of activity in the brain. Hanna Damasio and colleagues, in an article in the prestigious scientific journal *Nature*, reported finding activity in different brain locations according to different concepts which people were asked to recall (animal names, well-known people's names, and tools were used).

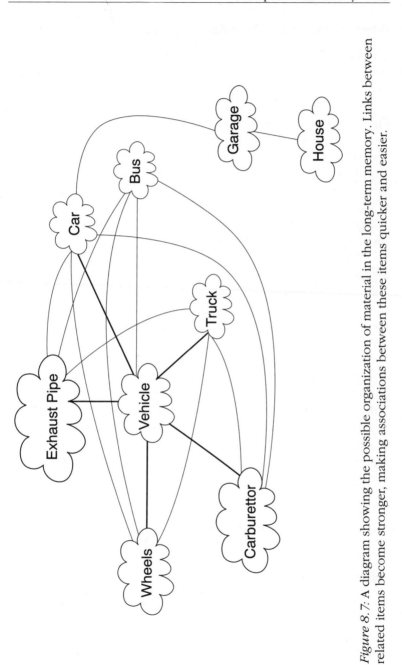

Figure 8.7: A diagram showing the possible organization of material in the long-term memory. Links between related items become stronger, making associations between these items quicker and easier.

What's wrong with the information processing model?

The simple explanation of memory, in terms of encoding, retention and retrieval which has been at the basis of our considerations so far, assumes that information transfer occurs in one direction only. However, telephone numbers appear in telephone directories in the form of black squiggles on a white background. You cannot encode a telephone number in the form of the sounds the digits would make if you said them (acoustic code), unless you have already learnt how to interpret the squiggles. This means that there must be information flowing from the long-term to the short-term memory as well as the other way round.

Another problem concerns the division of the storage system into two distinct parts. An alternative, suggested by Fergus Craik and Robert Lockhart, is that it is the *depth of processing* to which an item is subjected which determines how durable its memory will become. Shallow levels of analysis concern physical attributes such as shape, pitch and brightness; deeper levels may involve meanings or links with other stored items and will lead to more lasting memories.

Other alternatives to the explanation of short-term memory as a passive store of a very limited amount of information also seem to fit the evidence better. One such, proposed by Alan Baddeley and Graham Hitch emphasizes the active nature of short-term memory and renames it *working memory*. The idea is that there are in fact several component parts, including three separate stores based on different types of information, and a central executive which controls them all.

INTERESTING FACTS ABOUT REMEMBERING AND FORGETTING

Where did you learn it?

Successful memory can depend on contextual cues. Have you ever gone upstairs to get something only to forget what it was by the time you got there? Chances are that you went back to where you were when you thought of what you needed from upstairs and promptly remembered what it was.

Were you sober at the time?

A person's own internal state at the time of encoding can be important for later retrieval. The phenomenon whereby you may be told something when under the influence of alcohol or other drugs, be unable to recall it later when sober, but able to do so when again similarly intoxicated, is known as *state dependent learning*.

On the tip of your tongue?

The feeling that you can almost but not quite recall a word is probably a familiar one. Experiments with this *tip-of-the-tongue* phenomenon help us to understand how information is stored in memory. For example, it is a common experience to be able to recall the initial letter or a word related to the one we want, showing that we search by sound or meaning through our semantic memories. For recall of material in the episodic memory, on the other hand, we are more likely to reconstruct a familiar scene.

Is the material emotionally arousing?

Imagine watching a football match which includes a very famous but controversial player. You are a fond supporter of this player, whereas your friend is of the opinion that he plays a dirty game. When discussing the match the following day, would you and your friend describe the player's game in the same terms? Probably not. Our attitudes to things we see, read and so on affect the way we interpret and remember them. This has major implications for witnesses to crimes, as their memories will certainly be influenced by the, probably fearful, state they were in at the time the crime was perpetrated.

Do we only remember the good times?

Sigmund Freud argued that unpleasant experiences are repressed into the unconscious and not normally available for recall. Try writing down a list of important events which happened to you in your childhood and then label them as good, bad or neutral. The chances are that you will have more good than bad memories on your list. Perhaps this is because the bad experiences have been repressed, or it may be simply that there were more good than bad important things in your young life.

Did it really happen?

False memory syndrome has caused much trouble recently, particularly in the context of child sexual abuse. Brenda Maddox, writing in *The Times*, refers to false memory syndrome as 'a sorry bi-product of the awakening to the fact of adult–child sexual relations'. The question is, whether or not under hypnosis or psychoanalysis intended to uncover repressed memories from the subconscious, clients may confuse fantasy with reality. Work being carried out in America by Daniel Schacter and colleagues, again using PET scanning, offers some promise for controversial cases. Their research shows that sensory areas of the brain, in addition to those known to be involved in memory, were active only when authentic material was being recalled.

You can improve your memory

Strategies for improving memory include mentally allocating items from a 'to-be-remembered' list to different places. A mental 'walk' through the places in order will then allow you to recall the list of items. This is known as the *method of loci*. An example for remembering a shopping list of oranges, lettuce, milk, flour and eggs would be to picture your kitchen with oranges on the worktop by the door, a lettuce on the hob of the cooker, milk in the oven, flour in the sink and eggs on top of the microwave. This may sound silly but it works surprisingly well – try it and see.

The *peg word* method involves first learning a list of rhyming pairs ('One is a bun', and so on) and then imagining the first item of your list in association with the bun and so on. Another method, *story linkage*, involves building up a story around the items to be remembered. Still another requires one to make up a story using the initial letters of the words to be remembered. In order to remember the recent presidents of the United States, for example, with their election dates, your story might be something like this: 'One day *61 ke*ttles set out on a car journey. Unfortunately their car broke down and they had to use *63 j*acks to hold it up. *69 n*eighbours came out to help and after *74 p*ackets of *f*ries had been bought for everyone, they were on their way. They finally arrived in the *c*ountryside at *7* minutes past *7* and so on. (Kennedy, 19*61*; Johnson, 19*63*; Nixon, 19*69*; Ford, 19*74*; Carter, 19*77*).

Most of us will never be able to remember lists of 70 items as one exceptional mnemonist could do, but we might improve our memories a bit if we employ one of these strategies.

Interference leads to forgetting

Although we have said that long-term memory capacity is unlimited, we are all capable of forgetting or being unable to recall information when we want it. Forgetting in long-term memory seems to occur because of interference. This happens in two ways: new learning interferes with earlier memories (*retroactive interference*), and old memories interfere with the learning of new material (*proactive interference*).

An example of retroactive interference would be that if you have read lots of books in the last year, you may be unable to remember the title of the book you were reading in January. If, however, you haven't read anything since last January, you may very well remember the title you read then. You may have experienced proactive interference when attempting to communicate in a newly-learned language, such as German, and found that words from another language (say French), learned long ago in school, intrude.

The processes of perception, attention and memory discussed in this chapter can all be explained within the general framework of information processing. As we have seen, however, simplistic models showing flow of information in one direction (from sensory receptors via attention filters to the central nervous system, and from short-term to long-term memory stores) must be modified to recognize mental representations of knowledge and conscious thought processes.

References

Baddeley, A.D. and Hitch, G.J. (1974). Working memory. In Bower, G.H. (Ed.), *The Psychology of Learning and Motivation*, *Vol. 8*, 47–90. New York: Academic Press. [A reinterpretation of short term memory.]

Broadbent, D. (1954). The role of auditory localization in attention and memory span. *Journal of Experimental Psychology*, *47*, 191–196. [Single channel theory of attention.]

Craik, F.I.M. and Lockhart, R.S. (1972). Levels of processing: a framework for memory research. *Journal of Verbal Learning and Verbal Behaviour*, *11*, 671–684. [An alternative model of memory.]

Damasio, H., Grabowski, T.J., Tranel, D., Hichwa, R.D. and Damasio, A.R. (1996). A neural basis for lexical retrieval. *Nature, 380,* 499–505. [PET scanning study of memory concepts.]

Gibson, J.J. (1986). T*he Ecological Approach to Visual Perception* (reprint of 1979 edition). Hillsdale, New Jersey: Lawrence Erlbaum Associates. [Theory of direct perception.]

Gregory, R.L. (1966). *Eye and Brain.* London: Weidenfeld and Nicolson. [Theory of perceptual hypotheses.]

Hubel, D.H. and Wiesel, T.N. (1959). Receptive fields of single neurones in the cat's striate cortex. *Journal of Physiology, 148,* 574–591. [Discovery of feature detection cells.]

Maddox, B. (1996). The children's tales as yet untold. *The Times, May 29.* [Comment on false memory syndrome.]

Neisser, U. (1976.) *Cognition and Reality.* San Francisco: Freeman and Company. [Cyclical theory of perception.]

Schacter, D. L., Reiman, E., Curran, T., Yun, L. S., Bandy, D., McDermott, K.B. and Roedieger, H.L. III. (1996). Neuroanatomical correlates of veridical and illusory recognition memory: Evidence from positron emission tomography. *Neuron, 17,* 267– 274. [Brain activity when remembering.]

Treisman, A. (1964a). Verbal cues, language and meaning in selective attention. *American Journal of Psychology, 77,* 206–219. [Language, not just physical features is used in selection processes.]

Treisman, A. (1964b). Monitoring and storage of irrelevant messages in selective attention. *Journal of Verbal Learning and Verbal Behaviour, 3,* 449–459. [Experiments on selective attention.]

Recommended reading

Appignanesi, R. and Zarate, O. (1992). *Freud for Beginners.* Hounslow: Icon Books Ltd.

Eysenck, M.W. and Keane, M.T. (1990). *Cognitive Psychology: A Student's Handbook.* Hove: Lawrence Erlbaum Associates.

Smyth, M.M., Collins, A.F., Morris, P.E. and Levy, P. (1994). *Cognition in Action, 2nd edn.* Hove: Lawrence Erlbaum Associates.

LIMITATIONS OF SIZE CONSTANCY

INSTRUCTIONS
- Stretch your arms out in front of you, put your hands up with your palms facing away from you, and about a chest's distance apart.

- Look from one hand to the other and you will see that your two hands are much the same size.

- Now draw one hand in towards you, to about the level of the other elbow. Your hands will probably still appear to be about the same size.

- If you now move the nearer hand closer to the arm belonging to the other one until its outline begins to overlap with the other hand, keeping the wrists at the same height, are your hands still the same size?

WHAT YOU WILL SEE
Many people suddenly become aware when the outlines of the hands overlap, that the further away hand seems to be about half the size of the one held at elbow level.

AN EXPLANATION
As long as the retinal images of the two hands do not overlap, size constancy works, and the illusion that they look the same size is upheld. However, when the two retinal images overlap, a direct comparison of these images is forced on us and we can no longer use distance to compensate for size, so size constancy breaks down (after all, we know that our two hands are virtually the same size).

MEMORY, MEANING AND RHYME

INSTRUCTIONS

Look down the list of words below. For every word with an 'M' beside it, think of a different word related by meaning to the word given. The meaning need not be the same – 'knife' would do for 'fork', for example. For every word with an 'R' beside it, think of a word which rhymes with the word given. For example, 'pork' for 'fork'.

mouse (M)	car (R)
bag (R)	fence (M)
shed (M)	chair (M)
stone (R)	cup (R)
paper (R)	nose (M)
cloud (R)	brush (M)
tree (M)	rug (M)
pond (R)	bread (R)

Now put the list out of sight and write down as many of the original words as you can recall.

Check how many of your answers are 'M' words and how many are 'R' words.

YOUR FINDINGS

Probably you will have remembered more 'M' words than 'R' words.

AN EXPLANATION

The levels of processing theory predicts that we will remember more 'M' than 'R' words in this task because *semantic processing* (involving meaning) occurs at a deeper level than *acoustic processing* (using the sound the words make). This usually works, but there is an alternative to the explanation that it is the depth of processing that the two tasks require that leads to this effect. It usually takes people longer and is more difficult to think up synonyms than rhymes, so is it perhaps the time it takes or the effort involved which determines how well things are remembered?

9. *Learning and Thinking*

How do we learn? Almost every day we meet new people, learn their names and learn to recognize their faces and voices. We learn items of news from the media or from other people. We may also have learned our times tables 'by heart' as children; we learn all sorts of things as we move about in our daily environment. But how do we do this? Do we learn by forming associations between pairs of things, building on these and accumulating a big bank of linked items of information? If so, how come you can't 'teach an old dog new tricks'? Or can you? One group of early researchers thought that learning could be explained by the forming of associations.

LEARNING BY LINKING

Pavlov's dogs

A Russian physiologist investigating the digestive system of dogs was the first person to describe a form of learning by association, which became known as *classical conditioning*. In his study of the reflex salivation of dogs when food was present, Ivan Pavlov (1849–1936) was surprised to observe that dogs secreted saliva on some occasions when no food was there. He went on to investigate these *psychic secretions*, as he called them, and found that they were responses to cues which the dogs had come to associate with food. Food (which always induced salivation) was called an *unconditional stimulus* (*UCS*) and the response of salivation was called the *unconditional response* (*UCR*). In his experiments, Pavlov sounded a bell immediately before the dogs were fed. When this linking procedure had been repeated a number of times, he sounded the bell without giving the dogs any food, and still the dogs salivated. They had learnt that the sound of a bell heralded the arrival of food and responded accordingly. The bell had now become a *conditional stimulus* (*CS*) and the response to the bell (salivation which would not naturally follow hearing a bell) had become a *conditional response* (*CR*) (see *Figure 9.1*).

Further experiments showed that the classically conditioned response may be *generalized* to stimuli similar to the original CS, although following repeated exposure to one specific CS, animals may also show *discrimination* between possible CSs. This

Figure 9.1: Pavlov classically conditioned dogs to salivate in response to the sound of a bell.

discrimination in classical conditioning is shown by sheep in a field which may come to respond excitedly (CR) to the Landrover (CS) which normally brings their food (UCS) but not to every other vehicle which passes by on the same road (*neutral stimuli*). Following classical conditioning and whether generalization or discrimination occurs, the CR will be *extinguished* when the CS is presented a number of times without the UCS.

The time gap between the CS and the UCS during the conditioning period was thought from the early work to be very critical, suggesting a principle of *temporal contiguity*, or the need to be very close together in time, which, we will see later, does not quite fit all the evidence.

Watson's Behaviourism

The idea that behaviour could be explained as a series of learnt associations between stimuli and responses was the basis of a new school of psychology known as *Behaviourism*. Psychology in the late 1800s and early 1900s had depended on people's introspections concerning their feelings and sensations in order to gain understanding of consciousness. The new behaviourism was something of a reaction to this, and only considered behaviour which could be observed and recorded objectively as acceptable data for study in psychology. This new type of psychology was founded by an American called John B. Watson (1876–1958). Watson extended Pavlov's work and showed that classical conditioning worked in humans. He did this by inducing a conditioned fear of furry white animals in a child named Albert (see also Chapter 7).

Poor little Albert, who initially had no fear of a pet rat (a neutral stimulus), began to experience a loud banging noise (Watson banging a piece of metal just behind his head) whenever the rat came near him. This bang (a UCS) frightened Albert, who started and began to cry (UCR). After several pairings of the bang with the rat, the rat was presented alone and Albert's response was now to start (a CR). The formerly neutral stimulus had become a CS. Over the course of a few months, Albert's conditional fear response was shown to have generalized to a rabbit, a dog, a fur coat and a Santa Claus mask. The process of extinction was not studied, as Albert was taken away from the hospital where Watson had studied him. This was probably just as well, as one thing Watson considered trying was 'reconditioning' the child to remove his fear by showing him the fear producing objects while simultaneously stimulating his erogenous zones: first lips, then nipples, then sex organs. Not a procedure which would be considered ethical today!

Although we know now that the mechanistic kind of theory proposed by Watson is too simplistic and that we cannot explain all learning by stimulus response associations, we do know that this type of learning does occur in our everyday lives as well as in experiments. For example, if you revisit your old school or another place which you haven't been to for a long time, come across an odour which you haven't smelled since childhood, play a piece of music which you haven't heard for years, or look at an old school photograph, memories of people, emotions, place names, and conversations may all come flooding back. The conditional stimuli (such as a photograph, or music) are associated with actual events in your past (unconditional stimuli) and you respond with embarrassment, pleasure, anxiety and so on as you did on previous occasions when the UCSs were present.

LEARNING BY CONSEQUENCES

A puzzle for cats

Other pioneers of the new American psychology based on learning were Edward Thorndike (1874–1949) and the very well known Burrhus Skinner (1904–1990). Thorndike developed a puzzle box from which a cat had to escape by pulling a string or pressing a catch in order to get to food. Cats would take less and less time to escape over a series of trials in the box, which Thorndike explained as the gradual formation of an association between the stimulus situation of the box and the response which was instrumental in securing the cat's escape. This type of learning was known as *instrumental conditioning* and the explanation was, as with classical conditioning, in terms of stimulus–response associations. However, in this case, the animals' own actions are instrumental in their gaining the rewards, whereas in classical conditioning, two stimuli become linked so that either elicits the same reflex response. The emphasis has therefore shifted towards the consequences of action. Thorndike's other important contribution was his *Law of Effect* which holds that those behaviours which produce desirable outcomes will be those that are repeated. This was an important advance although we would now interpret Thorndike's findings rather differently.

The Skinner box

Burrhus Skinner investigated this type of learning in greater detail. The Skinner box (see *Figure 9.2*) is a piece of apparatus containing a lever which can be pressed or a button which can be pecked and a tray for the automatic delivery of food. The lever presses or button pecks are recorded automatically over time.

When an animal (for example, a rat) is first placed in the box, it may be given a food reward for moving around investigating the box. After this, it may be rewarded only if it approaches the lever; later, it will have to touch the lever in order to receive a reward; next, it will be rewarded only when it presses the lever. Versions of this process of *shaping* the desired behaviour can be seen in everyday life when we use money to increase the productivity of workers, or sweets to increase 'good' behaviour in children. Once the rat has learnt to press the lever or the pigeon has learnt to peck the button in order to gain food, its discriminatory abilities, for example, can be investigated. It could be rewarded for responding only when a red light shines or only when a triangle is illuminated.

The Skinner box method is generally known as *operant conditioning*, as the animal in the box performs some operation on the environment in order to bring about change. The changes which animals will work for are, as we know from Thorndike's work, changes that benefit the animal and are known as *reinforcement.* Operant conditioning has been particularly useful in the study of different forms and different schedules of reinforcement, among other things.

Punishment

The Skinner box may also be used to demonstrate the effects of punishment. If pressing a bar results in a rat receiving a mild electric shock, the rat will soon stop pressing the bar. However, following a punishment routine such as this, the rat may show signs of stress and stop performing *all* the behaviour that it was doing at the time or may start to perform in unpredictable ways. These

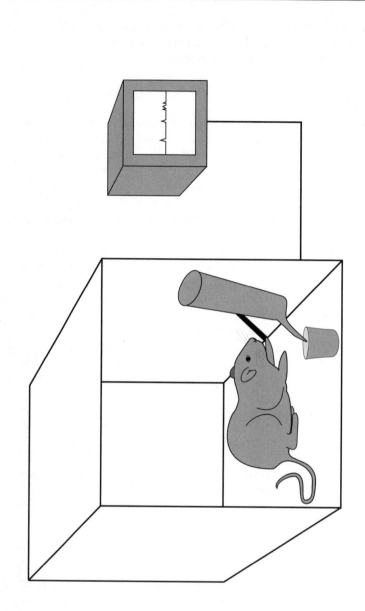

Figure 9.2: In a Skinner box, the rat (or other animal) receives a food pellet when it presses the bar. Bar presses and food delivery are recorded.

findings led Skinner to recommend reinforcement, rather than punishment, for shaping behaviour in humans as well as rats.

Perhaps the most important thing to come out of work with the Skinner box was as a result of the difficulty of explaining what was going on in terms of stimulus–response associations. It was unclear to Skinner what was acting as the stimulus in operant conditioning, and he dropped the idea of a stimulus eliciting a response from his explanation of conditioning. Instead, Skinner divided responses into *elicited* responses such as salivation in Pavlov's classical conditioning experiment, and *emitted* responses, such as touching a lever in a Skinner box. The latter was a freely performed response which an animal may carry out at any time. This dissent from hard-nosed behaviourism was also cropping up in other guises elsewhere as we will now see.

LEARNING WHAT TO EXPECT

Predicting behaviour

The approaches to learning considered so far in this chapter have been concerned with responses either elicited by stimuli or emitted because they are reinforced. There has been little thought of the processes involved between stimulus and response and no place for the cognitions or facts that animals may learn and use when faced with new situations. Work being carried out while S–R psychology (where S means stimulus and R means response) was still in its hey-day, by Edward Tolman (1886–1959), pointed to the conclusion that the behaviour of rats running mazes was purposive and flexible, not mechanistic as suggested by others. One experiment which led Tolman to this conclusion was performed by Donald Macfarlane in 1930.

Macfarlane's experiment involved training rats (which are good swimmers) to find their way through a maze which was flooded with water. When the rats had completed this task, the maze was drained and the rats once again placed at the start. Using a completely different set of responses (running instead of swimming) the rats were able to complete the maze without error. According to Tolman, the animals had learnt not a series of responses to be performed, but information about the experimental situation, such as 'turn towards the window at the T-junction, right by the window, then right again onto the path that brings you to the food'. In other words, the rat forms a *cognitive map* or internal representation of its environment which it stores in its brain. It is then able to use this information with the expectancy that it will reach its goal (*Figure 9.3*).

Many ingenious experiments have followed Tolman's early work and have allowed a new interpretation of classical and operant conditioning to be made. Without going into too much detail, the new interpretation states that the occurrence of an event, E1, can lead an animal to expect another event, E2. It is an animal's ability to form this E1→E2 expectancy that gives it an advantage as it goes about its daily life, as this is the ability that makes it able to form predictions about what is going to happen. Without the ability to predict events, the animal may not act in the most appropriate way.

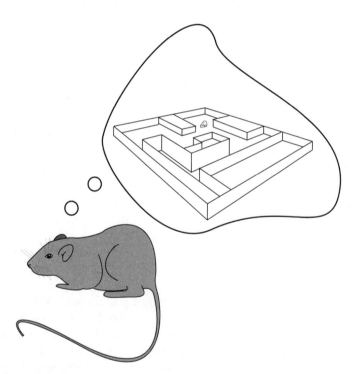

Figure 9.3: Edward Tolman suggested that animals form 'cognitive maps' of their environments, rather than learning their way around by simply stringing together responses to stimulus situations.

Can any event become a predictor for any other event?

An expectancy that a stimulus may, for example, be harmful, need not be based on experience of its immediate noxious effects, as would be predicted by the rule of temporal contiguity to which Pavlov, Watson and others subscribed. An animal's evolutionary background may make it impossible to establish certain events as predictors. These points are illustrated in the examples that follow.

Avoidance learning

A famous experiment by John Garcia and Robert Koelling in 1966 showed that if rats were ill several hours after consuming water flavoured with saccharine, they refused saccharine-flavoured water subsequently, apparently having learned to associate the taste of saccharine with their illness and to expect a nasty outcome to result from consuming something with this taste again (that is, E1, drink flavoured water →E2, feel ill). This expectancy can be formed despite a gap of several hours between Event 1 and Event 2. Also, the learning occurred after only one experience with the taste. It is rats' capacity for this type of learning which makes them so difficult for us to poison.

It is quite common for a very similar type of learning experience to occur in humans. Perhaps you were ill years ago after eating a particular food or drinking too much, and have been unable to face the same food or drink again? Even though you may know that the foodstuff was not the cause of your illness or that the drink in moderation is very unlikely to produce adverse consequences now, you are still unable to bring yourself to try it. Another very interesting finding which emerges from this work, and which also goes against the earlier understanding of classical conditioning, is that the rats will not learn an aversion to plain water. Our understanding of this is that it would not be biologically possible for rats to have evolved the capacity to associate water with illness and to avoid it, as there is no other adequate source of fluid for them. Avoiding harmless water would inevitably lead to death, whereas drinking possibly poisonous water may have no repercussions. As an omnivore though, the ability to reject a foodstuff which has once made one ill has obvious advantages. This shows that not everything can be taught to any animal (and that includes us).

Another series of examples of this constraint on learning comes from attempts to teach tricks to animals for show business or advertising purposes using operant conditioning. Keller and Margaret Breland (1961) were completely unable to persuade pigs to carry coins to a piggy bank and drop them into it, even though this would appear to be a simple task for a highly intelligent animal. The pigs repeatedly dropped the coins and rooted them along the ground. The point here is that an animal being reinforced with food will tend to graduate towards food-getting behaviour typical of its species, and will not learn to carry out a different behaviour in order to get food.

LEARNING FROM OTHERS

So far, the learning we have considered has involved one animal or person learning a likely outcome of an action or event. However, we know that a lot of learning takes place in a social context. The American psychologist Albert Bandura put forward the idea of *observational learning* which occurs without direct links to benefits (*reinforcement*). Bandura argued that if we pay attention to the actions of others, we remember what they do and can reproduce their behaviour ourselves at a later date.

Bandura's 'Bobo' doll

An experiment which Bandura published in 1961 and which is often quoted by those concerned about the effects of violence in the media involved groups of nursery school children. One group watched an adult playing with a set of small toys but ignoring a large inflated 'Bobo' doll which was in the room. Another group watched an adult hitting and shouting at the doll. When afterwards the children were allowed to play with the doll, those who had seen the adult being violent towards it acted in a similar way, whereas those in the first group played pleasantly with the doll. How much light this experiment throws on the effects of media violence is controversial and not the subject of this chapter; the point is that the children had learnt through observation and imitated their adult model's behaviour. Young chimpanzees have been filmed watching their mothers fishing for termites and subsequently trying the behaviour themselves, something they do not necessarily do without the adult model. But this learning by observation is not confined to highly intelligent primates. Hens (not generally thought of as being particularly clever) have been shown to peck more at red than blue food containers after seeing a video in which food was presented in red containers (or vice versa).

THINKING AND THE NATURE OF THOUGHT

What do we mean by 'thinking'? We use this word in a variety of ways. For example, we might say, 'Try to think where you put it', using the word as a synonym for 'remember', or, 'What do think about the present government?', meaning 'What is your opinion?', or, 'What do you think about God?' meaning 'What do you believe?'. 'Think what you're doing' means 'concentrate'. So what are we asking people to do by each of these questions? What is thought? What processes are involved in thinking?

Thought has been explained in different ways by psychologists who adopt different theoretical standpoints and we will look at some of these.

Where and what are thoughts?

Sigmund Freud (1856–1939), whose theory of *psychodynamics* put great emphasis on levels of consciousness, distinguished between rational conscious thought of which we are aware, and less logical, emotionally-based, repressed thoughts and fantasies stored at an unconscious level. The latter are only retrievable under the special conditions of psychoanalysis. Others have been more concerned with not where thought takes place, but in what form. Most importantly, the relationship between language and thought has been the topic of several significant theories. Do we need language in order to think? Or perhaps we need thought in order to be able to use language? Perhaps language is irrelevant and thought occurs in the form of visual or other sensory images?

In the 1920s and 1930s two men working independently came up with the idea that the way each of us thinks depends on the way we express concepts in our particular language. The theory has been named after the two linguists (one of them an amateur), Edward Sapir (1884–1939) and Benjamin Lee Whorf (1897–1941), and is known as the Sapir–Whorf hypothesis or the *linguistic relativity hypothesis*. The main idea, that language affects the way we think about things, can be supported by examples from the world's different cultures. For example, in European languages we have different tenses to indicate the passage of time (past, present and future), and we tend to regard time as an object rather like a tape which we can mark off in spaces or cut up. The Hopi Indians of North America, on the other hand, have no time referents in their language and apparently (consequently?) no use for the idea of the passage of time. Another often-quoted example is of the Inuit people, who have many words for snow in their language. The suggestion based on the Sapir–Whorf hypothesis is that this actually enables these people to perceive many different kinds of snow compared with people from other parts of the world.

Some experimental evidence also seems to support a relationship this way round between language and thought. If you show line drawings to people and then later ask them to reproduce the drawings, the outcome depends on the label given with the original drawing (see *Figure 9.4*). This experiment was originally performed as long ago as 1932. Participants were given either one of two different sets of labels with line drawings, or no labels at all. When asked to reproduce the line drawings from memory, what people actually drew was clearly influenced by the label they had read; the original ambiguous drawing having been modified to resemble the description given. The language in other words had influenced what the person thought they had seen.

But does it follow from examples such as these, that the whole nature of thought is based on language? Could it be the other way round?

The great developmental psychologist Jean Piaget (1896–1980) based his theory on universal stages in thought processes through which all children pass as they mature, regardless of the language they are learning to speak or the culture in which they live. For Piaget, then, language was secondary to thought, depending on maturation of thought processes and reflecting the complexity of thought of which the person was capable, according to their developmental stage. This idea is more or less the opposite to the *linguistic relativity hypothesis* which considers thought to depend on grasp of language. It is supported by an increasing body of evidence that non-human animals (so far as we know without language) may be capable of thinking through the consequences of their and others' actions.

Perhaps the true answer to 'Which comes first, language or thought?' is that neither does. The Russian psychologist Lev

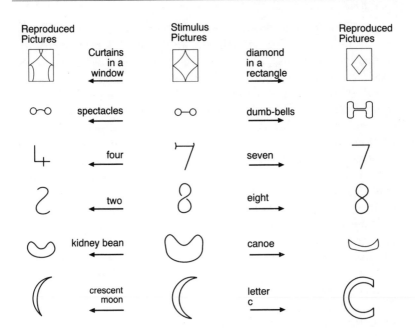

Figure 9.4: The label attached to a shape affects people's memory for the shape they have seen, as shown in the experiment illustrated here which was first performed by Carmichael, Hogan and Walter in 1932.

Vygotsky (1896–1934) was among the first (in the 1930s) to suggest that at least from the age of two, language, thought and social development are all inextricably linked. No one factor can be singled out as coming first and enabling the others.

An example of the consequences of problems arising somewhere in this three-way package is autism. The autistic child typically has problems with language and other aspects of communication, with relationships and interactions with others, and with flexibility of thought. It is not clear where the initial difficulties lie, but the spread of difficulties indicates that the three areas of language, thought and social interaction are tied up.

INDIVIDUAL DIFFERENCES IN THINKING

Do we all think in the same way? We are all capable of creative thinking in that we put together thoughts in unique and original ways. Some people though, seem to be more creative than others, thinking up ideas which are markedly different from anything already around. Although tests have been devised to assess creativity, it has been difficult to identify those who will produce the best ideas. Creativity has been linked by some with a tendency to mental illness, but here we are getting into the realms of abnormal psychology and personality and beyond the scope of this chapter. Our interest here is about the nature of the creative process. It was suggested by Graham Wallas, in 1926, that creative thinking occurs in four stages: *preparation, incubation, illumination* and *verification*. The idea of incubation in this context brings us back to the whereabouts of thought processes, as the idea indicates that the creative process is taking place outside conscious awareness. The evidence for this is the way that original ideas sometimes appear to pop up in our minds (the illumination stage) when we are carrying out some completely unrelated task.

We are not the only species experiencing this 'Eureka!' phenomenon and apparently able to solve problems using insight. Wolfgang Köhler reported an experiment in 1925 in which chimpanzees were able to reach pieces of fruit outside their cages. The chimps had two sticks available to them, which could be joined end to end, but neither stick was long enough to reach the fruit. Some chimps hit on the solution of joining the two sticks together. An interesting point here is that this insight was seen more often in chimps who had experience of handling the sticks; the general experience helped with the specific problem-solving. This reflects a finding reported from several studies in different species, that general enrichment of the environment and increase in experience alters behaviour, making individuals less timid, more adventurous and therefore better equipped to explore and learn. To come back to ourselves: do you think in colour? in pictures? in emotional feelings? in words? in musical sounds? For example, one of the authors thinks days of the week are different colours, and another is sometimes surprised when expressing thoughts because, although they seem well-formed, they do not come across well in words. Some of these modes of thought would be impossible without the appropriate experience. Perhaps our experience is important in determining how creatively we think?

References

Bandura, D.A., Ross, D. and Ross, S.A. (1961). Transmission of aggression through imitation of aggressive models. *Journal of Abnormal and Social Psychology, 63*, 575–582. ['Bobo' doll experiments.]

Breland, K. and Breland, M. (1961). The misbehaviour of organisms. *American Psychologist, 16*, 681–684. [What animals won't learn and why.]

Carmichael, L., Hogan, H.P. and Walter, A.A. (1932). An experimental study of the effect of language on the reproduction of visually perceived form. *Journal of Experimental Psychology, 15*, 73–86. [Experiment into the effect of language on thought.]

Carroll, J.B. (1956). *Language, Thought and Reality: Selected writings of Benjamin Lee Whorf*. New York: MIT Press and Wiley. [Linguistic relativity hypothesis.]

Freud, S. (1962). *Two Short Accounts of Psychoanalysis*. Translated and edited by James Strachey. Harmondsworth: Penguin. [Translations of some of Freud's own lectures.]

Garcia, J. and Koelling, R.A. (1966). Relation of cue to consequence in avoidance learning. *Psychonomic Science, 4*, 123–124. [Experiment with rats and saccharine solution, the results of which dismissed several rules of classical conditioning.]

Koehler, W. (1925). *The Mentality of Apes*. New York: Harcourt Brace Jovanovich. [Observations of chimpanzees showing them apparently to be capable of insight.]

Lynch, J.J., Hinch, G.N. and Adams, D.B. (1992). *The Behaviour of Sheep*. Wallingford, Oxford: C.A.B. International. [Reference to sheep behaviour.]

Macfarlane, D.A. (1930). The role of kinesthesis in maze learning. *University of California Publications in Psychology, 4*, 277–305. [Rats can run a maze previously learnt by swimming.]

Mcquoid, L.M. and Galef, B.G. (1993). Social stimuli influencing feeding behaviour of Burmese fowl: a video analysis. *Animal Behaviour, 46*, 13–22. [Hens learn from watching videos.]

Pavlov, I.P. (1927). *Conditioned Reflexes*. Oxford: Oxford University Press. [Original English language version of classical conditioning experiments.]

Piaget, J. (1967). Language and thought from the genetic point of view. In Piaget, J., *Six Psychological Studies*. New York: Random House. [The place of language in cognitive development according to Piaget.]

Skinner, B.F. (1974). *About Behaviourism*. London: Jonathan Cape. [A review by the famous American behaviourist.]

Thorndike, E.L. (1911). *Animal Intelligence*. New York: Macmillan. [Cats and puzzle boxes.]

Tolman, E.C., Ritchie, B.F. and Kalish, D. (1946). Studies in spatial learning: II. Place learning versus response learning. *Journal of Experimental Psychology, 36*, 221–229. [Cognitive maps.]

Vygotsky, L.S. (1962). *Thought and Language*. (Original Russian edition published 1934). Cambridge, MA: MIT Press. [The relationship between thought and language.]

Wallas, G. (1926). *The Art of Thought*. New York: Harcourt Brace Jovanovich. [Creative thinking and its four stages.]

Watson, J.B. and Rayner, R. (1920). Conditioned emotional reactions. *Journal of Experimental Psychology, 3*, 1–14. [Classical conditioning of little baby Albert.]

Recommended Reading

Association for the Study of Animal Behaviour (1995). *Stimulus Response Video.* Available from: ASAB Education Officer, Department of Biological Sciences, John Dalton Building, Manchester Metropolitan University, Chester Street, Manchester M1 5GD.

Hill, W.F. (1989). *Learning: A survey of psychological interpretations.* Harlow: Addison Wesley Longman Ltd.

Pearce, J.M. (1987). *An Introduction to Animal Cognition.* Hove: Lawrence Erlbaum Associates.

Weisberg, R.W. (1993). *Creativity: Beyond the myth of genius.* New York: W.H. Freeman and Company.

CLASSICAL CONDITIONING

WHAT YOU WILL NEED
You will need a small torch (it is important that it is not too bright), a bell or buzzer (a kitchen timer with seconds would do), and a willing friend.

WHAT YOU NEED TO DO
Position yourself so that you can hold the torch near to your friend's eye. Sound the buzzer and make sure that it doesn't make your friend blink. Also try flashing the torch in your friend's eye – hopefully your friend will blink.

Try sounding the buzzer and immediately afterwards flash the torch in your friend's eye. Repeat this pairing of buzzer and flash several times. Now sound the buzzer on its own. Did your friend blink in this last stage?

YOUR FINDINGS
If your friend blinked in the last stage you have turned an initially neutral stimulus (the buzzer) into a conditional stimulus for the eye blink response. This response is now a conditional response, having been originally an unconditional response to the unconditional stimulus (flash of light). In terms of expectancy, your friend has learned to expect that E1 (the buzzer) will be followed by E2 (the light).

THOUGHT AND LANGUAGE

WHAT YOU NEED TO DO
The words below are common English language words. Look through them and mark them according to whether you think they are linked to universal categories or whether they have meanings specific to the culture of a particular society.

male and female	child and adult	teenager
student	weekend	morning
afternoon	tea-time	mother
housewife	chair	magazine
book	treat	reward

WHAT YOU WILL SEE
This exercise makes us consider the relationship between language and thought. Just to look at one example: 'tea-time' has a clear meaning for most British families. To many people in the United States of America though, there is no such thing as 'tea-time'. Do Americans have difficulty conceiving of tea-time because they have no word for it, or do they have no word for it because it is a concept they do not have?

Why not try out this task on a few other people? Try to include some who are from cultures other than your own.

10. *Measurement and You*

In the UK, and probably in other countries as well, there is an increasing emphasis on *accountability* in different areas of working life. For better or for worse, teachers, doctors, managers and many other professionals are all expected to be more accountable for the work they do, which means establishing clear-cut objectives or 'performance indicators'. One clear example of this is in the field of education: the performance of British schools is now assessed to a considerable extent in terms of the examination performance of pupils, and so-called 'league tables', comparing the performance of different schools, are published and widely scrutinized.

Performance criteria such as these must be *transparent*: the ways in which individuals and organizations are assessed must be public and explicit. The whole question of *assessment* is clearly very important in this climate, and psychologists have an important contribution to make. *Psychometrics* is the name given to psychologists' attempts to measure, or quantify, different aspects of our behaviour. The emphasis upon measurement has always been strong in psychology, and the focus has largely been on the development of standardized psychological tests.

EARLY DEVELOPMENTS

The first intelligence test was devised by the British biologist Sir Francis Galton (1822–1911) over a century ago. Galton set up an 'anthropometric laboratory' at the International Exposition of 1884, in which visitors could receive a thorough analysis of their physical and psychological functions – vision and hearing, reaction times, and muscular strength – for the sum of threepence. The laboratory remained in operation for a while at London's South Kensington Museum, enabling Galton to build up a body of data on over 9000 people. Galton's view that intelligence was based on the ability to make sensory discriminations turned out to be misguided, though he undoubtedly pioneered the study of *individual differences* between people.

The development of psychological testing since those early days has been shaped by practical requirements rather than by theoretical developments. In 1904, the French government set up a commission to look at the particular problems faced by subnormal children attending schools in Paris, and Alfred Binet (1857–1911) was called in to devise a variety of sensory and perceptual tests which could be used to pinpoint deficiencies and serve as the basis for remedial programmes of education. Alfred Binet and Theodore Simon developed different test items, and Lewis Terman of Stanford University translated and adapted the test for use in the USA in 1916. The result was what was named the *Stanford–Binet Scale*, which became the model for most subsequent IQ tests.

When the USA entered the First World War, it was necessary to assign the vast numbers of new recruits to different types of service, and to make other administrative decisions about them, by screening them rapidly for intellectual level. This led to the development of the *Army Alpha* and *Army Beta* intelligence tests, which served as an early model for other group tests of intelligence. As with the *Stanford–Binet Scale*, these tests were devised in response to a pressing practical need.

PSYCHOLOGICAL TESTING TODAY

The number and variety of contemporary psychological tests available today are vast, and psychological as well as educational testing is routinely carried out on a large scale. Nearly all of us have taken a psychological test at some point in our lives, and this is probably the main way in which members of the general public are likely to come into direct contact with professional psychology.

The popularity of tests and testing has changed over time, varying according to prevailing climates of opinion. In the liberal, progressive 1960s, for example, the whole ideology behind testing was seen as elitist, competitive, and socially divisive, and the British '11-plus' examination provides some justification for this view. On the basis of written tests lasting no longer than a few hours, children were classified as having either passed or failed, and this determined the course of their secondary education (as well, in many cases, as their future careers). The obvious undesirability of labelling children as 'failures' at this early age led to the abolition of the 11-plus in many education authorities, although it survives even today in a few.

With the new emphasis on accountability and assessment, tests are very much in favour once again. In the USA, the concept of *competency-based* education is based on the explicit and continuous monitoring of the child's progress by means of routine, regular testing; in fact, the testing itself forms part of the instruction in some cases. In Great Britain, the introduction of the National Curriculum in 1988 made it mandatory for all children to study the same ten subjects at each of four 'key stages'. The original plan was that they should be tested in each subject at the end of each key stage – at the ages of 7, 11, 14 and 16 years. This programme of testing proved to be overwhelmingly time-consuming, and was later 'slimmed down'. However, the basic principle that children's progress should be regularly and routinely checked by standardized tests remains a fundamental principle of the British education system.

Of course, tests are neither good nor bad in themselves. A psychological test is simply a refined form of observation. By asking people standardized questions under similar conditions, psychologists try to obtain samples of behaviour which can be compared from one person to the next. As far as possible, they also try to obtain objective assessments of people's behaviour rather than relying on subjective interpretations (though this is not always a straightforward affair, as we shall see later). The usefulness or otherwise of tests depends on the reasons why they are administered, the setting in which they are given, and the uses to which the results are put. Let's examine some of these.

USES OF TESTS

Clinical

Clinical psychologists apply their knowledge of psychology to problems connected with health and illness. They rely upon tests to help them to pinpoint the nature of a particular person's problems. They might want to assess the precise intellectual deficits shown by people with head injuries from a car crash, for example; to analyse the moods and emotions of people with depression; or to assess the personalities of people with hallucinations and delusions. In each case, psychological tests may enable them to make a more accurate diagnosis of the current problem, and also possibly to predict what the likely outcome of treatment might be.

Educational

Educational psychologists are concerned with the diagnosis and treatment of behavioural problems shown by children at school. These might include learning difficulties, emotional problems, social anxieties, and so on. Here again, tests are used to provide basic background information about pupils' particular strengths and weaknesses, and this information is used in working out remedial strategies.

Occupational

The occupational or industrial psychologist uses tests in making decisions about people at work. One of the main applications is in vocational guidance counselling. Test results can help in deciding which careers might be suitable for the undecided school leaver, for example. They also help in making personnel selection and guidance decisions within the work environment – in fitting people into jobs, and in tailoring jobs to suit people. Occupational psychology is an area which has grown very rapidly over the last decade or so, and many privately-funded organizations now offer vocational testing services to commercial firms and organizations. Psychological tests are now used by managers, careers counsellors, consultants, training advisors and others, many of whom have received training in testing, but are not themselves registered occupational psychologists.

In 1990, Steven Blinkhorn and Charles Johnson published an article in the eminent science journal *Nature*, in which they questioned the usefulness of a good deal of personality testing in occupational selection. They suggested that the evidence of the predictive value of the tests for personnel decision-making was shaky at best, and questioned the methodology by which validation evidence was typically collected. This led to a great deal of controversy over the next few years, including a heated exchange of views in the pages of *The Psychologist*, in which Douglas Jackson and Mitchell Rothstein mounted a defence of the use of personality tests in occupational selection. In order to meet this kind of concern, in the UK at least, The British Psychological Society has formulated an explicit set of standards for the use of tests in occupational settings, and now issues certificates of competence to those who are able to demonstrate competence in their use.

POTENTIAL ABUSES OF TESTS

These varied examples show how important it is to safeguard against the possible abuse of test data, since they can be used to make decisions which are of vital importance to the lives of the individuals taking such tests. In all three areas of application, tests are essentially *tools* that are used by the psychologist, and the correct interpretation of the results requires skill and training. For this reason, the availability of tests is (by and large) restricted to appropriately-trained users, and the qualifying procedures are administered by professional bodies such as The British Psychological Society (BPS).

These bodies also publish technical and ethical guidelines for the construction and use of tests. In the UK, anyone who wants to purchase a test is asked for details of his or her psychological qualifications and test training, and is then graded accordingly. Less experienced users have access only to those tests requiring little technical expertise, such as those which might easily be administered with the help of the manual alone. They are not qualified to obtain those tests, for example, whose use requires the interpretative skills of the experienced psychometrician.

The dangers of misinterpretation

The reason for this kind of restriction is that test scores are very easy to misinterpret without adequate training and psychological knowledge. The information that a child scored 85 on a particular IQ test, for example, would be treated with great caution by an educational psychologist who was making a general assessment of the child. This score is only a very rough indicator of general ability. It is subject to many sources of error, and leaves out a great deal of information about the underlying *profile* of the child's particular strengths and weaknesses. The psychologist would also recognize that whilst a high IQ score undoubtedly indicates some form of ability, depending on how 'intelligence' is defined, a low score does not imply that the child lacks that ability. An off-day, a lack of willingness to comply with test instructions or a particular tester, tiredness, boredom, and many others factors can all give rise to a low score which is unrepresentative of actual ability.

In the mind of the unqualified layperson, however, these scores can easily take on a spurious air of scientific objectivity. A worried parent might easily regard an IQ score as a kind of precise, objective characteristic like height or weight. Because of the anxiety that this kind of misunderstanding might cause, not to mention the harmful misuses that might be made of confidential test scores were they to fall into the wrong hands, it is up to psychologists to make sure that their data remain confidential. This is all the more important at a time when there is public concern about who does and who does not have access to the large amounts of personal information that are held on centralized computer files.

VARIETIES OF PSYCHOLOGICAL TEST

Perhaps the most comprehensive guide to the vast range of psychological tests currently available is the *Mental Measurements Yearbook*, founded by Oscar Buros. This contains details and independent reviews of well over 1000 tests. A comprehensive British guide, *Tests in Education*, was published by Philip Levy and Harvey Goldstein in 1984. The British Psychological Society has also published reviews of tests edited by David Bartram and others. We will first try to convey a broad picture of this field by outlining the main types of test that psychologists use. In the rest of the chapter, we will look at two of the best-known varieties of ability test in more detail; that is, at tests of intelligence and creativity.

Typical versus maximum performance

One broad distinction is that made between tests of *maximum performance* and tests of *typical performance*. The first type are designed to measure people's ability to work at their limit – when they are trying as hard as possible to succeed on a task. Two of the most common tests of maximum performance types are those of *ability* and of *attainment*: an intelligence test and a school examination would be good examples of each of these. Tests of typical performance, on the other hand, are used to gain an impression of what people are usually like, rather than how they perform 'at their peak', and the two main varieties of these are tests of *personality* and of *interests and attitudes*. There are also four other ways of classifying the basic types of psychological test.

Individual versus group

First, there is the distinction between *group* tests and *individual* tests, which is fairly self-explanatory. In the interests of time-saving and efficiency, large-scale tests of ability and achievement are likely to be administered to people in groups, whereas more time-consuming diagnostic and clinical tests tend to be administered on an individual basis.

General versus specific

Second, tests can be described as being either *general* or *specific*. The former are designed to make overall assessments of people, such as tests of intelligence or personality. The latter make more detailed assessments within a narrower domain: a test of musical ability, or an inventory to measure social anxiety, would fall into this second category.

Self- versus other-reports

Some tests are based on *self-reports*, so that subjects make judgements or evaluative statements about themselves – attitude surveys or scales would be a typical example. These contrast with tests which use *other-reports*, such as ratings of the test subject by peers, supervisors, teachers, or other expert referees.

Pencil-and-paper, performance, and automated tests

The distinction between *pencil-and-paper* and *performance* tests has been made for many years. The former involve the person taking the test in writing, or in other types of form-filling (with pens as well as pencils!), and consequently require a certain level of basic literacy. Performance tests, on the other hand, are specifically designed to eliminate this requirement. It would be impossible to test very young children, or people with certain special needs, on pencil-and-paper measures, for example, and tests would be used which might involve the manipulation of toys, coloured blocks, or pictures. Responses can be spoken, physically acted or indicated rather than being written down. Finally, recent technological developments mean that tests are increasingly being administered and scored automatically, using computers. In some cases the person being tested presses a computer key or operates a mouse, and more sophisticated systems are developing the use of touch-sensitive screens.

TESTS OF ABILITY AND ATTAINMENT

Ability (or aptitude) tests are designed to measure people's capabilities as independently as possible from their experience of the tasks in question. These can be general abilities, such as general intelligence, or more specific ones such as spatial, verbal, mathematical or musical skills. A person's overall score on a general intelligence test (some of the best-known of which are mentioned later) is supposed to reflect the 'pure' intelligence of that person, regardless of learning, experience, or good or bad teaching. In practice, this is well-nigh impossible. Any test score is bound to be influenced at least to some degree by the person's previous experiences of similar tasks, and the tests simply strive to keep these influences to a minimum.

Tests of attainment (or achievement), on the other hand, are specifically designed to measure learning, and school examinations provide a good example. When you take an examination in history, algebra or French, your examiners want to find out how much of your course of instruction has sunk in, and how well you have understood the material. Of course, this is also affected by your general ability in the subject. Scores on an exam paper are not pure measures of learning any more than scores on an ability test are pure measures of ability. However, attainment tests are geared to the assessment of particular courses of instruction, and they are designed to cover the syllabuses and objectives of these courses as accurately and comprehensively as possible.

TESTS OF PERSONALITY, INTERESTS AND ATTITUDES

Self-reports

As we said earlier, *personality tests* are designed to assess what the person is typically like. Probably the best-known ones are *self-report* inventories, such as the *Minnesota Multiphasic Personality Inventory* (MMPI), the *Eysenck Personality Questionnaire* (EPQ), or *Cattell's 16PF* test, in which people are typically asked to answer questions such as, 'Are you mostly quiet when you are with other people?' or, 'Do you always practise what you preach?' On the basis of their answers, people obtain scores on a number of *personality dimensions*, and these scores can then be used to form profiles of individuals, and thus to make direct comparisons between them.

The questionnaire items are stringently selected so as to give very pure measures of the personality dimensions in question. This is often done by using the technique of *factor analysis*, which statistically identifies the main dimensions in the pattern of responses. Different tests are based on theories which propose that personality is based on different numbers of dimensions: Cattell's test is based on 16 dimensions (or *factors*, hence the name 16PF), for example, whereas the Eysenck test is based on just three. There seems to be some convergence of current opinion that five factors can explain most of the variation in most personality tests: these so-called 'Big Five' factors are *extraversion, agreeableness, conscientiousness, neuroticism,* and *openness to experience.* Although tests have been devised which are based on the 'Big Five' (for example, Paul Costa and Robert McCrae's *NEO Personality Inventory*), there is still some debate on the topic.

Projective tests

Another well-known method of personality assessment is by the use of *projective tests*. Most people have heard of the *Rorschach Inkblots Test*, in which individuals are questioned systematically about their perceptions and interpretations of a series of visually ambiguous, symmetrical grey/black and coloured inkblots. These responses are used by the tester as a basis for personality assessment.

A number of other instruments are used in projective testing. These include the *Thematic Apperception Test* (TAT), in which the person creates a story about what is going on in a series of pictures showing human figures in ambiguous situations; open-ended word association; sentence completion tasks; and projective doll play, in which children are asked to make up stories about a set of dolls placed before them which might, for example, represent their immediate family members. All of these techniques rely on the skills of the tester in making what are essentially subjective judgements about the responses of the person being tested. This subjectivity is an obvious disadvantage in comparison with the more objective techniques of the self-report inventories, but the corresponding advantage is that the person's responses are less constrained by the format of the test itself, and may therefore be more likely to convey real feelings and attitudes.

Tests of interests and attitudes

Tests of interests and attitudes are designed to map out a comprehensive picture of the person's expressed preferences for different activities, such as work activities, hobbies, and other leisure pursuits, and they tend also to use self-reports. The *Strong Vocational Interest Blank* (SVIB), for example, is used in careers counselling. Statements about the test-taker's interests and hobbies are compared with the typical profiles obtained by a wide variety of different occupational groups, and these comparisons can then be used to guide the person towards an appropriate career choice. The well-known *Allport–Vernon–Lindzey Scale of Values* takes a rather more general approach. People are asked to answer 45 questions such as, 'If you had some time to spend in a waiting room and there were only two magazines to choose from, would you prefer (a) *Scientific Age* or (b) *Arts and Decorations?*' Their responses to these questions give rise to a profile of values on six scales, which are designated as *theoretical, economic, aesthetic, social, political* and *religious.*

MEASURING INTELLIGENCE

What is intelligence?

Although most people are familiar with the idea of intelligence (IQ) tests, and today a vast number of them are routinely carried out, there is still no generally agreed definition of intelligence. In a famous symposium reported in the *Journal of Educational Psychology* in 1921, 14 eminent experts were asked to explain their understanding of the meaning of intelligence. Fourteen quite different views emerged. These included:

'the ability to give responses that are true or factual'
'the ability to adjust oneself to the environment'
'the ability to learn or profit by experience'

. . . and so on. Generally speaking, we could say that intelligence involves the ability to think, and that this is typically displayed in *verbal* intelligence, *problem-solving*, and *practical* intelligence, but views still differ about its precise nature.

One of the main stumbling blocks is that intelligence is often conceived in the abstract, as a kind of general property that can be defined independently of the activity in which it is displayed. Many psychologists would now argue that intelligence can only be defined in relation to particular activities. You may be very intelligent in the way you plan your finances, or in reading a railway timetable, yet you may, at the same time, be very unintelligent in the way in which you go about building a garden shed, or mending your car. The problem is that certain types of activity, in Western society, are seen as requiring more general intelligence than others. Intelligence tends to be defined in terms of one's ability to perform the skills valued by the educational system – the ability to read, write, compute, speak foreign languages, and so on.

This is readily apparent when we examine the contents of a typical IQ test. *Exercise 10.1* (p.249) shows 12 items from Part 1 of the 1968 revision of the AH4, a well-known IQ test designed by Alice Heim for use with the general adult population. It is easy to see that the abilities required to do well on these 12 questions are those which are cultivated in the school system: logical reasoning, knowing the precise meanings of words, being good with numbers, and so on. The test obviously does not measure intelligence of the type that is needed in getting on well with other people or in doing practical jobs, for instance; and this leads to a circular argument. Intelligence is defined in terms of abilities that are needed for scholastic success, but the validity of intelligence tests is often assessed in terms of their ability to predict that success. You might say (only half-jokingly) that the safest definition is that 'intelligence is what intelligence tests measure'.

Some recent developments

Some of the more recent attempts to understand intelligence are now in fact beginning to move away from this circular, *operational* definition, in two ways. First, they try to identify the general processes involved in intelligence; and second, they try to investigate all its manifestations in practical settings. Robert Sternberg has proposed a *triarchic theory* which defines intelligence in terms of three components: (a) the internal world of the individual, which includes the ways in which people acquire knowledge and process information; (b) the external world of the individual, which involves the ways in which people adapt to their existing environments, or move into new ones; and (c) the individual's experience in the world. This latter component also involves the idea of *practical intelligence*, which can be observed in people's everyday activities rather than in academic settings.

Howard Gardner's *multiple intelligence* theory has certain features in common with Sternberg's view. He agrees with the idea that academic abilities constitute only one part of what ought to be a much broader conception of intelligence, and also that intelligence must be defined in terms of a wider range of practical activities carried out in real-life cultural settings. Gardner proposes that there are seven 'intelligences' – *musical, bodily-kinaesthetic, logical-mathematical, linguistic, spatial, interpersonal,* and *intrapersonal,* and suggests that these are all essentially independent of one another.

The last two of Gardner's 'intelligences' may be at the heart of the recent idea of 'emotional intelligence', which has been popularized in a best-selling book by the science writer Daniel

Goleman. Goleman's idea is that qualities such as persistence, self-motivation, and the ability to work with others can be just as, if not more, important than IQ in determining success in life, and that these reflect the individual's ability to maintain an optimal balance between reason and emotion. This is clearly in tune with the thinking of Sternberg and Gardner, and seems to be a natural reaction against the traditional dominance of the IQ. Whether the concept of emotional intelligence will lead to new insights remains to be seen, but in the meantime IQ tests will continue to be administered in increasing numbers, and so we will return to these.

Intelligence tests

We mentioned the *Stanford–Binet Scale* earlier in the chapter, and this is still one of the most widely-used individual IQ tests for children. A child's IQ is calculated by comparing his or her score on the test with an *age norm*; that is, with the average score that other children of the same age obtain. Binet introduced the idea of the child's 'mental age', which is where his or her score falls in relation to the test's age norms. If the child's mental age is higher than his or her chronological age, the IQ score will be higher than average, and lower than average if these are the other way round. The average, where a child's mental age is the same as the chronological age, is usually set at IQ = 100, and there are different ways of computing IQ.

Amongst the other better-known individual tests are the *Wechsler Intelligence Scale for Children* (WISC), which is accompanied by the *Wechsler Preschool and Primary Scale of Intelligence* (WPPSI) and the *Wechsler Adult Intelligence Scale* (WAIS). The better-known group tests of intelligence in the UK include *Raven's Progressive Matrices* and the *Mill Hill Vocabulary Scale*. Many British adults are also likely to have encountered the *Moray House* and *NFER* tests at some point in their school careers. In North America, the *Lorge–Thorndike* tests, the *School and College Ability Tests* (SCAT), and the *Scholastic Aptitude Test* (SAT) are amongst the better-known measures.

Another significant development in Great Britain has been the publication of the *British Ability Scales* (BAS), the first edition of which appeared in 1979. These scales are the product of a project based at the University of Manchester which used educational psychologists all over the country to pilot the tests on a massive and comprehensive sample of schoolchildren. There are 12 separate scales on the test, including some innovative features such as divergent or 'creativity' tests (see next section), and Piagetian developmental tasks. The general IQ scores derived from these 12 scales are good predictors of scholastic and academic attainment.

RELIABILITY AND VALIDITY

Scores on all of these tests are subject to many sources of error. If the person taking the test is having an off-day, happens to be very familiar with some of the test items, or if there is a noisy road outside the test room, then the test score will not give an accurate reading of his or her true ability. Because of this, testers try to assess the *reliability* of different tests. Reliability is the extent to which the test measures what it is supposed to in a consistent manner, and there are different ways of measuring it.

One way is to give the test to the same group of people on two separate occasions, to see how closely the two sets of scores agree. This is known as *test–retest* reliability. Another measure of reliability is the *internal consistency* of the test. We can compare how well a group's scores on half of the test items agree with those on the other half, for example. A good test should be reliable over time, and also be internally consistent.

The other vital property of a test is its *validity* – the extent to which it measures what it is supposed to measure. Validity is usually assessed by comparing peoples' scores on the test with their scores on some external *criterion* measure. Tests of musical ability, for example, which might involve making pitch judgements, analysing chords, memorizing melodies, and so on, are sometimes used in guiding children towards an appropriate musical career. Such tests might be validated by comparing test scores with assessments of real-life musical abilities, such as the ability to play an instrument, to sing or to improvise. The tests would be regarded as valid if they gave an accurate prediction of real-life musical ability.

MEASURING CREATIVITY

Before reading further, try to answer the questions in *Exercise 10.2*, on p.250.

Convergent and divergent thinking

Some common answers to the first 'Uses for Objects' item are that a brick might be used as a doorstop, as a hammer, as a weapon, or 'to stand on if short'. These questions require you to use your imagination, and to generate plenty of ideas. This ability has been called 'divergent' thinking – your thinking branches out, or diverges, from a given starting point. This is rather like the idea of 'lateral thinking', popularized by Edward de Bono. In contrast, the thinking skills that were required in *Exercise 10.1* involve *convergent* abilities: you are required to converge on the one correct solution to a problem. Convergent and divergent thinking have sometimes been equated with 'intelligence' and 'creativity' respectively. Is this equation realistic?

Intelligence and creativity

The study of creativity arose in the 1960s from a general dissatisfaction with the narrow concept of 'giftedness' that was implicit in the educational selection procedures in existence at the time. Joy Guilford's presidential address to the American Psychological Association on the subject of creativity in 1950 started off the idea that there might be a whole realm of creative abilities which were not being tapped by traditional examination procedures. If these abilities were independent of convergent intelligence, and if they were important in children's development and education, their omission was presumably a serious one. Many of the child-centred, informal, teaching methods that were being developed around this time put creative abilities in a much more central position.

Jacob Getzels and Philip Jackson carried out a pioneering and controversial study in 1962 which looked at the relationship between intelligence and creativity in a sample of 533 Chicago schoolchildren. They found that a 'high creative' subgroup who had high scores on what were described as 'creativity tests', but low scores on IQ tests performed just as well on measures of educational success as a 'high intelligence' group whose scores were biased in the opposite direction. This seemed to indicate that creative abilities were just as important as intelligence in school attainment.

Unfortunately, this study was riddled with problems of methodology and experimental design, and so the results were inconclusive. However, the educational importance of Getzels and

Jackson's conclusion served to stimulate an immense amount of further research, which has generally confirmed the importance of creative thinking abilities. Creativity has now become an established and respectable part of psychometrics, and divergent thinking tests are a recognized part of general ability tests (as in the *British Ability Scales*, for example).

Science and the arts

However, we must be very careful not to equate convergent and divergent thinking with intelligence and creativity respectively. It is nowadays more accurate to say that convergent and divergent thinking are generally regarded as distinct abilities in their own right; that both have a part to play in real-life intelligence and creativity; and that both can be used to predict educational success. It is even more important to keep these distinctions clear when we consider the suggestion that convergent and divergent thinking abilities tend to be at a premium in science and arts subjects respectively, since an erroneous confusion of these different concepts could imply that artists tend to be unintelligent and scientists uncreative.

This confusion sometimes arises from the failure to distinguish between creative *potential*, which divergent tests are supposed to measure, and *real-life* creativity, which is of course displayed in the works of scientists as well as of artists. We might hazard a guess that both convergent and divergent thinking skills are involved in creative work in both domains. When we prepare for a piece of creative work by gathering together materials, doing background reading, and mulling over the problems, it is very likely that divergent abilities will be brought into play. Once the ideas are crystallized and the course of the work is set, whether it be an essay, a picture, a musical composition or a piece of scientific research, convergent skills are called into operation in formalizing, or realizing it and in working out the final details. In other words, divergent tests do not measure creativity, but they might well give psychologists clues about some of the processes that are involved in it, and this is probably typical of the whole enterprise of psychological testing. Human beings are such complex, ever-changing creatures that it is impossible to measure them in the same way that the properties of physical objects can be measured, and we must also remember that it is the human beings themselves who are doing the measuring. So long as we keep a clear idea of what they *cannot* do, there is no doubt that psychological tests have many valuable practical uses.

References

Blinkhorn, S. and Johnson, C.E. (1990). The insignificance of personality testing. *Nature, 348*, 671–672. [Wide-ranging critique.]

British Psychological Society Professional Affairs Board (1980). Technical recommendations for psychological tests. *Bulletin of the British Psychological Society, 33*, 161–164. [Official statement by the BPS.]

Bartram, D., Lindley, P., Marshall, L. and Foster, J. (1992). *Review of Psychometric Tests for Assessment in Vocational Training* (including update). Leicester: BPS Books (The British Psychological Society). [Independent reviews of tests.]

Bartram, D., Anderson, N., Kellett, D., Lindley, P. and Robertson, I. (1995). *Review of Personality Assessment Instruments (Level B) for Use in Occupational Settings*. Leicester: BPS Books (The British Psychological Society). [Independent reviews of tests.]

Bartram, D., Burke, E., Kandola, B., Lindley, P., Marshall, L. and Rasch, P. (In press) *Review of Ability and Aptitude Tests (Level A)*. Leicester: BPS Books (The British Psychological Society). [Independent reviews of tests.]

Buros, O.K. (1978) (Ed.). *The VIII Mental Measurement Yearbook*. Highland Park: Gryphon Press. [The standard reference guide to psychological tests, which includes independent reviews of each one. Since Buros' death, this volume has continued to be issued. The latest edition is Kramer, J.J. and Conoley, J.C. (Eds.) (1992). *The 11th Mental Measurements Yearbook*. Lincoln, Neb.: Institute of Mental Measurement. The latest supplement is Conoley,J.C. and Impara, U.D. (Eds) (1994). *Supplement to the 11th Mental Measurements Yearbook*. Lincoln, Neb: Institute of Mental Measurement. You may be able to consult these in university libraries.]

Gardner, H. (1983). *Frames of Mind*. London: Paladin. [Gardner's theory of multiple intelligences.]

Getzels, J.W. and Jackson, P.W. (1962). *Creativity and Intelligence*. New York: John Wiley. [A pioneering, though heavily criticized research study.]

Goleman, D. (1995). *Emotional Intelligence: Why it can matter more than IQ*. London: Bloomsbury.

Guilford, J.P. (1950). Creativity. *American Psychologist, 5*, 444–454. [Guilford's presidential address to the American Psychological Association.]

Jackson, D.N. and Rothstein, M. (1993). Evaluating personality testing in personnel selection. *The Psychologist, 6*, 8–11. [A reply to the critics.]

Levy, P.and Goldstein, H. (1984). *Tests in Education: A book of critical reviews*. London: Academic Press. [A comprehensive guide to some psychological as well as educational tests.]

Sternberg, R.J. (1985). *Beyond IQ: A triarchic theory of human intelligence*. New York: W.H. Freeman. [Sternberg's triarchic theory.]

Thorndike, E.L. *et al*. (1921). Intelligence and its measurement. *Journal of Educational Psychology, 12*, 123ff. [A report of the famous 1921 symposium on defining intelligence.]

Recommended Reading

Anastasi, A. (1988). *Psychological Testing, 6th edn.* New York: Macmillan.

Jackson, C. (1996). *Understanding Psychological Testing.* Leicester: BPS Books (The British Psychological Society).

Kline, P. (1992). *The Handbook of Psychological Testing.* London: Routledge.

Kline, P. (1993). *Personality: The psychometric view.* London: Routledge.

Rust, J. and Golombok, S. (1989). *Modern Psychometrics: The science of psychological assessment.* London: Routledge.

PART OF THE AH4 IQ TEST

AH4

AHF
QUESTION BOOK
(1968 REVISION)

INSTRUCTIONS

Below are some examples of the test. Do them now.
Write your answers on the answer sheet. Write the *number*, not the word.
Some of the examples are already done for you.

DO NOT WRITE ANYTHING ON THIS PAPER
PART 1. EXAMPLES

Q1	1, 2, 3, 4, 5, 6, 7, 8, 9. Write down the largest of these figures.	**Q1**
Q2	1, 2, 3, 4, 5, 6, 7, 8, 9. Write down the middle one of these figures.	**Q2**
Q3	*Late* means the opposite of . . . 　　　1　　　2　　　3　　　4　　　5 appointment, early, behind, postponed, immediate.	**Q3**
Q4	1　2　3　4　5 *Big* means the opposite of . . . tall, large, place, small, high.	**Q4**
Q5	1, 4, 7, 10, 13 . . . What number comes next?	**Q5**
Q6	2, 4, 8, 16, 32 . . . What number comes next?	**Q6**
Q7	*Fish* is to *swim* as *bird* is to . . . 　1　　2　　3　　　4　　　　5 man, fly, walk, aeroplane, sparrow.	**Q7**
Q8	1　　2　　3　　4　　5 *Low* is to *high* as *bad* is to . . . evil, red, try, good, right.	**Q8**
Q9	Here are three figures: 325. Add the largest two figures together and divide the total by the smallest figure.	**Q9**
Q10	Here are three figures: 594. Subtract the smallest figure from the biggest and multiply the result by the figure printed immediately before the biggest figure.	**Q10**
Q11	*Young* means the same as . . . 　1　　　2　　　3　　　4　　5 youthful, ancient, vigorous, hot, baby.	**Q11**
Q12	*Gift* means the same as . . . parcel, toy, birthday, buy, present.	**Q12**

If there is anything you do not understand, please ask the tester *now*.

DO NOT TURN OVER UNTIL YOU ARE TOLD TO DO SO.

(From Part 1 of the AH4 test, N.F.E.R. Publishing Co., 1968. Reprinted by permission.)

A TEST OF CREATIVITY

USES FOR OBJECTS
1. How many uses can you think of for a brick?
2. How many uses can you think of for a paper clip?
3. How many uses can you think of for a blanket?
4. How many uses can you think of for a jam jar?

PATTERN MEANINGS
Think of all the things that each of these patterns might be:

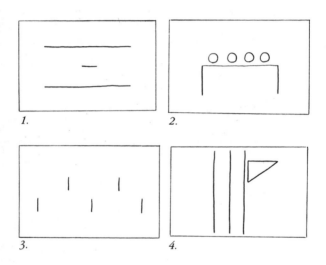

1.

2.

3.

4.

SIMILARITIES
Think of all the ways in which the following pairs of objects are alike:
1. An apple and a pear.
2. A radio and a telephone.
3. A violin and a piano.
4. A cat and a mouse.

11. *You and Other Animals*

Why should a book essentially about people include a section on our links with other animals? There are several different rationales that we could use to answer such a question. Firstly, we are animals. Thus, by studying ourselves in relation to other animals, we may gain insights into our place in the scheme of things within the animal kingdom. Of course the idea that we are animals is relatively new. In the past we set ourselves apart from the animal kingdom, but Charles Darwin's ideas changed this view profoundly. In *The Descent of Man*, he put forward the notion that we evolved from other animals and were not a distinct and separate creation. This view is now as much a part of our everyday thinking as that the world is round rather than flat. But the nature of the 'difference' between us and other animals is still very much discussed.

Comparative psychology is a branch of psychology in which animal species are investigated with the emphasis on finding similarities between them. In this, humans are seen as just one important species among many. However, research on animal behaviour is not as fashionable as it once was, due in part to the very strong reaction against research on animals which burgeoned in

251

the 1970s and 80s. Many people began to feel that much animal research was unethical and this led to a reduction in this type of work within psychology in Britain and elsewhere. Rightly or wrongly, the end result has been a move away from the belief that much can be gained from research on animal behaviour as a means of increasing our understanding of human behaviour. Psychologists' extensive interest in the rat in the early and middle part of this century probably fuelled this view. Most humans do not wish to be compared with rats even if we can see points of comparison. This reduction in animal behaviour research in psychology has had its impact on how we see the place of animals in the discipline.

A wholly different way of looking at this issue is to recognize that other animals play a significant part in the lives of many people. We work with them, live with them and play with them. Animals are farmed for food and a range of other products such as wool and silk. They play a vital role in research (for example, medical and pharmacological), and we use them for pleasure as pets and in recreation in a multitude of different ways (in horse racing, jumping and hunting, greyhound racing, bull fighting, and circuses to name just a handful of ways). Viewed in this way, our relationships with animals, how we interact with them, and why, can be seen as just another part of our psychology.

A third view is to see psychology as more than just a 'human science', but as a subject that is essentially about behaviour, emotion and cognition and which includes *all* species that display these characteristics.

Whatever perspective you take, there seems to us to be a good argument for considering other animals in an introductory text. And so, before reading further, you might like to pause and think about your answers to the questions in *Exercise 11.1* (p.270), which deal with some commonly-held views about the differences between humans and other animals.

This chapter explores some of the issues raised in *Exercise 11.1*. We shall look at the research evidence on areas of difference between humans and other animals, and the unique and special characteristics which other animals have, and which we lack, will also be highlighted. The ethical issues involved in using other animals will be discussed, and, finally, we shall look at our relationships with other animals.

IS LANGUAGE UNIQUE TO HUMANS?

Language has been said to be unique to humans, but what do we mean by the term 'language'? It is not easy to define because it has many characteristics. *The Shorter Oxford Dictionary* mentions 'speech' and 'words and methods of combining them in the expression of thought' in its definition. Psychologists have tried to tease out the various qualities of language:

– Language is symbolic and the symbols are arbitrary.
– It enables us to communicate about things remote in time and space.
– Language is learned and is passed on by tradition.
– Language enables us to express our thoughts honestly or to prevaricate.
– By using language we can reflect on the nature of language itself.

And there are many more qualities; indeed, Charles Hockett and others have identified 16 qualities or 'design features' in language. But if you take these features one by one, many are also found in communication systems among other animals.

Take communication in honey bees. Bees, on returning to the hive, can convey information about the distance and location of a food source, by performing a 'waggle dance'. The dance seems to be symbolic, although some suggest that since the rate of waggling is related to the distance of the food source, the relationship is not truly symbolic. In fact, different bees have different dialects. For a given distance, a German bee waggles more slowly than an Egyptian one.

The ability to communicate about something remote in space is found in other animals. A dog's marking behaviour enables it to convey information when it is no longer present. This 'displacement', as it is called, is also found in the alarm calls of some species, which can indicate whether a predator is in the air or on the ground.

The fact that language is *learned* and *passed on by tradition* is not exclusive to human language either. Chaffinches, for example, learn their local dialect song from other chaffinches in a particular critical period during development. Thus the song is passed from one generation to the next. Fostered birds reared by chaffinches from another locality learn the song of their foster parents; they do not sing like their biological parents.

So we see that some of the qualities of human language are found in the communication systems of other species. However, there are other qualities over which there is still much debate and these are highlighted next.

Language in Chimpanzees?

Numerous attempts have been made to teach other animals to speak our language. Most of these have proved to be fairly unsuccessful. For example, after much effort a chimpanzee called Vicki managed to utter the words 'mama', 'papa', 'cup' and 'up', but it became clear that the chimpanzee larynx is simply not designed for producing the range of sounds needed. Since speech is not essential in language communication – deaf people communicate linguistically using signs – later attempts at teaching apes used this and other non-vocal methods.

Washoe, Nim, Sarah and Lana

Washoe and Nim are two chimpanzees who became famous during this research. They each learned over 100 signs from Ameslan (American Sign Language) and were able to associate accurately sounds and visual cues, and could sign appropriately when asked to name these cues. On a few occasions the chimps combined the signs in novel ways. Thus 'water bird' and 'candy drink' were created.

The language quality of 'openness', or the ability to coin new phrases (and new meanings) by making new combinations of words, appeared to have been found. But more careful analysis of the signing of these chimpanzees raised doubts. Records of sign combinations showed that combinations were not produced grammatically (syntactically). One of Nim's longest utterances, 'Give orange me give eat orange me eat orange give me eat orange give me you', shows this clearly. Like Washoe, Nim also used novel combinations but some of these, such as 'banana toothbrush', were not felt to be indicative of true 'openness'. Although children also play with words to some extent and make nonsense phrases, the new phrases generated by the chimps formed such a tiny proportion of their total range of combinations, that it was felt that they may have occurred purely by chance. Thus the ability to display 'openness' remains in doubt. Other approaches with chimps included using plastic (arbitrary) symbols to represent words, which a chimp called Sarah learned to use by placing them on a board in answer to questions. She became proficient with 120 plastic symbols and could also carry out commands given in these symbols.

A chimp called Lana was taught to operate a computer keyboard that displayed words and symbols on a screen – she was trained to converse with the computer. There is no doubt that all these apes showed truly exceptional abilities and were able to learn language to the level of a young child. Chimps could learn to use arbitrary symbols and they could refer to objects not present; indeed their abilities went well beyond that which was previously thought possible.

As David McFarland points out, *'Language should not be defined as a uniquely human activity because there are many features of animal communication that are language like'*, and he goes on to say that *'Apes cannot learn to speak, but they can learn to communicate with humans using symbols to represent words.'*

CAN OTHER ANIMALS THINK?

Darwin believed that animals possess some powers of reasoning, but his views were strongly contested by Conway Lloyd Morgan whose famous canon states that, *'In no case may we interpret an action as the outcome of the exercise of a higher physical faculty, if it can be interpreted as the outcome of one which stands lower in the psychological scale'*. Who was right?

Donald Griffin, in his book *The Question of Animal Awareness*, suggests that mental experiences are 'the objects and events that are remote in space and time' which we think about, or have in mind. A mental image of a future event in which the 'intender pictures himself as a participant' is what he means by intention, and this is another quality which has often been said to be uniquely human. Human language and thought are often considered to be so closely linked that some would argue that one cannot exist without the other; however, studies in other animals make this assumption questionable.

Non-human animals can solve a variety of abstract problems. Fredrick Rohles and James Devine demonstrated that chimpanzees can learn the concept of 'middleness'; they could learn to select the middle one from various numbers of objects arranged in different ways. Children aged between four and six can also solve this type of problem. A number of researchers report evidence of counting in non-human animals – examples come from a range of bird and mammal species, including parrots, ravens, magpies, pigeons, monkeys, chimpanzees and gorillas. Hank Davis and John Memmott, in a critical evaluation of this research, believe that counting *can and does occur in infrahuman animals*. In a recent study by Sarah Boysen and colleagues, a chimpanzee, trained in counting arrays of 0–7 items and also to comprehend number symbols, was able to show behaviour *comparable to similar behaviours observed in children in the early stages of learning to count*.

The use of mental images by other animals is hard to demonstrate and a study of pigeons raises more questions than it answers. Pigeons were taught to discriminate between geometric shapes, and their mirror images were presented in various orientations. They were then required to indicate which of two symbols a sample symbol most resembled. Humans given this task were found to have a similar accuracy rate to pigeons but the pigeons were *quicker* at selecting the correct response than were humans. The humans' reaction times increased with the angular disparity between the sample and comparisons, but this was not the case with the pigeons. Humans appear to require some form of mental representation in order to do this task but it is not clear if this is so in pigeons. If not, in what way can this ability in pigeons be explained? At present the best way for us to explain this ability in other animals is to consider it in terms of thinking, but thinking that may not include mental images and language.

If intention requires imagery, as Donald Griffin believes, then if it can be shown to occur in other animals this too would indicate 'thinking' in these creatures. A number of birds will feign injury. The broken wing display of the sandpiper is one such example, and it is shown by incubating birds as they move away from the nest when a predator threatens. This behaviour has been accounted for in terms of a ritualized display characteristic of a species, but it is possible that intentionality may play a part. Donald Griffin points out that primates and members of the dog family can show intention, because they can learn to 'mislead' in a situation where there is competition for food. If so, then the goal of the behaviour is not what it outwardly appears to be, and evidence for thinking in Griffin's terms, and one further 'design feature' of human language, will have been found to occur in other animals.

INTELLIGENCE

Reasoning power is often said to be central to the concept of intelligence. Although psychologists argue over the definition of intelligence, problem-solving ability is frequently included in any assessment of an individual's intelligence. Experiments comparing problem-solving abilities in humans and other animals have been devised. For example, Morton Bitterman used a fish, a reptile, a bird and two mammals (a rat and a monkey) in various learning tasks. He found that the fish was least successful and the two mammals showed the best performance.

On the face of it, this kind of experiment may seem perfectly sensible as a way to compare intelligence in different species but, in reality, it is fraught with problems. Every species is uniquely adapted to a particular environment and way of life. A deep sea fish, for example, is likely to rely much less on eyesight than do birds, and it has probably never encountered a vertical face, such as the wall of a fish tank, in its natural setting. A rat is used to walls and confined spaces – it lives in tunnels and can readily learn routes through a maze to a food source. Psychologists in the past frequently used maze learning tests when comparing learning abilities in different species, but such a test is quite inappropriate for many species. Once we find problems that are appropriate for each species it then becomes hard to equate the degree of difficulty of each problem in any comparison.

The notion that humans are at the top of an evolutionary scale is highly misleading. Evolution is not a simple progression; mammals and birds, for instance, evolved at the same time from different groups of reptiles. Birds did not evolve before mammals, as is often thought. Because each species is uniquely adapted, it is not possible to arrange them in a linear hierarchy from least to most intelligent.

If we use the kinds of non-verbal problems that are used in intelligence tests for humans on other mammals we are likely to find that cats and dogs are less competent at solving these problems than non-human primates are. But, since we ourselves are primates, it should be no surprise to find that our adaptations are more like theirs. In our terms, we are undoubtedly the most intelligent, but we may ignore or disregard qualities in other animals simply because we do not share them.

Clever Hans

At the turn of the twentieth century, a retired German mathematics professor had an exceptional horse, so exceptional that he was called 'Clever Hans'. Anyone could ask Hans a complicated arithmetical problem and he would miraculously stamp out the correct answer with his hoof. Hans amazed the people who flocked to see him. Could Hans really count? For some time it was believed so, until one keen observer noted that, at dusk, Hans made mistakes. Careful manipulation of the circumstances in which Hans was questioned showed that if no one present knew the answer, then Hans didn't either. Hans' intelligence was in his ability to detect minute changes in his audience as they awaited his answer. As he stamped, when he reached the correct number, he observed a slight increase in tension in his audience and ceased stamping. Hans had learned, not to count, but to observe his audience very closely. He was indeed an amazing horse, but was he intelligent?

TOOL-USE AND CULTURE

Extending the body with a tool, in order to attain a goal, has often been viewed as intelligent behaviour. Human culture has been built on this ability and yet it is not uniquely human. Other primates have been observed using tools. Chimpanzees use twigs to gouge insects from cracks and crevices, and leaves as 'sponges' to soak up drinking water from inaccessible sources. Elephants may use a stick to scratch their backs. Sea otters use two stones to crack open shellfish – one stone is used as the anvil and the other as the hammer. Crows sometimes use a stick such as a matchstick to aid grooming and the woodpecker finch uses sticks to find its insect prey.

Some forms of tool use in non-human animals seem to be passed on by genetic means – the woodpecker finch may be an example of an innate predisposition to tool use (although not all authorities accept this) – however, other forms of tool use do *not* appear to be 'built-in' adaptations, but are spontaneous solutions to problems confronting particular individuals which are then passed on to others by observation and imitation. This seems closer to our idea of intelligence or reasoning behaviour.

Some delightful examples of cultural traditions have been recorded in Japanese macaques. In a macaque colony, whose diet was supplemented with sweet potatoes by scientists, one female was observed to wash the sand from her potatoes in a stream. Soon other macaques imitated her and over some years this new practice was established virtually throughout the population of the area. Another example concerns snowball-making, also in macaques. Again, this practice was started by one monkey and it rapidly spread throughout the population and became a characteristic of their winter behaviour.

Although these examples of tool use and culture are quite limited in type and range, it is clear that other animals, and in particular other primates, share the ability to solve problems which we believe characterize intelligent behaviour. Whilst the reasoning abilities of humans may go far beyond what is demonstrable in other animals, it is clear that the basis of this behaviour *is* found in these creatures. Probably the major difference between us and other primates is that whilst tool use is essential for our survival, it has only a minor place in the life of other primates.

SENSORY SENSITIVITY

We are very aware of the sights, sounds and smells around us, so it is perhaps surprising to learn that our sensory sensitivity is not exceptional in the animal world. Many animals are more aware than we are in one or other sensory modality, and some creatures have senses about which we know nothing.

Seeing other colours

Honey bees see a world in colours that we cannot see. For example, they can see ultraviolet, a colour invisible to us, but they are less sensitive to the red end of the spectrum. Honey bees can orient themselves using the polarization patterns of the blue sky, an ability totally lacking in humans.

Long distance smelling

Although we might expect to be able to see another person at a distance of perhaps half a mile, the idea that we could smell them at such a distance seems laughable and yet such an ability would be nothing to the male silk moth. It can detect the presence of the female moth, by odour alone, at a distance of several miles. Similar feats of sensitivity exist in the salmon, which can identify the tributary of its birth, after travelling across the ocean, by smell alone. It appears that salmon learn the exact olfactory character-istics of their native stream and this enables them to relocate these waters quite precisely later in life.

Hearing other sounds

Many animals have the ability to hear sounds well outside our audible range – they may also communicate using ultrasonic cries. Rodents, for instance, make ultrasonic cries which are audible to cats. A pet parrot perplexed its owners by its imitative ability. They believed that their television was changing channel by itself until they realized that the bird was imitating the ultrasonic signals of the TV remote control. Bats, whales, dolphins and porpoises all have hearing outside our audible range, and they can produce signals which enable them to echolocate obstacles or prey. A bat can locate and catch its insect prey *entirely* by echolocation.

Sensing electricity

Sensitivity to electric fields is another sense beyond our imagining. Electric fish can produce an electric current from special organs and are so sensitive to electric fields that they can locate the objects around them in dark and muddy waters. They can also identify other electric fish species and their own mates by this means.

Telepathy?

The ability in humans to know what someone else is thinking is an area of parapsychology that has been researched and evidence indicates that experiments can demonstrate an above chance like-lihood that some people have this ability. Can the same be said of non-human animals?

Recent research on dogs suggests that some may have the ability to predict when their owner is coming home. Careful study of a number of dogs indicated this ability. In one particular case, a dog called Jaytee participated in over 150 trials where the owner's time of returning home was varied; Jaytee was accurate on 80 per cent of trials, typically going to the door ten minutes before her owner started her return journey. It is hard to explain this unlikely behaviour, but is it indicative of a telepathic ability?

There are many more examples of the exceptional nature of animals' senses but those given serve to demonstrate that our perceptual abilities are in some respects quite limited compared with other animals.

AWARENESS AND CONSCIOUSNESS

According to McFarland, awareness is a form of perception, while consciousness involves a special kind of self-awareness. It involves '*a proportional awareness that it is I who am feeling or thinking, I am the animal aware of the circumstances*'.

Of course, sensitivity to the environment tells us nothing about how *self-aware* other animals are, but there are experiments which show that animals can be made aware of what they are doing. A rat can be trained to press one of four levers depending on which of four activities it is engaged in when a buzzer is sounded. Thus, if the buzzer sounds when it is grooming, it can press the 'grooming' lever to receive a food reward.

Self-awareness and mirrors

A dog will bark at itself in a mirror, treating its reflection as another dog, but chimpanzees and orang-utans can look in a mirror and recognize themselves if they have a little time to become used to mirrors. Gordon Gallup painted small red patches on lightly anaesthetized chimpanzees in places which could not be seen unaided. These animals looked long and hard at the patches when later they were given mirrors. Chimpanzees will also use mirrors to groom parts of their bodies which they cannot otherwise see.

Consciousness and self-awareness are not thought to be identical. Donald Griffin suggests that consciousness involves the presence of mental images to regulate behaviour. Evidence of intentional behaviour would therefore in his view be a sign of consciousness. The issue of how other animals feel about themselves is a very difficult field of study. One person cannot really know whether another person's experience is the same as their own. We have evidence, however, that some non-human primates can recognize themselves and this is perhaps very close to, if not the same as, our own consciousness. Indeed Gallup goes so far as to suggest that if a chimpanzee can contemplate itself, and hence perhaps its own existence, this is not far from the contemplation of its non-existence or mortality.

Consciousness, suffering and empathy

We have no idea of what the conscious experience of other animals might be, and we must avoid being anthropomorphic about how they feel. We cannot assume that 'they' feel as we do when they appear to show facial expressions or postures that we associate with particular feelings in ourselves.

Nevertheless, we do tend to assume that, if other people react or behave as we do when we experience a particular emotion, then their experiences are like ours. We give people the benefit of the doubt. When it comes to suffering in other animals, whilst we may still wish to avoid being anthropomorphic, should we not also, as McFarland suggests, give them the benefit of the doubt? Should we not strive to help other animals in distress, or to prevent their distress?

If non-humans animals have some self-awareness as the Gallup research suggests, then it is argued that they may also show some empathy. Research on humans shows that between the ages of 16 and 24 months children come to show mirror recognition, and at the same time as this they show the beginnings of empathy – an awareness that others have feelings similar to their own.

There are a number of interesting anecdotal cases of non-human animals helping distressed humans (see *Exercise 11.2*, p.272). It is hard to know how we can explain these examples, but an explanation involving empathy may perhaps be one possibility. Alternatively, such responses may be seen as merely being elicited by cries or distress, or bodily postures indicating injury, and the species which is showing the 'helping' responds to these just as a robin will attack a bunch of red feathers placed in its territory. It is said that redness has evolved as a 'sign stimulus' eliciting aggression because redness is the key feature of robins (and evokes this response despite the fact that a bunch of red feathers bears little resemblance to a robin).

ARE HUMANS 'BETTER' THAN OTHER ANIMALS?

To say someone behaved 'like an animal' often means that they are cruel, but is there evidence that humans are different from other animals in this respect?

Killing for pleasure

Let us consider two examples. A fox in a chicken run may 'kill for pleasure'; it will kill in excess of its needs, and may leave many dead chickens in its wake. How can this behaviour be explained? The fox's prey in this example is captive. It cannot escape as a wild animal would be able to. Human intervention in the breeding of fowl has provided an unnaturally dense source of prey, which would rarely, if ever, be encountered by a fox in a natural setting. In the evolution of prey-catching the fox probably showed this excess killing beyond need, which appears to be wasteful of energy, so rarely that it made no impact on the survival of the species. Whatever the explanation for foxes, we must also bear in mind that humans also kill for pleasure in excess of their needs. Hunting and shooting as sports are just two examples that are widespread pastimes for humans.

Infanticide

Male lions taking over a pride by displacing aged or diseased lions may kill most or all of the cubs of the pride. Infanticide is explained by sociobiologists as an adaptation which reduces the survival of the genes of competing males, and enables the males showing this behaviour to take over the females and impregnate them. A lioness will care for her cubs for two years; whilst lactating she does not ovulate and so the removal of her young returns her rapidly to a state in which she can be impregnated again.

Infanticide is also found in humans. Violent acts towards children are more common in families where a child is not biologically related to the parent who rears it. Infanticide is also practised as a means of fertility control and it is sometimes directed towards female infants in societies where the male is valued more highly than the female, and where a female requires a large dowry from her parents before she can be married.

Whatever our views are on the acceptability, morally or legally, of these forms of behaviour in humans, we cannot deny that they occur. Any claim that such behaviour is animal-like, whilst not recognizing ourselves as animals, would be absurd. Such behaviour is part of what we observe in humans; it does not distinguish us from other animals. But, it should be borne in mind that recognizing that such behaviour may occur is not the same as claiming that it is inevitable. Most of us accept that being rational beings we should be able to learn to control this aspect of human behaviour.

HUMAN USES OF OTHER ANIMALS

Ethical issues involved in using other animals for food and in research cover many areas, two of which we will briefly consider. The first issue concerns whether there is any moral justification for placing ourselves before all other animals, and the second issue revolves around the problem of how such animals should be used, if they are used, to ensure that they do not suffer.

The Bible tells Christians that 'man' has 'dominion' over all animals – this view has been used by some Christians to justify using animals in any way they choose. 'Speciesism' is a term coined by Richard Ryder to describe the view that humans are uniquely important in the scheme of things and discrimination against other species is possible simply because they are other species. Ryder suggests that speciesism, like racism or sexism, has no moral justification.

Another less extreme form of speciesism is 'speciesism with a reason'. Here discrimination is practised because other animals are held either to lack, or to possess to a lesser extent, attributes which we have. An example might be that other animals lack consciousness, or feel no pain. The problem here is to justify the reason, for as we have seen, it is hard to differentiate between other animals and humans on clear-cut grounds.

If we accept the use of animals, for instance, for food or research, then how can we ensure minimal suffering or distress? Knowing when an animal suffers is not always easy. It is often said of domesticated animals that if they breed, then their living conditions must be adequate for their needs. Similarly, that given a choice between its usual living conditions, for example, a battery cage, or a free range environment in the case of domestic fowl, then if the animal prefers what it has this is a sign that it cannot be suffering. Marion Dawkins has investigated habitat preferences in domestic fowl and her work is described in her book *Animal Suffering*.

Marion Dawkins studied hens' preferences for a battery house environment versus an outdoor run in a garden. Hens in the study lived in one or the other of these environments. Dawkins found that given a choice, each group chose the familiar environment. Battery hens chose batteries, those who had lived outside chose outside runs. But after repeated choice tests, battery hens started choosing the outside runs, whereas the hens who already lived in such runs continued with their initial choice.

Thus brief experience of outside runs was sufficient to alter the battery hens' choices, but experience of batteries did not alter the choices of hens from outside runs. This study highlights the importance of careful research to establish appropriate rearing conditions for animals which humans use – whether as pets, as farm animals or in research. Only by research of this type can we establish ways of using them humanely.

ARE ANIMALS GOOD FOR YOU?

Humans can form close associations with other animals as companions or pets. All human societies have tamed and domesticated animals, and this close association between two or more species is not unique. Ant and aphid species benefit by a close association, as do the honey guide (a small bird) and the honey badger. Ants 'farm' aphids for their honeydew (a substance similar to cuckoo spit), whilst the aphid gains protection from predators. The honey guide leads the badger to a nest of bees, the badger opens the nest, and then both can feed. Humans and other animals living together often exchange food for protection, or milk, or wool, and the latter need not be harmed by such an association. It is likely that there has been no time in our evolution when humans have not enjoyed other animals as pets, and today pets play a large part in life in Western societies.

Relationships with pets

Studies of pet owners reveal that people may feel very strongly about their pets. Research on Swedish dog owners found that 93 per cent agreed that 'the dog gives me love and affection', and 63 per cent agreed that the dog gave them someone 'to lavish love on'. Feelings involved in the pet–owner relationship were very strong indeed. Research by two of us (Julia Berryman and Kevin Howells) on the relationships that people have with their pets produced some intriguing findings.

In our pet research we used a modified version of the repertory grid technique (described in Chapter 2). This technique allows the assessment of people's individual perceptions of what is important to them in their relationships with others. In our study we used 30 pet owners, and we took six relationships with humans and two with pets for each participant. Each participant compared relationships in threes (or *triads*); this enabled us to find out what was important to each of our participants in their relationships. The 'important things' are termed 'personal constructs'. An example might be that one relationship was 'fun', whilst another was

Figure 11.1: Humans can form close associations with other animals as companions or pets.

'serious'; thus the construct would be 'fun–serious'. Constructs are very personal and no two people produce the same ones.

All the people we tested were able to make comparisons between relationships with humans and relationships with other animals. Statistical analysis of the results revealed that for about one third of our participants, the pet(s) were rated as *more important* on a whole range of constructs when compared with significant human relationships. A dog might be more loved, easier to talk to, or missed more, than a spouse, for example. Not all our subjects described themselves as pet lovers, and for these the pets were not rated so highly; they occupied an intermediate position in relation to the human relationship explored.

Over all 30 participants no constructs emerged which could not be applied to the pets, and all those tested found that they could easily compare relationships with humans with those with pets. To put it another way, *the important things in relationships with other people were evidently not dependent on 'higher human attributes'*, according to our study. We may be capable of intellectual discussion but this does not seem to be central in an important human relationship. It follows from this, if our study reflects a general tendency, that the potential of pets to satisfy many of our needs is just as great as that of friends, parents or partners. Obviously much more research is needed, but our findings suggest that the important things for humans in their relationships with other humans are not necessarily unique to us as humans, but are very much the qualities that relationships with other animals can provide – if we choose to have a pet. This is not of course the same as saying that people *should* have pets, or that pets are 'people substitutes'.

THE HUMAN: A UNIQUE ANIMAL

In conclusion, the human animal is undoubtedly a very special one, but many qualities that were once thought to be uniquely human do not now appear to be so. Some of the qualities of language are found in other animals and yet our use of language goes far beyond anything that has been observed in other species. Human language is a highly complex communication system: it can be written, spoken, communicated through gestures and, with 'tools', any message can be conveyed around the world, by telephone, radio, fax or the internet to name only a few ways.

Our ability to solve problems by thinking or with the use of tools exceeds that shown by other animals. Tool use has become essential to our survival; it is central to our way of life. Our thinking powers also appear to be beyond those of any other creature. We can reflect on our nature and mortality, the reason why we are here, and the possible existence of an all-powerful deity. Our quest for understanding appears to be greatly in excess of that shown by other animals, for, although we may observe curiosity in other animals, our need to explore and find out appears to go so very much further. However, having an ability to solve problems does not mean we have found all the answers!

We are very special animals, but we still have many problems to solve and not least of these is the solution to the problem of our inhumanity to our own kind and to other animals.

References

Beninger, R.J., Kendall, S.B. and Vanderwoof, C.H. (1974). The ability of rats to discriminate their own behaviour. *Canadian Journal of Psychology, 28*, 79–91. [Self-awareness in rats.]

Berryman, J.C. (1981). Animal communication. In A. Colman (Ed.), *Co-operation and Competition in Humans and Animals*. Wokingham: Van Nostrand Reinhold [General coverage of communication in non-human animals.]

Berryman, J.C., Howells, K. and Lloyd-Evans, M. (1985). Pet owner attitudes to pets and people: a psychological study. *Veterinary Record, 117*, 659–661. [Relationships between people and pets.]

Bitterman, M.E. (1965). The evolution of intelligence. *Scientific American*. London: W.H. Freeman. [Intelligence compared in a variety of animals.]

Boysen, S.T., Berntson, G.G., Shreyer, T.A, and Hannan, M. B. (1995). Indicating acts during counting by a chimpanzee (Pan troglodytes). *Journal of Comparative Psychology, 109(1)*, 47–51. [Chimpanzee counting.]

Crocker, J. (1985). Respect of feathered friends. *New Scientist, 1477*, 47–50. [Tool use in crows and the 'talking' parrot are discussed.]

Darwin, C. (1871). *The Descent of Man and Selection in Relation to Sex*. John Murray: London. [Discusses human evolution.]

Davis, H and Memmott, J. (1982). Counting behaviour in animals: a critical evaluation. *Psychological Bulletin, 92(3)*, 547–571. [Counting behaviour; quotation on p. 547.]

Dawkins, M.S. (1980). *Animal Suffering: The science of animal welfare*. London: Chapman & Hall. [Research on hens' preferences.]

Dickemann, M. (1985). Human sociobiology: the first decade. *New Scientist, 1477*, 38–42. [Female infanticide in humans.]

Eaton, G.C,.(1976). Social order of Japanese macaques. *Scientific American, 235(4)*, 96–106. [Cultural transmission in macaques.]

Gallup, G.G. Jr (1979). Self-awareness in primates. *American Scientist, 67*, 417–421. [Use of mirrors by chimpanzees.]

Griffin, D.R. (1976). *A Question of Animal Awareness*. New York: Rockefeller University Press. [Discussion of mental experiences.]

Holland, V.D. and Delius, J.D. (1983). Rotational invariance in visual pattern recognition by pigeons and humans. *Science, 218*, 804–806. [Pigeons and pattern recognition.]

McFarland, D. (1993). *Animal Behaviour: Ethology and evolution*. London: Pitman. [Wide ranging coverage; Lloyd Morgan quotation on p. 8, McFarland quotation on p. 506.]

Rohles, F.H. and Devine, J.V. (1966). Chimpanzee performance on a problem involving the concept of middleness. *Animal Behaviour, 14*, 159–162. [Chimpanzees and the concept of middleness.]

Ryder, R.D. (1975). *Victims of Science*. London: Davis-Poynter. [Speciesism and animal experimentation considered.]

Thorpe, W.H. (1974). *Animal Nature and Human Nature*. London: Methuen. [Hockett and the qualities of language.]

Recommended Reading

Dawkins, M.S. (1980). *Animal Suffering: The science of animal welfare*. London: Chapman & Hall.

Gould, J.L. (1982). *Ethology, the Mechanisms and Evolution of Behaviour*. London: W.W. Norton.

Griffin, D.R. (1976). *A Question of Animal Awareness*. New York: Rockefeller University Press.

McFarland, D. (1993). *Animal Behaviour: Ethology and evolution*. London: Pitman.

Serpell, J. (1986). *In the Company of Animals*. Oxford: Basil Blackwell.

HUMAN AND OTHER ANIMALS COMPARED

Read the following statements. Do you agree with them? Tick 'Yes' or 'No' as appropriate.

- Humans are the peak of evolution.   Yes   No

- Humans are capable of intelligent behaviour, other animals are not.   Yes   No

- Humans have a mental life, other animals do not.   Yes   No

- Humans can think about abstract problems, other animals cannot.   Yes   No

- Language is unique to humans.   Yes   No

- Communication in other animals is unlearned.   Yes   No

- Communication in other animals is straightforward. Only humans can lie about their thoughts and feelings.   Yes   No

- Humans can show intention in their behaviour, other animals cannot.   Yes   No

- Cultural transmission of ideas/behaviour is unique to humans.   Yes   No

- Only humans have a sense of themselves – a self-awareness.   Yes   No

- Humans are more sensitive than other creatures, and are more aware of the world around them.   Yes   No

- Other animals cannot feel pain to the extent that humans can.   Yes   No

- Humans can show empathy with others, other animals cannot.   Yes   No

continued

continued --

HUMAN AND OTHER ANIMALS COMPARED

- Any relationship that a human has with
  another animal is on an entirely different
  level to that of a human–human relationship.　　Yes　No

Conclusion

There is no universal agreement on the views outlined in this
list – many are, as yet, a matter of debate, but when you read
this chapter you will find out our current state of knowledge
on the answers to each of these questions.

EMPATHY AND ALTRUISM TOWARDS HUMANS
BY OTHER ANIMALS

Consider the following true newspaper reports. How can we explain this behaviour towards humans by other animals?

Gorilla saves injured boy

A female gorilla picked up a three-year-old boy who fell into her enclosure at Brookfield Zoo, Chicago. The boy, who suffered serious injuries when he plunged 18 feet into the compound after climbing over the barrier, was cradled in the arms of the gorilla. She carried him to the door of the enclosure where paramedics and zoo keepers treated him. The gorilla, Binti Jua was also carrying her 17-month-old infant on her back.
[An anonymous report, (1996). Gorilla saves boy at zoo. *The Times*, 19 August, 9.]

Monkey saves man's life

Cyril Jones, a former Japanese prisoner of war, told how a monkey kept him alive for 12 days by feeding him on bananas. In 1942, then Sergeant Jones was a member of the Royal Artillery Airbourne Division. He parachuted into Sumatra but his parachute became caught in the branches of a tree where he hung for 12 days. A monkey came up to him and 'we became very close friends', Mr Jones reported. The monkey fed him on bananas and other fruit keeping him alive during this period. Finally he managed to cut himself down but was caught by Japanese soldiers.
[Smith, M. (1996). My life was saved by a monkey, says POW. *The Daily Telegraph*, 27 August, 5.]

Man saved from shark by dolphins

Three bottlenose dolphins saved Martin Richardson from a shark in the Red Sea. Mr Richardson was swimming with dolphins off the Sinai peninsula when a shark bit his side and

continued

continued ---

EMPATHY AND ALTRUISM TOWARDS HUMANS
BY OTHER ANIMALS

arm. The dolphins encircled him, flapping their tails to scare off the shark. A statement issued by the Israel Recanati Centre for Maritime Studies at the University of Haifa indicated that this behaviour is common in dolphins when mothers are protecting their young from predators.
[An anonymous report. (1996). Man saved from shark by dolphins. *The Times*, 25 July, 13.]

Cows protect farmer
Donald Mothram, a farmer, was protected from an enraged bull by his cows. The farmer, who had been tossed by the bull, blacked out, but the cows saved his life by forming a protective ring around him.
[An anonymous report. (1996). Herd instinct. *The Times*, 30 August, 2]

COMMENT: Are these animals showing empathy for the plight of the human? Or can we explain this behaviour much more simply? For instance:

- Are the non-human animals responding to a 'sign stimulus' from the human that automatically elicits some form of caring or protective response (such as the robin's response to red feathers discussed in the chapter)?

- Are the non-human animals responding just as they would towards their own offspring, and thus this is a form of maternal or parental behaviour?

- Have the early experiences of the non-human animals in these examples altered their behaviour in some important way? For example, the gorilla, Binti Jua, was hand-reared, so she will have formed strong attachment(s) to her human carers early in life. Research on animals hand-reared in this way indicates that such animals display

-- *continued*

continued --

EMPATHY AND ALTRUISM TOWARDS HUMANS BY OTHER ANIMALS

social and sexual behaviour towards their 'adopted' species as they get older. In other words, is Binti Jua reacting to the boy because she identifies herself with the human species, just as much as with gorillas?

- What other explanations can you offer?

12. *Psychological Research Methods and You*

If you volunteered to take part in some psychological research what would be expected of you?

In writing this book we have endeavoured to give you examples of psychological research which has increased our understanding of the underlying causes and mechanisms controlling what we do, think and feel. The methods which psychologists use in carrying out research have only been dealt with briefly because we feel that, for those who are new to this subject, knowing the findings of the research is probably more interesting than discussing the methods used to produce those findings. In other words, the goal of research – the results – is more exciting than the means of achieving that goal. Nevertheless, the methods used by psychologists are of enormous importance, and over the last century methods in psychology have been refined and improved. After a long period during which the scientific approach had been seen as central to the methodology, today there is an increasing interest in more qualitative approaches. This chapter illustrates examples of some of the main methods used by psychologists today, and, if you volunteered to take part in some psychological research, it is likely that one of the methods outlined here would be used.

Repeatable and scientific

All psychologists are trained in research methods and an important feature of these methods is *replication*. If psychologists can repeat a piece of research and reproduce the earlier findings then they are justified in believing that the two sets of results are more than just a chance occurrence. This scientific approach to the study of people and other animals has many advantages, but it also has some limitations: there are some areas of human experience with which this approach cannot deal adequately and which we shall discuss later.

Psychoanalysis

The scientific approach within psychology came, in part, as a reaction to some of the earlier approaches, in particular to that of Sigmund Freud. We noted, in the Introduction, that Freud's psychoanalytic theory explained the basis of human behaviour in terms of instincts housed in an unconscious area of mind. By concentrating on this aspect of the mind, Freud's theory, by its very nature, could not be proved or disproved in any scientific sense and, as a result, many psychologists rejected his views as not useful.

Behaviourism

The approach of John Watson, the main instigator of behaviourism (see Chapter 9), was in total contrast to that of Freud. Behaviourists are concerned with the stimuli which act on an organism to change or shape its behaviour. The organism is viewed from the outside; its behaviour, the readily observable acts, form the data for this school of psychology. The stimulus–response connection, or S–R connection as it came to be known, is central to this approach. The mind plays no part because it can not be observed directly.

Watson found that much learning in humans and other animals could be explained in terms of these observable connections, as he showed with 'Little Albert' (in Chapter 9), and he went so far as to say that, given the appropriate environment, any normal child could be *made* into a lawyer, artist or beggar. In many ways Watson's views were very optimistic – almost anything is possible

– whereas for Freud, because the most basic drives were thought to be inbuilt, they formed and shaped the person in ways that could not be escaped.

Psychoanalysis and behaviourism can be seen as at the two extremes of the influences on psychology. Other theories and schools of psychology have developed which also play an important part in contemporary psychology, but these cannot be detailed here. Nevertheless, all the approaches have contributed to the methodology of the discipline, and it is to these methods that we now turn our attention. We begin with the *experimental method* described in the Introduction.

EXPERIMENTAL, CORRELATIONAL AND OBSERVATIONAL METHODS

The psychological experiment described at the start of the book (on p.9) illustrates one form of a typical experiment in psychology. It was designed to answer a specific question: 'Do underarm (axillary) secretions from human males influence menstrual cycle length and regularity in females?'. The experiment included an experimental group to whom the chemical secretions in ethanol, the *independent variable*, were administered, and a control group who received a placebo, ethanol alone, instead of ethanol plus axillary secretions. The independent variable is so called because it is the variable which the psychologist chooses to manipulate. The thing (behaviour, emotion, thought and so on) which is measured following the treatment, in this case menstrual cycle length and regularity, is called the *dependent variable* because it is assumed to be dependent on the treatment which the experimental group receives. A comparison of the menstrual cycles of women in the experimental and control groups enables the psychologist to measure the effect of male secretions; the experiment has been planned so that the only difference between the groups is the presence or absence of the male secretions, and the control group provides a baseline level of response with which the effects of the secretions can be compared.

Control groups

A control group of this kind is not always essential in the design of an experiment. In some cases the psychologist may simply use two or more dose levels of the independent variable (in this case male secretions), because these also enable a comparison to be made. Psychological experiments are described throughout this book and include the Purdue University 'touching' experiment in Chapter 1, the Stanley Milgram experiment concerning TV violence in Chapter 4, and the learning and recall experiment in *Exercise 8.2* in Chapter 8.

Useful though the experimental method is, it has its limitations. An experiment is only appropriate when we have a specific hypothesis to test. But even with a hypothesis we are not always willing or able to perform experiments. The Milgram experiment, supposedly on the effects of punishment on memory (in Chapter 4), is an example of an experiment which today we would *not* be willing to perform because it would be regarded as unethical. There are also other situations in which a hypothesis cannot be tested experimentally.

Correlational studies

Research on gender difference is a case in point, because it is not possible to compare two groups of people identical in all but sex. Thus, in attempting to answer the question 'Are females more intelligent than males?', the *independent variable* of sex cannot be assigned by the psychologist to one group as can the axillary secretions in the study outlined earlier. All that can be done is to compare groups of males and females who share a number of similarities (age, class, education, and so on) and compare the results. This is a *correlational study* and one result might be that the females performed at level A and the males performed at level B on a given test of intelligence. Such a finding tells us nothing about whether our biology (in this case sex) determines our performance on intelligence tests. There is a common tendency to confuse correlational findings with causal links between two factors.

'Natural' experiments

Alternatively, a hypothesis might be, 'Are the frontal lobes of the brain the part which is concerned with self-awareness?' Once again this is an example where an experiment would be considered unethical. But sometimes 'natural' experiments arise which permit a comparison to be made between those with and without a particular part of the brain. Tragically, the 1939–45 war resulted in many severely brain-damaged people, and, by studying these people, neurophysiologists and psychologists came to understand much more about the relationships between parts of the brain, behaviour and experience.

Another example of a 'natural experiment' is found in the research on children who have been orphaned. Much of the research on love and attachment (see Chapter 5) arose out of comparing such orphaned children with those who lived with their parents.

How objective are the 'facts'?

One problem for psychologists is the nature of the questions asked or hypotheses generated. Ideally these should be objective and not evaluative. But this can be quite difficult to achieve, as values are often implicit in what we accept as 'facts'.

Feminist psychologists, for instance, have argued that the questions posed in psychology (and other disciplines) are bound to be value-laden in a patriarchal society. Male dominance or superiority is, they suggest, implicit in our view of the sexes, and male and female roles are often assumed to be determined in great part by biology (as we saw in Chapter 3). Thus, for example, since women tend to do most child care, questions about maternal feelings and behaviour lack objectivity because implicit in such questions is an assumption that it is right that women should be maternal. Females lacking such feelings are thought to lack an essential feminine quality, whereas males lacking paternal feelings do not have their masculinity questioned. Indeed, fathers who take on the role of primary carer in a single parent family are often shunned or pitied by other men.

Observation

At times a psychologist may begin research without any specific question or hypothesis in mind. She or he may wish to study a particular topic within psychology which has not been researched, or where little research has been undertaken. For instance, at one time play in children was little studied and a psychologist wanting to understand more about this activity may have had few specific questions. The first phase in investigating such a topic is observation – the psychologist simply observes the behaviour in as many naturally occurring situations as possible. Once this is done, a variety of questions are likely to be generated and it may then be possible to investigate play more rigorously, perhaps by an experiment or correlational study. Thus, questions such as 'Do boys and girls differ in play behaviour?', or 'Does play experience influence performance in a learning task?' could be tackled.

Observational methods are a vital first stage in research but on their own they can rarely answer our questions about behaviour. The majority of research on non-human animals described in Chapter 11 began with careful observation of the animals in their natural habitats, but after the initial observations we need to control the variables involved, changing one thing at a time, before we can see the individual effect of a given factor on the behaviour under scrutiny. In natural circumstances there are usually too many uncontrolled variables for us to be able to identify how one event influences another.

SURVEYS AND TESTS

Other methods used by psychologists include *surveys* and *tests*. The psychologists may, for example, wish to find out what people do, think or feel in an area in which there are little or no data. The survey includes questions and perhaps interviews. One of the most famous surveys was that by Alfred Kinsey and his co-workers on sexual behaviour, mentioned in Chapters 3 and 7. Prior to this little was known about the average person's sexual experiences and this survey was an attempt to find such information at a time when observational methods were considered inappropriate. Since Kinsey, other researchers, such as William Masters and Virginia Johnson, have studied sexual behaviour in the laboratory. Volunteers prepared to participate have been observed and recorded during sexual activity. Whilst such research may seem to be voyeuristic to some readers, it produced a much greater understanding of this aspect of human behaviour. As a result of this research, many people who have sexual problems have been helped.

Finding the norm

Charting what is average or 'normal' for humans is one important aspect of psychological research. We all tend to think of ourselves

Figure 12.1: Psychologists often use surveys and tests to gather information. (*From Dave Roberts.*)

as 'normal' (providing that we are not too obviously different from our peers) and discovering that others' experience may be very unlike our own is important in increasing our understanding of others. The primary purpose of much research on child development, as we saw in Chapter 6, has been to establish what the average child, in a given culture, is capable of at a given age. A parent with little contact with other parents may worry greatly at a child's nightmares, bed-wetting, thumb-sucking or nail-biting, but all these are common at a particular stage in development and are thus quite 'normal'. This knowledge can bring relief to the parent. Normal is not, of course, necessarily 'desirable' or 'good'. Having nightmares is distressing whether or not other children also have them and it should not prevent us from searching for their cause or finding some way to alleviate them.

Tests are conducted in psychology to measure a variety of aspects of human behaviour – personality and intelligence are just two examples which are considered in Chapters 2 and 10. Tests are carefully constructed so that the aspect of humans in question can be systematically examined in large numbers of people. As we saw in Chapter 10, intelligence tests are made up of a range of questions, or exercises, which people are asked to complete under specified conditions. The variations in the people tested can then be correlated with their test performance. If it is found that children who are educationally disadvantaged do less well on intelligence tests, then such a finding may lead to the suggestion that their education should be changed. If improved education makes for no improvement in the children's performance then other causes need to be investigated.

THE INDIVIDUAL IN PSYCHOLOGY

Many of the psychologist's methods are concerned with the study of participants who are grouped on the basis of some similarity. But all of us know that we are unique individuals – even identical twins, who may look indistinguishable to others, have different environments, and as people they may be very aware of their uniqueness. Much of scientific psychology seems to overlook this individuality; indeed, the humanistic approach in psychology stresses that science is not the total answer to our understanding of people; rigorous observation and experiment excludes important aspects of the individual's subjective experience. Today, psychologists are much more aware of the need to look at subjective experience, but there has always been a place in psychology for the *case study* and it is to this that we shall turn first.

A case study is an individual case history. The life of a person is reconstructed at a given point in time through the memories of that person and others, plus the aid of recordings of events such as diaries. The clinical psychologist might use this technique to find out whether an earlier life event is a significant factor in the precipitation of a later problem. Personal Construct Theory is also a technique which seeks to explore the subjective experience of the individual. An example of this can be found in Chapter 11.

QUALITATIVE RESEARCH IN PSYCHOLOGY

As we have already noted, feminist psychologists have been critical of some of the questions posed in psychology and these criticisms have extended beyond just the questions. Concern has also been voiced over the methods used by psychologists – the emphasis on 'scientific methods' and the relatively minor place of qualitative data gathering, as we saw earlier. This issue is illustrated clearly in considering issues that relate to girls and women only. The following example illustrates the point.

Jane Ussher, as a young Ph.D. student, was interested in carrying out research on the menstrual cycle and its effect on women. However, she was dismayed to discover that as a topic for research this was not taken seriously; indeed, it was seen almost as a form of deviance by some. Surrounded by academics who saw the empirical positivistic approach as the only way forward for real psychological research (that is, the application of the scientific method) Jane Ussher found herself studying 'Psychological change, performance on computer tests and mood during the menstrual cycle'. 'Subjects' were tested and an extensive and elaborate statistical analysis was carried out.

'What's wrong with that?', you may be asking. For Jane Ussher it was only a small part of the story. Interview data that she collected at the pilot phase of her study was seen to be of little relevance; this 'subjective' data was viewed as of secondary interest relative to the 'objective' information obtained through tests and psychological measures traditionally used in quantitative research. It was not seen as important or relevant to her work. In fact, many feminist psychologists have felt that psychology is dominated by males at all levels (except the undergraduate level) and this has led to the subject matter of psychology, and the methodology, being determined by males. Perception, learning, memory, physiology are all areas that have had a dominant role within psychology; those areas that are of real concern to people, such as love, relationships, being a mother, father or friend were, and still are, to a great extent, under-researched. The objectivity required by the 'scientific method' meant that the methods of psychology simply could not handle adequately the experiences of women and men. To return to Ussher's dilemma, when she started her research she wanted to capture how women themselves felt about the menstrual cycle and menstruation, how it felt for them and what their experience was. But somehow she became sidetracked by the methods she was required to use. Although she achieved her Ph.D., Ussher felt angry that for her it lacked real meaning. She noted: *The content of the work did not have to be particularly meaningful – in fact it seemed to me that the more removed from human experience (and particularly women's experience) the research was, the more acceptable it was'* to those who assessed it. These are angry words indeed. Ussher felt that psychology was letting her down, and letting itself down by its disregard for the more subjective and qualitative data.

In recent years there have been clear moves within psychology to tackle this problem. An issue of *The Psychologist* in 1995 focused on qualitative research in psychology and possible ways forward, but many textbooks on psychology still make no reference to the new interest in qualitative research. How do psychologists now endeavour to capture subjectivity? As we have noted, psychology has had a chink in its armour in the idiographic approach – dealing with the unique aspects of the individual, through, for example, the case study. But we need to learn from other disciplines such as sociology and anthropology. For example, *discourse analysis* is a method which examines how language itself shapes our understanding of social reality by looking at the linguistic content, structure and formation of what is said. *Verbal protocol analysis* is another way in which subjective data can be examined. This is used as a means of inferring thought processes. Participants in such research are required to express their thoughts but not to infer the processes that produced them; the latter is the task of the researcher. These are just some of the ways in which more qualitative data can be examined.

The traditional approach in psychology, with the emphasis on the experimental method, is not wrong but it should perhaps be viewed as an important aspect of methodological repertoire within psychology. The future for psychology lies in achieving a balance between 'objectivity' and 'subjectivity', and in developing and refining qualitative approaches and methods.

WHAT PSYCHOLOGISTS DO

In this book the emphasis has been on describing the findings of psychologists who have carried out research in each of the areas covered by a chapter. Our understanding of people has been greatly enhanced by psychological research but not all psychologists do research, as we shall see.

In Britain, becoming a psychologist is achieved by taking a qualification in psychology that is recognized by The British Psychological Society (BPS) as being equivalent to the BPS Qualifying Examination, or by being a graduate who has passed the BPS Qualifying Examination. Once a person has achieved either of these qualifications they can become a Graduate Member of the BPS. However, in order to become eligible for Registration as a Chartered Psychologist, further BPS-accredited postgraduate training in an area of applied psychology must be undertaken. The BPS is the professional body of psychologists in Britain and as such sets standards for the profession.

In the first half of the twentieth century most psychologists worked either as researchers or teachers of their subject. Today psychologists can be found in a wide range of settings and the majority of graduates will not go on to take up either of these areas. However, for those who do pursue a research and teaching career (for example in universities, lecturers will generally do both), they will usually work within specific areas of psychology, each with its own particular methods of study. Physiological psychologists study the brain, nervous system, and other bodily processes to discover how each influences the others. The study of brain-damaged patients mentioned earlier is carried out by them. Experimental psychology and comparative psychology are both fields in which experimental methods are applied to assist in understanding the behaviour of humans and other animals. Traditionally experimental psychology is often used to explain how people respond to external stimuli (as in visual perception) but the use of experimental methods is not confined to this area as the numerous examples throughout this book show.

Human development is the province of developmental psychologists who are concerned with explaining development throughout life. This topic may seem to embrace every aspect of human psychology, but, in fact, personality, cognition and social psychology are generally considered to be separate specialities, though interrelated. Influences in human development shape our personalities, but the latter field has become so specialized and is often concerned with devising methods of personality assessment that the field is generally considered to be a separate one of individual differences. Cognitive psychologists study how the mind processes the information which is received – processes involved in memory or problem-solving, for example. The influence of others on the individual is the concern of social psychologists and, as we saw, a person's behaviour can be greatly challenged by the social context within which it occurs.

Clinical psychologists are occupied with people who have psychological problems. Their concern ranges from the treatment of relatively minor stresses to major forms of mental illness, such as schizophrenia. Their aims are to diagnose the nature of the illness and to effect its treatment. Clinical psychologists may work within universities in teaching and research or outside in the Health Service or private health care. Under certain circumstances, they may also work within Young Offenders institutions or in Penal Reform units/Special Care units.

Outside academic research and teaching today psychologists are found in many applied fields; for instance, there are educational psychologists, prison psychologists, occupational psychologists and psychologists working in advertising and marketing. Because psychology is about people, and most occupations, especially the larger organizations, are concerned with managing people – the employees – it is likely that there will be someone around who is knowledgeable about this area.

Let us look briefly at some of these applied areas. *Educational psychologists* specialize in helping children both in the classroom and in the home. They are qualified in both psychology and education (having training and experience as teachers) and one of their most important functions is the assessment and diagnosis of children who are not doing well at school and where there is concern about a possible problem. For example, a child who has difficulties in reading, but otherwise seems able and bright, might be diagnosed as having dyslexia. The educational psychologist will be the person assessing the child and once he or she has diagnosed the problem, s/he may also be involved in the treatment.

In the prison setting, or other penal institutions, again the *forensic psychologist's* role is concerned with assessment and diagnosis. Prison inmates, like the rest of the population, may suffer from a range of psychological disorders, and their particular circumstances are likely to add to the stresses they experience. Being isolated from family and friends, feeling guilt, and the stresses associated with being incarcerated with people one would not necessarily choose to be with, are just some of the problems that prison itself causes. The psychologist's role is to identify such

Figure 12.2: An educational psychologist at work.

problems and to help to treat them. They will also work closely with prison staff and medical practitioners.

In addition to the work of clinical psychologists already discussed, some psychologists specialize in *counselling psychology.* Such psychologists work with individuals as well as with couples, families and groups. Their aim is to help people improve their sense of well-being and cope better with the difficulties of everyday life. *Health psychology* is another burgeoning area of psychology which seeks to promote changes in people's attitudes and thinking about health. They may work in a number of settings such as hospitals, health authorities and academic departments.

Occupational psychologists, or *industrial psychologists,* work in a wide variety of areas. They may work as independent consultants, who are called in by organizations from time to time, or they may be based in-house and be involved with almost any aspect of the concerns of employed staff. They could be employed as personnel psychologists primarily concerned with selection of staff and staff training, or they may be involved with problems in the workplace concerned with staff motivation or job satisfaction and ways of improving both. Some occupational psychologists work in the area of ergonomics, 'fitting jobs for people'. One aspect of their work might be to ensure that workstations are designed to maximize employee comfort and well-being as well as to maximize performance in the job. They will also be interested in reducing boredom and fatigue in employees. Occupational psychologists may often work at an organizational level rather than just at the level of individual employees. Here they are concerned with how the organization itself works, how it is managed, the structures within the organization (such as board or committees) that are part of the administration.

Another well-known area where psychologists may be employed is in advertising and marketing. A subject that enables people to learn more about people's needs, wishes and aspirations is likely to be one that can assist in promoting product. Most large companies will call on experts to help them sell their products, and psychologists are likely to be bought in to research how best to do this. Selling a product is not the only way a psychologist may be used in advertising. Selling an idea or an image may be very much part of this too. One of the authors was recently consulted by a top hairdresser on the psychology of hair colour. The hairdresser wanted to be able to sell his hair colouring products by being able to tell his clients what image they would achieve, according to psychological research, if they chose to dye their hair a particular colour. In fact there is very little research on this topic (see Chapter 1 for details), so this is an area about which relatively little can be said but it is one that could form a basis of research.

We have covered just a few areas in which the psychologist may work; space does not permit a more detailed examination of this topic, but for those who are interested, the Recommended Reading section includes appropriate books.

Psychology and you

As you are approaching the end of this book you may be wondering, 'What next?' If you are on the brink of a psychology course for which this book was recommended then your immediate future is clear. We hope that this book has whetted your appetite for more psychology. If you chanced upon this book without any specific plan to read more psychology, you may be wondering how best to satisfy your interest. In Britain, you can join a GCSE, or A-level course in psychology or, even better, an initial way to find out more is to join an adult education class in psychology. Many universities and colleges of further and higher education run such courses and all the authors of this text have taught these classes. Adult education is an ideal way to plunge further into psychology and if you are captivated by psychology, classes also provide a way of gaining qualifications. At Leicester University, UK, for example, the Department of Adult Education runs courses in psychology for general interest, through to certificate courses, a diploma in psychology, and for those who want a degree, psychology can also be taken as part of the part-time degree programme.

How far you want to take your interest in psychology, whether as just an enjoyable pastime or hobby, or as a serious career choice, we hope that *Psychology and You* has provided a stimulating and enjoyable read. We also hope that we have shown you that psychology is a subject that seeks to throw light on every facet of human behaviour, thought and emotion. Of course, however much we may know about people in general, there is at least one question which is never likely to be fully answered by psychologists, and that is: *What makes you the unique individual that you are?*

References

British Psychological Society (1996). *Careers in Psychology*. Leicester: The British Psychological Society. [Free leaflet.]

Burman, E. (1990). *Feminists and Psychological Practice*. London: Sage. [Jane Ussher discusses her Ph.D. research here; quotations are on pages 49 and 50.]

Cutler, W.B., Preti, G., Krieger, A., Huggins, G.R., Garcia, C.R. and Lawley, H.J. (1986). Human axillary secretions influence women's menstrual cycles: The role of donor extract from men. *Hormones and Behaviour, 20*, 463–473. [The experiment using male axillary secretions.]

Green, A. (1995). Verbal protocol analysis. *The Psychologist, 8(3)*, 126–129. [Qualitative research using verbal protocol analysis.]

Henwood, K. and Nicolson, P. (1995). Qualitative research. *The Psychologist, 8 (3)*, 109–110. [Discuss the development of qualitative analysis.]

Kinsey, A.C., Pomeroy, W.B. and Martin, C.E. (1953). *Sexual Behaviour in the Human Female*. Philadelphia: W.B. Saunders. [One of the first major studies of female sexual behaviour.]

Masters, W.H. and Johnson, V.E. (1966). *Human Sexual Responses*. Boston: Little, Brown. [The first major study of human sexual responses.]

Recommended Reading

Boring, E.G. (1957). *A History of Experimental Psychology*. New York: Appleton Century Crofts.

Coleman, A.M. (1993). *What is Psychology?* London: Routledge.

Foster, J. and Parker, I. (1995). *Carrying Out Investigations in Psychology: Methods and statistics.* Leicester: BPS Books (The British Psychological Society).

Richardson, J. T. (1996). *Handbook of Qualitative Research Methods in Statistics for Psychology and the Social Sciences.* Leicester: BPS Books (The British Psychological Society).

Thomson, R. (1968). *The Pelican History of Psychology.* Harmondsworth: Penguin.

GLOSSARY

Ability tests: tests designed to measure people's maximum performance, independent of their learning.

Adrenal gland: a hormone-producing, or endocrine gland situated over the kidneys.

Adrenaline: hormone secreted by the adrenal gland and active in emotional excitement.

Age norms: the average scores obtained on psychological tests by people at given age levels.

Aggregation: a summing together of different instances of behaviour.

Agoraphobia: one of the more common forms of irrational fear or phobia in clinical groups. Strong fear and panic may occur in a range of situations such as crowds, public places, travelling on trains or buses.

Androgens: a collective term for the hormones produced chiefly by the testes, the chief one of which is testosterone. Responsible for the maintenance and development of many male sexual characteristics.

Androgyny: the combination of masculine and feminine characteristics within an individual male or female.

Attachment behaviour: behaviour which promotes proximity and physical contact with the object of the attachment.

Attainment tests: tests designed to measure people's progress, or learning, on a given course of instruction.

Attribution: the perception of the cause of an event.

Authoritarian personality: a constellation of personality characteristics which characterize people with prejudiced attitudes centring on respect for authority.

Autism: a form of disordered behaviour which arises in early childhood and is characterized by communication difficulties.

Autonomic nervous system (ANS): a system of nerve cells and nerve fibres which control the functions of smooth muscles and glands.

Behaviourism: a school of psychology associated with John B. Watson. It defined psychology as the study of behaviour, and limited the data in psychology to observable activities. Mental events were excluded.

Behaviour modification: therapeutic techniques, often involving the use of rewards and punishments, based on operant conditioning.

Catharsis: the purging or release of an emotion through direct or indirect expression.

Causality: this refers to the person's perception of what the cause of an event was, that is, 'Why did this occur?'

Central nervous system: the brain and spinal cord.

Cerebral cortex: that part of the brain responsible for many 'higher' human mental activities.

Chromosome: microscopic body found in a cell nucleus containing genes, the individual's hereditary material.

Classical conditioning: the learning of a response through association with a previously neutral stimulus, studied by Pavlov.

Cognition: a person's thoughts, knowledge and ideas about him/herself and the environment.

Cognitive dissonance theory: one of the best-known cognitive consistency theories which was proposed by Leon Festinger, and which explains how people resolve inconsistencies in their knowledge, beliefs and behaviour.

Cognitive processes: refers to mental activities involving evaluation and appraisal. It can sometimes be used as equivalent to thought.

Cones: receptive cells in the retina responsive to coloured light.

Consciousness: a state in which an individual is aware of, or is 'inside', what is happening. Often used synonymously with 'awareness', but generally thought to be rather more than this.

Conservation: a cognitive advance which Piaget proposed as a central feature of concrete operational thinking acquired at around the age of seven.

Constructive alternativism: the theory that the world may be construed in very different ways, without any one view being 'correct' in an absolute sense.

Control group: a group in an experiment that is not given the treatment whose effect is being studied (see *Experimental group*).

Convergent thinking: the ability to focus on the correct solution to a problem.

Correlational study: a study which is designed to find out the degree of correspondence between two sets of measures.

Dependent variable: the behaviour or response measured in a psychological experiment which is believed to be changed by the independent variable.

Discrimination: the process of learning to differentiate between various stimuli in order to produce the correct response.

Divergent thinking: the ability to generate different ideas from a given proposition, or problem.

Echolocation: the emission by an animal of high frequency sounds which can be heard and timed by that animal as they are reflected off solid objects in the vicinity. Used by bats for flight in darkness and the location of food.

Ecological approach: a research strategy in developmental psychology which takes account of all the interacting social and environmental influences upon humans.

Egocentrism: the tendency to see the world only from one's own point of view, which Piaget believed was an essential feature of early childhood.

Electra complex: The Freudian notion that at a certain stage a girl becomes aware that she lack a penis. She is said to feel 'penis envy' and blame her mother for her feelings of castration. A girl then rejects her mother and turns to her father. The complex is named after the Greek myth in which Electra connives at the death of her mother who had murdered her father.

Emotional leakage: occurs when the facial expressions commonly associated with an emotion are suppressed and the emotion is shown, or 'leaks' out, elsewhere in other parts of the body below the head (such as feet and hands). Also known as *leakage*.

Encoding: the transformation of a sensory input into a form (code) for storage in memory.

Episodic memory: the part of the memory which holds details of people, places and events.

Ethologist: one who researches the behaviour of animals, and who works primarily in their natural habitats rather than in the laboratory.

Experimental group: a group in an experiment that is given the treatment whose effect is being studied (see *Control group*).

Extinction: the gradual fading of behaviour when it fails to produce a reinforcing consequence.

Extravert: a psychological type who is more concerned with social life and the external world than with inner experience.

Facial primacy: this refers to the fact that the face is viewed by people as the most important part of the body for conveying information about emotions.

Factor analysis: a statistical technique which reduces a large number of test interrelationships to a small number of factors.

False memory syndrome: apparent memories for events usually of a disturbing nature, which did not actually occur.

Family therapy: treatments taking the whole family, rather than the individual, as a focus.

Free association: a form of word association in which a subject reports any word which comes to mind in response to a stimulus. Also the reporting of anything that comes to mind, without modification.

Gender identity: the concept of oneself as either feminine or masculine.

Gene: transmission of individual hereditary traits contained in a chromosome.

Generalization: the production of a response by a stimulus similar, but not identical, to the original stimulus when learning took place.

Generalized anxiety disorder: chronic long-term high anxiety. The individual is continually anxious and frightened.

Hermaphrodite: an individual who has both male and female reproductive organs, also applied to individuals in whom there is a contradiction between their external genitals and/or secondary sexual characteristics and various internal structures, for example, gonads.

Hypothalamus: a part of the base of the brain concerned in particular emotions, motivation and sleep.

Iconic memory: the sensory memory system for vision.

Identification: a process of personality development involving taking on the characteristics of other people.

Imprinting: learning that occurs within a limited period early in life (usually in relation to the mother and likened by Lorenz to a pathological fixation), and which is relatively unmodifiable.

Independent variable: the variable in a psychological experiment which is under the control of the psychologist and is varied by her or him.

Insight: the discovery of the solution to a problem.

Intelligence: a general ability whose definition remains elusive.

Interactionism: the view that both person and situation are important in determining behaviour.

Introvert: a psychological type who is more concerned with the inner life and reflection than with social life and the external world.

IQ tests: tests designed to measure the 'intelligence quotient', that is, intelligence defined in some operational manner.

Lateral geniculate body: a part of the brain which acts as a relay for visual information from the eye to the visual cortex (area striata).

Long-term memory: the relatively permanent part of the memory system.

Moderator variable *(use of):* using a second measure in conjunction with a particular score to make a better prediction: for example, the prediction of school achievement from an intelligence test might be improved if a measure of motivation were also used.

Mnemonist: a person specializing in the use of memory.

Monotropism: an idea put forward by John Bowlby that an infant has an innate tendency to become attached to one particular individual with the implication that this attachment is different in kind from any other subsequent attachments formed.

Motivation: the readiness to act to achieve certain goals and outcomes.

Motor reproduction: the physical carrying out of behaviours learned through observation.

Mutual gaze: when two people look at each other simultaneously.

Object permanence: the concept that objects still exist when they are out of sight, and which Piaget proposed was acquired in infancy.

Oedipus complex: the Freudian notion that at a certain stage boys experience a conflict between sexual desire for the mother and punishment (castration) by the father, and which derives from a famous Greek myth.

Oestrogen: a sex hormone produced by the ovaries and responsible for the development and maintenance of many female characteristics.

Operant behaviour: any behaviour which, following the established setting conditions, leads to reinforcement.

Optic chiasma: the point in the brain which is a cross-over junction for the optic nerves.

Ovary: the sex gland in the female which produces ova and sex hormones.

Panic disorder: a disorder in which severe fear escalates to a full-blown panic, typically 'out of the blue', rather than in response to any specific feared object or situation.

Paranormal: any psychological phenomenon that cannot be explained by current psychological theories, including telepathy, psychokinesis, poltergeists, clairvoyance and many others.

Parasympathetic nervous system: the cranial and sacral parts of the autonomic nervous system. Active in relaxed or quiescent states of the body.

Perceptual defence: the apparent refusal to see words which might be upsetting or taboo.

Perceptual hypotheses: Testable predictions based on previous experience about the identity of an object or situation.

Personal construct: an important way in which an individual views his or her world. A pattern or template which the individual uses to make sense of his or her experience (from George Kelly's Personal Construct Theory).

Personal Construct Theory: a theory of the mind put forward by George Kelly.

PET scanning: position emission tomography scanning is a computer-aided scanning technique which can be used to show which area(s) of the brain is active under different stimulus and response conditions.

Pituitary gland: a hormone-producing, or endocrine gland located at the base of the brain. Its secretions influence sexual development, metabolism and growth.

Placebo: an inert substance used in place of an active drug, given to a control group in an experiment.

Positivity bias: the bias towards viewing a situation in such a way as to enhance self-esteem.

Posture mimicry: the adoption, often without the person being aware of it, of a posture shown by someone s/he likes or loves; thus two friends may be seen to display the same posture.

Prejudice: negative or hostile attitudes towards groups of people which are based on overgeneralized stereotypes (see *Stereotypes*).

Presumed central tendency: the expectation that others will respond with the average or 'normal' response.

Proactive interference: the interference of items stored in memory with the learning and recall of new items.

Progesterone: a sex hormone produced by the ovaries and responsible for preparing the uterus for pregnancy and the breasts for lactation.

Projective tests: open-ended personality tests whose results rely on the subjective interpretation of the tester.

Psychoanalysis: a method developed by Freud and his followers concerning the treatment of mental and nervous disorders in which the role of the unconscious is emphasized.

Psychodynamics: the psychological approach which Freud began. This approach is based on the idea that the unconscious is a source of drive or motivation.

Psychometrics: the theory and practice of psychological testing.

Qualitative research: research methods that contrast with the quantitative approach and are concerned with subjective data. This research might include verbal or written reports, use of open-ended questions (that have not been converted into points on numerical scales) and case studies.

Quantitative research: analysing data as numerical values. This approach is used in traditional psychology, with the emphasis on objectivity and 'the scientific method'.

Reflex: a physiological reaction, such as eye-blink to a bright light, over which we have no control.

Reinforcement: any outcome of a behaviour which either maintains or increases the frequency of the behaviour.

Reliability: a statistical index of the degree to which a test provides consistent measurements.

Repertory grid: a technique devised by George Kelly to assess personal constructs.

Respondent behaviour: a type of behaviour which, unlike operant behaviour, corresponds to a reflex action.

Reticular activating system: (*also* known as the reticular formation) a network of cells running up through the brain stem. It receives inputs from all sensory pathways and is closely connected to the spinal cord, thalamus and cortex. Thought to play an important role in arousal.

Retina: the part of the eye which is sensitive to light and contains the rods and cones.

Retroactive interference: the interference in memory of items memorized earlier, by items subsequently learned.

Rods: elements of the retina for black-and-white vision.

Role-taking: the process of imitating and identifying with the behaviour of other people or role models.

Schedules of reinforcement: the rate at which behaviour produces the reward – the weekly pay packet, for example.

Schema (plural **schemata**): cognitive structures which are abstract representations of events, people and relationships from the real physical world.

Schizophrenia: one of the most severe forms of mental disorder often accompanied by hallucinations and disordered thinking.

Semantic memory: the part of memory which holds knowledge.

Sensory threshold: the level at which low levels of stimulation are first perceived.

Shaping-up: the gradual production of a complex behaviour by initially rewarding more and more accurate approximations to it.

Short-term memory: the part of the memory system taken to be of limited capacity and only able to hold material for relatively short periods of time.

Social comparison: people's constant need to validate their opinions by comparing them with those of others.

Social facilitation: the increase in speed of a response as a result of social stimuli from others.

Socialization: the process whereby newborns gradually become fully-fledged members of society.

Speciesism: a term used to describe the view that one species is more important than any other. Usually used in relation to humans versus other animals.

S–R Psychology: the branch of psychology concerned with scientific study of the relationship between what is done to an organism (**s**timulus) and what the organism does (**r**esponse).

State-dependent memory: memory that is formed in a particular biological state, such as when drunk, and so is best recalled when the person is in a similar state.

Stereotypes: generalized sets of beliefs or attitudes about groups of people which are usually inaccurate.

Symbolism: a major developmental acquisition of the second year of life which enables the child to internally represent objects not immediately present.

Sympathetic nervous system: the part of the automatic nervous system made up of the ganglionic chain lying outside, and parallel to, the spinal cord. Active in emotional excitement.

Transsexual: a person with a disorder of sexual identity. For example, a transsexual man typically feels himself to be a female trapped in a male body and may want to live as a woman and to have surgery to feminize the body.

Transparencies: non-realistic aspects of young children's drawings where some parts of the scene or objects portrayed are visible through other parts.

Unconditional response: a behaviour, such as a reflex, which naturally occurs following a given stimulus.

Validity: a statistical index of the degree to which a test measures that which it is supposed to measure.

COPYRIGHT ACKNOWLEDGEMENTS

INDEX